MW00451499

Secularism Soviet Style

New Anthropologies of Europe
Daphne Berdahl, Matti Bunzl, and Michael Herzfeld, founding editors

SECULARISM
Soviet Style

Teaching Atheism and Religion in a Volga Republic

Sonja Luehrmann

Indiana University Press
Bloomington and Indianapolis

Publication of this book is made possible in part with the assistance of a Challenge Grant from the National Endowment for the Humanities, a federal agency that supports research, education, and public programming in the humanities. Any views, findings, conclusions, or recommendations expressed in this publication do not necessarily reflect those of the National Endowment for the Humanities.

This book is a publication of

Indiana University Press
601 North Morton Street
Bloomington, Indiana 47404-3797 USA

iupress.indiana.edu

Telephone orders   800-842-6796
Fax orders   812-855-7931

© 2011 by Sonja Luehrmann
All rights reserved

No part of this book may be reproduced or utilized in any form or by any means, electronic or mechanical, including photocopying and recording, or by any information storage and retrieval system, without permission in writing from the publisher. The Association of American University Presses' Resolution on Permissions constitutes the only exception to this prohibition.

∞ The paper used in this publication meets the minimum requirements of the American National Standard for Information Sciences—Permanence of Paper for Printed Library Materials, ANSI Z39.48-1992.

Manufactured in the United States of America

Library of Congress Cataloging-in-Publication Data

Luehrmann, Sonja.
Secularism Soviet style : teaching atheism and religion in a Volga republic / Sonja Luehrmann.
p. cm. — (New anthropologies of Europe)
Includes bibliographical references (p.   ) and index.
ISBN 978-0-253-35698-7 (cloth : alk. paper)—ISBN 978-0-253-22355-5 (pbk. : alk. paper)—ISBN 978-0-253-00542-7 (e-book)
1. Volga-Ural Region (Russia)—Religion.   2. Secularism—Volga-Ural Region (Russia)
3. Atheism—Volga-Ural Region (Russia)
I. Title.

BL980.R8.L84 2011
211'.8094746—dc23

2011024150

1 2 3 4 5 16 15 14 13 12 11

In memory of my grandparents
Karl Lührmann (1892–1978)
and
Käte Lührmann *née* **Emkes** (1907–1997),
who were, among other things, rural school teachers, and who
bequeathed to me a riddle about what happens to people as they
move between ideological systems.

Contents

Preface

On the evening of January 18, 2006, over tea between vespers and the midnight mass in honor of the feast of the Baptism of Christ, the Russian Orthodox priest of one of Marij El's district centers questioned the German-born anthropologist about her views on intellectual influence. "You have probably read all three volumes of *Capital,* in the original?" Some of it, I cautiously admitted. "Do you think Marx wrote it himself?" I supposed so. "And I tell you, it was Satan who wrote it through his hand." I made a feeble defense in the name of secular interpretation, saying that it seemed safer to assume that human authors were capable of their own errors, but could not always foresee the full consequences of their ideas. The priest remained unimpressed, but was otherwise kind enough to sound almost apologetic when he reminded me that, as a non-Orthodox Christian, I had to leave the church after the prayers for the catechumens, at the beginning of the liturgy of communion. Most priests in larger cities were quick to relegate that rule to ancient liturgical custom, but the rarer that actual appearances of heterodox visitors were in a church, the more literally clergy seemed to take it. During this particular mass, the dismissal of the uninitiated would come around 2 a.m., and since it was thirty below outside, the priest gave me permission to sit on a bench at the back of the church instead of actually leaving the building, and told me to be sure to stay for tea and breakfast after the service.

Among the many debts I incurred while writing this book, I am most thankful to the hosts who were honest about the suspicions that my eclectic interests raised in them but almost invariably willing to go a little further in their hospitality than their understanding of duty allowed. In a no less welcome contrast, archivists in Joshkar-Ola, Moscow, and Saint Petersburg provided professional help and respite from the opinionated worlds of religious and anti-religious activism. My special thanks go to Valentina Pavlovna Shomina and Valentina Ivanovna Orekhovskaja at the State Archives of the Republic of Marij El, Dina Nikolaevna Nokhotovich and Ljudmila Gennad'evna Kiseleva at the State Archives of the Russian Federation, and Ekaterina Aleksandrovna Terjukova, Petr Fedotov, and Elena Denisova of the State Museum of the History of Religion. In two of Marij El's district museums, Galina Nikolaevna Novikova (Novyj Tor"jal) and Galina Evgen'evna Selëdkina (Sovetskij) provided both work space and warmhearted hospitality, a combination for which I am doubly grateful.

A number of people and institutions facilitated my entry into the religious and social life of the Volga region. If the Bosch Foundation had not sent me to Mari State University as an instructor of German in 2000–2001, I might never have heard of the Republic of Marij El. Subsequent visits were made possible by reliable visa support from the International Office of Mari State University, in particular its director, Alexey Fominykh, and the vice rector for international relations, Andrey Andreevich Yarygin. Among local specialists in problems of religion and atheism, Nikandr Semënovich Popov and Viktor Stepanovich Solov'ev gave generously of their time and insights. Writer-folklorist-filmmaker Marina Kopylova shared the contents of her address book as generously as those of her fridge, and facilitated a wealth of initial contacts. Svetlana and Veronika Semënovy and Svetlana Algaeva assisted me in transcribing and translating Mari-language recordings. In a friendship that goes back long before my first trip to Marij El, Olga Nyrkova and, more recently, Andrey Nyrkov (Moscow) taught me how to move through Russian Orthodox services, and they continue to improve my understanding of what goes on there.

Financially, my research travel was made possible by grants from the German Academic Exchange Service, the Wenner-Gren Foundation, and various institutions at the University of Michigan: the International Institute, the Center for Russian and East European Studies, the Department of Anthropology, and the Doctoral Program in Anthropology and History. Crucial support for periods of writing came from a Humanities Research Candidacy Fellowship (Rackham Graduate School, University of Michigan), a Charlotte W. Newcombe Dissertation Fellowship (Woodrow Wilson Foundation), an SSRC Eurasia Program Fellowship (with Title VIII funds provided by the U.S. State Department), and an Izaak Walton Killam Postdoctoral Fellowship at the University of British Columbia.

Intellectually, this book owes much to the vibrant community of the Doctoral Program in Anthropology and History at the University of Michigan, and especially to the students and faculty in the 2003 installment of the core seminar: Dan Birchok, Dong Ju Kim, Ken Maclean, Oana Mateescu, Kate McClellan, Ed Murphy, Eric Stein, Nancy Hunt, and Ann Stoler. My dissertation committee, Alaina Lemon, Webb Keane, Douglas Northrop, and William Rosenberg, made a perfect team for all occasions, and I am grateful for their presence in these pages.

Heather Coleman and Bruce Grant were generously non-anonymous readers for Indiana University Press. Their enthusiasm, doubts, and practical suggestions helped to make this a better book, as did the wise editing of Rebecca Tolen and Merryl Sloane's thoughtful copyediting. For asking questions that stayed in my mind while writing, I also thank Danna Agmon, Michael Bergmann, Frank Cody, David William Cohen, Susanne Cohen, Maria Couroucli, Victoria Frede, Kate Graber, Chris Hann, Stephen Headley, Angie Heo, Paul Christopher Johnson, Sergei Kan, John Kelly, Valerie Kivelson, Julia Klimova, Jeanne Kormina, Michael Lambek, Ritty Lukose, Andrea Muehlebach, Vlad Naumescu, David Pedersen, Brian Porter-Szűcs, Justine Buck Quijada, Joel Robbins, Daromir Rudnyckyj, Danilyn Rutherford, Sergey Shtyrkov, Michael Silverstein, Ron Suny, Nikolai Vakhtin, Katherine Verdery, Ilya Vinkovetsky, and Mayfair Yang. Doug Rogers has been a source of many stimulating conversations on things religious in Russia, and provided much collegial aid. Rudolf Mrázek was a good spirit who always appeared at the right moment, and Christian Feest set high standards for a scholarship that takes itself seriously at all stages, from research to publication. At the University of British Columbia, I am grateful to Alexia Bloch, John Barker, Julie Cruikshank, Anne Gorsuch, and the members of the Eurasia reading group for a congenial writing home.

Parts of this book were published earlier in different form, and I thank the publishers for permission to reprint them here. Materials from chapter 2 appeared as "On the Importance of Having a Method, or What Does Archival Work on Soviet Atheism Have to Do with Ethnography of Post-Soviet Religion?" in *Anthrohistory: Unsettling Knowledge and the Question of Disciplines*, edited by Edward Murphy et al. (Ann Arbor: University of Michigan Press, 2011). Materials from chapter 5 appeared as "A Dual Struggle of Images on Russia's Middle Volga: Icon Veneration in the Face of Protestant and Pagan Critique," in *Eastern Christians in Anthropological Perspective*, edited by Chris Hann and Hermann Goltz (Berkeley: University of California Press, 2010).

For making clear that practicing a religion involves the courage to live with difficult questions, I owe thanks to my parents, Renate and Dieter Lührmann, and to the communities of Lord of Light Lutheran Church (Ann Arbor) and Christ Church Cathedral (Vancouver). Silke Lührmann and the other significant atheists in my life remind me that, as Soviet sociologists well knew, it is very difficult to say what difference religiosity or areligiosity actually makes. Jona, Philipp, and Vera set effective deadlines for various stages of writing, and Philipp also made excellent company on a wrap-up visit to Marij El in September 2008. Thanks to big brother Fyodor for patience and good humor, and most of all, to Ilya Vinkovetsky for a life that has room for all of this.

Note on Translation, Transliteration, and Names

The original archival and interview materials used in this book were predominantly in Russian and to some degree in Mari, a Finno-Ugric language of the Volga-Finnish branch. All translations are my own unless otherwise noted. A glossary at the end of the book explains the meaning and origin of Mari and Russian terms.

In contemporary Russia, Mari is written in the same Cyrillic script as Russian, with three additional letters: ӱ (transliteration: ü), pronounced like French *u* or German *ü*; ö (transliteration: ö), pronounced like French *eu* or German *ö*; and ҥ (transliteration: ng), pronounced roughly like *ng* in the English "sing." To avoid discrepancies between transliterations of Russian and Mari, I modified the Library of Congress system in the text, using *j* (pronounced like the *y* in the English "yes") to transliterate the letter й (i-kratkoe) and to indicate the beginning of soft vowels: *jazyk, jumo*. The standard Library of Congress spelling is used in the bibliography to enable readers to locate references in North American library catalogs.

Like English, Russian and Mari orthography requires capitalization only for proper names, leaving open its optional use in nouns and adjectives to indicate respect. Whether or not to capitalize the names of divinities, religious denominations, or sacred scriptures is a matter of ideological preference in atheist and religious literatures. When translating written texts, I follow the choices of capitalization made in the original; when quoting oral speech, I capitalize in those cases where I imagine the speaker would have done so.

In an effort to both respect local sensibilities and avoid making myself into a spokesperson for any of my interlocutors' mutually conflicting projects, I depart somewhat from common conventions of naming in Anglophone anthropology. Having met many people in Russia who found the idea of assigning pseudonyms deceitful and suspect, I decided against using them. Some interviewees would probably have given me permission to use their real names if I had asked for it. But I preferred not to do that either, not being sure that I would fulfill the implicit expectation of what the final text would look like. Instead, I only use the real names of publicly known figures from whose published work I am also quoting. Everyone else is referred to by a description of the role in which I encountered them, e.g., "the dormitory supervisor," "the Baptist minister," "the lecturer," etc. Since my work was with very recent archival documents, here, too, I only use the names of people who were acting in official capacities for which they are still remembered today, while anonymizing more incidental voices.

Secularism Soviet Style

Introduction: Atheism, Secularity, and Postsecular Religion

When political activists engage in anti-religious struggle, what are they fighting against? At a time when the return of religion to the public sphere makes more headlines than its long-expected withdrawal, this may seem a naïve way of posing the question. When considering contemporary religious revivals and the challenges they pose to the predictions of modernization theory, observers more commonly ask why these predictions once seemed so plausible and how to formulate more adequate understandings of modernity. But nineteenth- and twentieth-century theories of modernization bred not only expectations of the gradual disappearance of religion from public life, but also movements that actively sought to help this process along, through education, restrictive legislation, or the physical elimination of believers and sacred objects. For people caught up in secularist movements as strategists or participants, religion was a powerful adversary, not merely a remnant of a disappearing past. Rather than investigating the implications of religious revival for secular concepts of modernity, this book starts from the late Soviet atheist campaigns to reverse the question: what can the apprehensions and intuitions of secularist modernizers contribute to our understanding of religion?

Any possible answers need to take into account that Soviet citizens rarely engaged in atheist activism out of their own initiative, but because their professional or party position required them to do so. One of the first legislative acts of the Bolshevik government was a decree in January 1918 on the separation of the church from the state and the school from the church, and the so-called Stalin constitution of 1936 guaranteed freedom of religious confession, but gave only atheists the right to propagate their views (Corley 1996). Several waves of violent anti-religious campaigns in the 1920s and '30s destroyed the institutional power of the Russian Orthodox Church and other religious confessions by murdering clergy and lay believers (Husband 2000; Mitrofanov 2002). During the decades following the end of the Second World War and Stalin's death in 1953, which form the focus of this book, atheist propaganda remained a duty that members

1

of the Communist Party, teachers, doctors, scientists, and others in positions of authority might be called upon to perform. The strategies they were trained in were based on the double premise that religion had become institutionally obsolete, but remained a force in the lives of many citizens. When such not-quite-voluntary activists groped for the right language to denounce religious attachments, it became apparent that some of them were not immune to this force themselves. The following quote from a speech by a female factory worker at the height of a new anti-religious campaign under Stalin's successor, Nikita Khrushchev, illustrates the resulting ambiguities:

> From eight years of age I was alone, my parents died in 1933. Hungry and cold, I had to wander alone among people in search of food and shelter. Hunger forced me to steal vegetables from gardens so as not to die of hunger, and "god," he also forgot about me for some reason. He gave me neither food nor shelter, where was he at that time? He was silent, watched, but did nothing. No, he did not exist [*Net, ne bylo ego*]. Only our people and our Motherland helped me. They found me a place in an orphanage, put me through school, brought me out into society [*vyveli v ljudi*], this is what I always believed in and will believe, this is to whom I owe all my conscience and my life.[1]

This woman is speaking in 1960 in favor of the closing of the last Russian Orthodox church in Joshkar-Ola, the capital of the Mari Autonomous Soviet Socialist Republic (ASSR) in Russia's Volga region. When she remembers her hungry childhood, the God who did not help her seems real enough to still merit her anger. Even the phrase *ne bylo ego*, translated here as "he did not exist," is ambiguous—it might also mean "he was absent." While she seems uncertain if God is an illusion or simply unreliable, it is obvious which alternative object of trust the speaker seeks to promote: the community of human beings and human institutions that make up "our people" and "our Motherland." She credits this community not only with helping her survive, but also with making her a social being, educated and with a place in society. When she had no one but God to look to, the child was forced into antisocial behavior (stealing, wandering without a fixed residence), but being rescued by a state orphanage connected her to a saving web of human care. Even if her own atheism remains incomplete, this worker has correctly grasped the central contrast of Soviet atheist propaganda: asocial, treacherous religion was set against human collective accomplishments, which were the only deserving objects of faith.

Even in this short narrative, some pitfalls of this faith in people become apparent: if the speaker's parents died in 1933 because of the famine that ravaged the Volga region along with Ukraine and southern Russia that year, they were arguably victims of the hurried collectivization campaigns of the same Soviet state that their daughter lauds as her lifesaver (Davies and Wheatcroft 2004). More generally, to conflate "our people" with state institutions, such as an orphanage, means to credit an abstraction with the warmth and help received from other human beings, in a move of transference not unlike the one that critics since Ludwig Feuerbach (1841) have analyzed as the root of all religion. The state here seems to take the place of God, equally sacralized and lifted out of the realm of human questioning. Such structural similarities between religious and secular efforts to provide people with a transcendent purpose were painfully apparent to atheist strategists. But the latter also insisted on a critique of religion as something fundamentally opposed to socialist visions of society. This critique deserves to be interrogated more closely for what it says about late Soviet society and about the problems of religious community-building in the post-Soviet era.

A Century of Transformations

During the late twentieth and early twenty-first centuries, headscarf debates in France, disputes over stem-cell research in the United States, and the continued strength of religiously inspired international charity networks cast doubt on earlier expectations that religion would gradually lose its relevance to public life.[2] In turn, growing numbers of social scientists and philosophers have begun to direct their attention to secularism—the body of political doctrines and moral sensibilities that make it seem necessary for religion to be detached from modern public life—making it into an object of analysis in its own right instead of a normative background assumption. Perhaps because the bulk of this scholarship focuses on Western Europe, North America, and the Middle East, its authors tend to treat secularism as a corollary of political liberalism, linking it to liberal doctrines that see society as a collection of autonomous individuals, and politics as a negotiation of personal interests.[3]

Although some of these academic discussions were stimulated by clashes between secularist and religious politics in India (Bhargava 1998) and Turkey (Navaro-Yashin 2002; Özyürek 2006), those political movements of the twentieth century that made secularism part of a deliberate program of accelerated, collective modernization are seldom included in the wider debate on what it means to be secular. Also conspicuously absent is the state-sponsored atheism of socialist Eastern Europe and northern Asia, despite a growing body of historical and ethnographic work addressing changes in religious life under the influence of militant atheism (Berglund and Porter-Szűcs 2010; H. Coleman 2005; Ghodsee 2009; Khalid 2007; Pelkmans 2006, 2009; Rogers 2009; Wanner 2007; Yang 2008). Ironically, attempts to "provincialize" a European secular perspective on history (Chakrabarty 2000) seem to have made it harder to appreciate the global reach of secularism and to analyze the constellations of local interests and pressures to keep up with an ideal image of the West that led a variety of political movements to adopt it.

This book seeks to contribute to a more transnational view of attempts to banish gods and spirits from social life by bringing approaches to liberal and postcolonial secularisms into dialogue with the history of Soviet atheism, as it played itself out in the Middle Volga region. In this part of Russia, religion had long served as a marker of differentiation between imperial subjects. A border zone between the Muslim Khanate of Kazan' and Orthodox Christian Muscovy, inhabited by peasants who spoke Finno-Ugric and Turkic languages and worshiped agricultural deities in sacred groves, this region came under Russian rule in the sixteenth century. Until the Bolshevik Revolution of 1917, religious confession (in shifting combination with other criteria, such as noble or commoner status, native language, and place of residence) remained a decisive factor in determining a person's legal rights and obligations (Kappeler 1982, 1992; Werth 2002). For the communists governing this region, doing away with religion thus also meant doing away with the religious boundaries and norms that, they felt, inappropriately separated people by ethnic group, gender, or age. By making the shift from trusting in God to trusting the state, Soviet citizens declared allegiance to a new, overarching social body in which older particularities lost their force.

Others have traced the tortuous and often contradictory processes by which social planners in the early decades of Soviet rule sought to replace religious identifications with secular ethnic cultures that would relate to one another in a harmonious "friendship of the peoples" (Hirsch 2005; T. Martin 2001; Werth 2000). My aim is to ask why religion seemed to stand in the way of such commensurability, and how anti-religious efforts reshaped religious life. The answer to the first question has to do with assumptions about religion which Soviet communists inherited from classical Marxist thought; but these assumptions were also reworked under the pressures of shaping a new society under conditions of rapid technological and political change.

In the stretch of woodland, meadow, and bog on both sides of the Volga that was organized into the Mari Autonomous Region in 1921 (upgraded to an autonomous republic in 1936), the rhythms of life changed drastically. Marginal agriculture, hunting, and seasonal wage labor in logging or shipping were replaced by work in large-scale, mechanized farms and in the industrial enterprises of the urbanizing capital. The royalist name of that town, Tsarevo-Kokshajsk, was first revolutionized into Krasnokok-shajsk (Russian for Red City on the Kokshaga), and finally indigenized into Joshkar-Ola (Mari for Red City). New settlements along the railroad branch that connected Joshkar-Ola to the Moscow-Kazan' line from 1928 onward were ethnically mixed, different from the older confessionally and linguistically segregated villages. New educational institutions made literacy rates rise from 18 percent among Maris (only 7 percent among Mari women) and 37.8 percent among Russians in 1920 to near-universal levels in postwar generations, while also detaching the acquisition of knowledge from church authority. A teachers college founded in 1919 was the first-ever institution of higher learning in the republic, and rural primary schools replaced four-year instruction funded through Orthodox parishes (Iantemir 2006 [1928]: 89; Sanukov et al. 2004). During the Second World War, the evacuation of weapons factories from areas threatened by German occupation further accelerated the process of industrialization and urbanization. Adults who participated in atheist propaganda and church closures in the 1960s and '70s had not only lived lives increasingly remote from institutionalized religion, they had also been immersed in promises of constant change and unheard-of possibilities since childhood.

Shedding religious attachments—and the hierarchies and divisions connected to them—was a condition of entering this ongoing process of change. In this sense, one might see Soviet atheism as part of an exit strategy from imperial forms of governance in which different communities of subjects had been endowed with different rights. New comparative studies of empires suggest that secularists in Kemalist Turkey and post-independence India faced comparable legacies.[4] In all three contexts, rapidly modernizing, "mobilizational" states (Khalid 2006) sought to establish control over internally diverse populations, and feared that allegiance to nonhuman agents could present a threat to the new collective of equal citizens. While this comparison awaits more careful exploration, keeping in mind that the secularisms of the twentieth century were about building new communities as much as new selves provides an important corrective to the idea that secularism and liberal individualism are somehow inherently linked.[5] In fact, the extended and refocused forms of sociality that secularism promises may be part of its most enduring appeal.

If we are to understand the "thick texture of affinities, prejudices, and attachments" that continues to give secularist commitments "visceral force" within and outside of academia (Mahmood 2008: 451), surely the narrative of transformation of a hungry thief abandoned by all into a useful and grateful member of society deserves our attention. But if the collective she joins presents itself as an absolute savior, can it be called secular? Thinking about the sense in which a secular society existed in the Soviet Union requires some sorting through the intellectual baggage that Soviet Marxist thinkers brought to the topic, and through some common definitions of *secularity* and *religion*.

Was Soviet Society Secular?

When Soviet atheists thought about the relationship of their activities to religious practice, two outwardly contradictory models seemed able to coexist. One was an idea of functional replacement, where secular forms superseded their earlier, religious equivalents. The other was that of constructing a qualitatively new society that relied on and celebrated human action. Cultural planners of the 1920s and '30s acted out the logic of replacement by turning houses of worship into cinemas, and graveyards into parks (Dragadze 1993), and by introducing socialist holidays to coincide with commonly observed religious ones (Petrone 2000; Rolf 2006). As Leon Trotsky, who was one of the driving figures of Soviet cultural policy before his falling-out with Stalin, put it concisely in a 1923 essay: "The cinema competes not only with the tavern, but also with the church. And this rivalry may become fatal for the church if we make up for the separation of the church from the socialist state by the fusion of the socialist state and the cinema" (Trotsky 1973 [1923]: 39).

This view, in which secular spectacle replaces religious tools for community-building, was taken up by many outside analysts of the Soviet Union, who speak of Soviet state "rituals" (Lane 1981) or a "cult" of Soviet leaders (Tumarkin 1983). Though not always culminating in the charge that communism was in fact a substitute religion,[6] these analyses are similarly grounded in a Durkheimian view of the sacred, which is not defined by assumptions about the existence of divine or spiritual beings, but by virtue of being set apart from the profane (Durkheim 1998 [1914]; see also Moore and Myerhoff 1977). A state that appropriates some of this set-apart character for its own symbols and rituals is then no longer quite secular, but can be said to be placing itself at the center of its own "civil religion" (Bellah 1967).

If a secular society is one in which nothing is held sacred, the official Soviet culture of the 1960s and '70s might be better described as religious, dominated as it was by the invention and promotion of secular festivals and ritualizations of life-cycle events (Smolkin 2009). But it is perhaps no accident that Soviet theorists of religion never adopted the Durkheimian definition of religion as based on the contrast between the sacred and the profane, but always defined it as faith in God or spiritual beings.[7] Restricting our view to the intentional and unintentional equivalences between church and cinema, divine and bureaucratic helpers, would be to overlook the importance of this choice of definition. Striving to eradicate attachment to superhuman powers, Soviet atheists saw the creation of an exclusively human community as the ultimate goal of secularization.

To generate enthusiasm for this new community, festival planners might strategically exploit popular reverence for state symbols and try to approximate the appeal of religious rituals. But those in charge of atheist education also recognized that such parallels could compromise the message that religion and communism were incompatible. Postwar training materials on atheist propaganda thus called for approaches that focused not on replacing religious narratives but on spreading what was known as a "scientific world view" among the population (Powell 1975). Some of these materials explicitly addressed the need for atheism to be substantially different from the religious sensibilities it sought to replace. In this sense, theorists of Soviet scientific atheism might have agreed with Talal Asad (2003: 25) that the secular is not simply religion in another garb, but has a more elusive relationship to previous cultural forms. Rather than merely substituting earthly absolutes for heavenly ones, being secular in the late Soviet Union meant living in a society governed by different affective regimes and different communicative possibilities than those imagined to hold sway in religious societies.

New socialist holidays, though deliberately timed to coincide with and replace religious (mainly Russian Orthodox Christian) holidays or periods of fasting, were nonetheless said to have a different emotional tone. Where, in the words of a 1963 lecture about new Soviet traditions, religious holidays were characterized by a pessimistic mood of submission "to an imaginary god, fear of the afterlife, disbelief in the power of science and the strength of the human being" (Anonymous 1963: 25), Soviet holidays were joyful and optimistic, inspiring creativity and confidence in the future. The emotional switch from fear to joy, passivity to activity, becomes possible through events that materialize the collaboration of human contemporaries as a driving force of history.

Soviet secularization was thus not only about replacing the church with the cinema and appropriating the cinema's cultural power to the state. It was also about accustoming people to social relations in which there were no significant nonhuman agents. Rather than a notion of individualism or privatized religion, it is this "exclusive humanism," whose emergence in modern Western European thought has been described by Charles Taylor

(2004, 2007), that provides a link between the secularist traditions of Western Europe and state-enforced atheism.

The demands of exclusive humanism placed limits on strategies for the functional replacement of religious forms. From Marx and his contemporaries, who criticized religious faith as an expression of mystified social realities, Soviet communists inherited an ethical commitment to demonstrating that only living human agents made history. But if religion was "the sigh of the oppressed" (Marx 1957 [1844]: 378), it became harder to understand why religious attachments did not fade away as socialist society developed. To explain "the vitality of religion under socialism," as the titles of books and conferences in the 1960s framed the problem,[8] atheist theorists made a link between religiosity and enduring forces of social division. Sociological studies showed statistical correlations between proclaimed religious belief and either a status of pensioner and housewife or a lack of access to cultural facilities, such as libraries and cinemas. Researchers in the Volga region also argued that being part of an ethnic minority attempting to maintain a separate identity strengthened religious attachments (Solov'ev 1977, 1987). In a striking reversal of Emile Durkheim's analysis of society as the true referent of religious ritual, Soviet sociologists and propagandists went to great lengths to cast religion as antisocial, associated with isolation and fragmentation.

This emergent critique helps to explain some of the contradictions of the Soviet secularization process. On the one hand, atheist planners recognized and sometimes sought to imitate religious methods of achieving social cohesion. On the other, they suspected that the alternative relationships with divinities, saints, and spirits implied in religious ritual threatened human solidarity. The society they were engaged in building derived its claim to secularity from the exclusion of such alternative relationships, making human contemporaries the only possible partners in action. But since nonhuman interlocutors remained real to significant parts of the population, the exclusively human society often presented itself as a didactic goal.

Joining the Didactic Public

After the Second World War, there was no organization in the Soviet Union solely devoted to atheist propaganda. The League of the Militant Godless, founded in 1925 and formally dissolved in 1947, was replaced that same year by the newly founded Society for the Dissemination of Political and Scientific Knowledge. Renamed the Knowledge Society (Obshchestvo Znanie) in 1963, this association of scholars and intellectuals engaged in atheist propaganda as part of a broader mandate, since it was also heir to prewar organizations involved in popularizing science and technology (Andrews 2003; Peris 1998: 222). In the wake of wartime relaxations of anti-religious policy, the League of the Godless was condemned for crude anticlericalism and counterproductive attacks on the feelings of believers. The premise of atheist work within the Knowledge Society, by contrast, was that confrontation with the discoveries of modern science was the most effective tool for weaning people from reliance on supernatural agents (Powell 1975: 48–51).

For members of the Knowledge Society and lecturers of regional party organizations, conducting atheist propaganda always involved movement. Since religiosity was assumed to reside in more peripheral places, and enlightened knowledge in more central ones, lecturers from regional capitals traveled to Moscow for training, then were sent out to collective farms and enterprises in their regions. On the lowest rung of the pyramid, teachers from rural schools visited outlying hamlets to conduct lectures for milkmaids and combine drivers. Teachers and academics might also recruit their students to join them in lecture circuits. One prominent atheist activist of the Mari republic, the biologist Mikhail Nekhoroshkov, organized students from the teachers college into an atheist club and traveled with them to village houses of culture (Nekhoroshkov 1964). Their performances included skits and songs, but also demonstrations of chemical and physical experiments designed to convince audiences of the power of the natural sciences to explain unusual occurrences. These Evenings of Miracles without Miracles were not an original invention of the Mari club, but a form that was popularized through the network of trainings and publications of the Knowledge Society. The intricate movement of people and scripts geared toward making atheist arguments more persuasive says something about the kind of society atheist propaganda was intended to construct, which I call a *didactic public*.

Rejecting the liberal idea of the privatization of religion in modern society, Soviet policymakers never thought of anyone's convictions as a private matter. To be sure, the constitution guaranteed freedom of conscience, and legal restrictions barring religious associations from educational and social work left the family as the only legitimate place for the transmission of religious values (Pospielovsky 1987a, b). But the same constitution also guaranteed freedom of anti-religious propaganda, meaning that the domestic arrangements of citizens could become targets of didactic intervention. For this reason, the anthropologist Tamara Dragadze (1993) speaks of the "domestication" of religion in the Soviet Union, rather than its privatization. Religious practice was increasingly restricted to in-group contexts, and religious expertise became a more heavily feminized domain. The publicly

A lecture in the fields, Ronga district, ca. 1972. [From the album "Relay of Good Deeds," courtesy of Sovetskij District Museum, Republic of Marij El]

visible lives of household members, by contrast, were immersed in interactions that pointedly excluded any reference to more-than-human agents.

In a society in which few things were private in the sense of being protected from state intervention, the "sovereign subject" or "bounded self" of the liberal political imagination (Mahmood 2005: 32; Taylor 2007: 37) was replaced by a malleable self, open to the influence of outside forces (Kharkhordin 1999; Oushakine 2004). Training people to be atheists was part of this larger transformative effort. But the language of the "new man" notwithstanding, the primary object of intervention was often society as a whole, rather than individual selves. Efforts to become a new person were inseparably tied to learning how to change others. What is more, integration into networks of teaching and learning often motivated people to engage with official ideology as well as with their fellow citizens. Even during the decades known as the era of "stagnation," Soviet secular culture retained a measure of dynamism by offering people ways to change their own places in the world through participation in didactic initiatives (Benn 1989).

Where might one locate the social effects of such training efforts? The Knowledge Society and party-sponsored propaganda operated through networks that were designed to be centrally directed but use a minimal amount of central resources. This meant, for instance, that atheist concerts or lectures were centrally mandated, but rarely fully scripted, relying on a great deal of local improvisation. Soviet propagandists received direction through lists of recommended lecture titles and schematic descriptions of performative genres, rather than memorizing texts composed in the center. This system presupposed local activists skilled in reading the intentions behind titles and able to assemble the necessary materials and human talents to animate the preapproved forms. In its material organization, Soviet propaganda relied on a population not necessarily of convinced or enthusiastic followers, but of people who applied their own creativity to generate dogmatically correct statements and politically desirable events.

Such reliance on the generative competence of local performers was probably due in part to the need to save on printed materials in a socialist "economy of shortage" (Kornai 1992). But post-Soviet evidence shows that such material constraints may have helped to give Soviet propaganda more lasting effects. When interviewing people now active in religious organizations, I encountered many memories of their being drawn into propaganda activities based on particular skills. A Lutheran pastor remembered being asked to participate in the Evenings of Miracles during his student years because of his skill in reciting poetry; an artist and woodcarver now working on the restoration of churches remembered being put in charge of painting posters and wall newspapers during his time as a factory worker; and one of the Knowledge Society's few remaining lecturers talked about the gift of tactfully approaching diverse audiences that had made her a good lecturer. These people differed in their retrospective evaluations of the contents of their work, but shared a sense of pride in their skills.

Lecturers, painters, and student agitators were part of the Soviet didactic public, different from the egalitarian and open-ended communicative sphere imagined by liberal theorists. The didactic public was unapologetically directed by party-controlled organs that insisted on setting standards of truth. But like the liberal public, it allowed for a new scope of connectedness with strangers in a network constituted not through connections of kinship or residence, but "through mere attention" (Warner 2002: 87; see also Habermas 1988). Participants in this network faced the intellectual and practical challenge of making known truths and proclaimed goals comprehensible and meaningful to audiences. A radio report described the Evening of Miracles without Miracles as "interesting and joyful, and without a doubt . . . useful for those present."[9] Memories of the difficulties of making events "interesting" (*interesno*), "joyful" (*veselo*), and "useful" (*polezno*), and of the satisfaction of finding the right props and striking the right tone, contain important clues to the reasons that certain people find ideological activism attractive.

Keeping in mind that skills and methods can become preoccupations in their own right, we can understand some of the astonishing ideological versatility of members of the final Soviet generations. Though their relation to official ideology is often described as cynical or "pure pro forma," people who came of age under Khrushchev or Brezhnev nonetheless appear to have been profoundly shaped by their involvement in the official culture of their day, often taking models of behavior with them into post-Soviet careers (Yurchak 2006; see also Derluguian 2005). Since, for some of these people, post-Soviet careers include religious activism, this is testimony that engagement in the didactic public did not presuppose deep atheist convictions. But for teachers and learners in the Soviet Union as well as for secularists elsewhere (Ozouf and Ozouf 1992), there was also a more substantive connection between didactic engagement and secular values. As long as expanding systems of public education gave access to real chances of social mobility, they provided one of the most palpable proofs that people could transcend their circumstances with the help of other humans. For the hungry girl abandoned by God, human teachers and school administrators were not only temporary survival aids, but also forces of lasting transformation.

Permutations of Method

Through the networks of the Communist Party, the Knowledge Society, the Komsomol youth organization, and Young Pioneer palaces, institutions throughout the Soviet Union put a great deal of effort into training professionals and volunteers to reproduce ideological discourse. By the time the Soviet Union collapsed, the didactic skills of adapting content to particular audiences, creating visual aids, and collecting facts and illustrations were widespread among the population. In this book, I call people with such didactic expertise *methodicians,* a neologism inspired by the Russian term *metodist,* a professional designation for a person in charge of programming and events planning at a culture club, library, house of political enlightenment, or other such institution.

Also from Soviet terminology, I borrow a distinction between *methodology,* as a general theory of how to approach the task of convincing and transforming others, and *method,* as a more practical representation of steps to take toward that goal. In Russian, these two nouns correspond to two adjectives, *metodologicheskij* and *metodicheskij.* In an effort to keep the distinction visible in English, I speak of "methodical" skills or "methodical" guidance when referring to the practical sense of how to get things done, and only use "methodological" in reference to more abstract debates. As analysts of Soviet propaganda have noted, a preoccupation with the practicalities of method soon replaced both psychological inquiries into the effects of propaganda campaigns on target audiences and questions about underlying goals and principles (Benn 1989; Kenez 1985; Peris 1998). By the time of the postwar "developed socialism," participants at training sessions for atheist propagandists might ask *how* to interest rural audiences in the achievements of Soviet space flights, but they were never encouraged to question *if* someone who learned about the age and extent of the universe would necessarily abandon religious faith. Since I wish to draw attention to situations where *methodical* practicalities offer an alternative arena for debate when ideological regulation makes it impossible to question *methodological* premises, the distinction between the two adjectives is worth importing into English.

As I became immersed in religious life in Marij El, as the former Mari ASSR has been known since 1991, I encountered former professional or amateur methodicians in leadership positions among all denominations. Retired teachers, journalists, college instructors, actors, and trade union activists were now serving as clergy, organizing Mari sacrificial ceremonies, leading Bible studies, and teaching Quranic reading. The irony was that many of them had belonged to professional groups that were required to profess and promote atheism. After the end of the bloody persecutions of the prewar decades, a collective farm worker who was not a member of the Communist Party usually faced little censure for having a child baptized or circumcised or for keeping religious paraphernalia at home. A teacher who did the same, however, risked losing her job. What is more, many of the converts I encountered had never even faced such problems, because they recalled having been convinced communists. One Tatar woman who used to be a trade union activist and now taught Arabic to women at Joshkar-Ola's mosque had even been too conscientious to join the party, although that would have helped her advance to administrative jobs: "I would rather be a true communist outside the party than a careerist within it," she said.

Ethnographers of religious life in other parts of the former Soviet Union describe activists with comparable backgrounds (Rogers 2009; Wanner 2007). These religious methodicians bring a particular didactic orientation to their new work; they view words, images, and events in terms of their potential to catch the attention of others and influence them toward desired changes in opinion and behavior. I have argued above that drawing ever-new participants into didactic networks was one of the major ways in which Soviet society secularized itself. In a strange twist of history, the orientation toward change through persuasion that such networks promoted has now become a point of convergence with global forms of religiosity that some observers label "postsecular."

The term *postsecular* emerged from dialogues between social sciences and theology, and refers to situations where the ongoing public importance of religious commitments is increasingly recognized, while the society remains secular in the sense that holding such commitments is not a condition for membership. Citizens who engage in religious practices are aware that not everyone around them does the same (Höhn 2007; Schweidler 2007). As analysts of religious life in secularizing societies have noted, the possibility of observing no religion at all has an impact even on those who consider themselves religious. Religious organizations compete for people's commitment with one another as well as with more secular offerings, leading them to adjust their styles of self-presentation and epistemological claims (Casanova 1994; Habermas 2005). This can result in more event-centered, emotionally charged, and "seeker-friendly" forms of congregational life (Buckser 1996; Cox 1984; Hervieu-Léger 1997). When the prestige of religious expertise declines, such expertise sometimes becomes the domain of those marginalized in public life, such as housewives and pensioners (Brown 2001; Dragadze 1993).

But the relationship between religious life and a secularizing society is not a one-way street where religion is always on the defensive. When secular concepts become "theologized" (Assmann 2002) and endowed with sacred meaning, this can result in unforeseen transformations of religious as well as social possibilities. As individual paths of "believing without belonging" (Davie 1994) defy older doctrinal boundaries, techniques for attracting and cultivating the attention of potential converts acquire new ethical and theological significance. As shown by ethnographies of the use of new media in so-called fundamentalist movements, the quest for attention makes religious leaders adapt their messages and personas to the demands of film and voice recording, but also draws on older ways in which seeing and listening were valued theologically (S. Coleman 2000; Harding 2000; Meyer 2006).

Charles Hirschkind's study of the circulation of tape-recorded sermons among Egyptian Muslims, for example, points to a subtle shift where paying attention, once thought of as a virtue incumbent on the listener, now becomes a measure of the skill of a preacher in attracting an audience (2006: 40). At the same time, this shift is far from complete, because listeners continue to work on themselves to be able to better absorb and respond to a preacher's message. Among religious responses to the Soviet obsession with finding the right method to engage and persuade, there is a similar mix of mutual appropriation and friction, part of a much longer relationship between religious and secular settings of learning in Europe that is best described by the Weberian term *elective affinity*.

The Riddle of Elective Affinity

Former cultural workers who use their Soviet methodical training to promote religious causes extend principles of Soviet mobilizations into religious life, but they are also part of a long shared history of religious practice and human learning. All religions face the problem of knowledge transmission, and those with bodies of sacred writings in particular have developed elaborate systems of formalized schooling (Ong 1982; Whitehouse 2000). Arguably, many modern pedagogical methodologies have a religious history, notably in colonial missions and parish schools (Comaroff and Comaroff 1997; Ozouf and Ozouf 1992). But where state schools expand, they also introduce new methods and principles of learning that have an impact on religious life, as Dale Eickelman (1992) and Brinkley Messick (1993) have noted for countries dominated by Islam. Histories of schooling and literacy in imperial Russia suggest a comparable cross-fertilization between religious and secular institutions (Brooks 1985; Eklof 1993).

After 1917, the contributions of religious institutions to Russian popular education were intentionally stopped. Instead, methodological reflections on how to open education to groups that had previously been excluded from it—workers, peasants, women, young children—drew on pedagogical reform movements of the nineteenth century with their search for experiential approaches to learning (L. Froese 1963; Kirschenbaum 2001). But the service ethic of descendants of Russian Orthodox clergy and the interest in all-around human development of various esoteric movements have also been identified as influential in early Soviet pedagogy, showing the continued entanglement of religious and secular quests for personal and social transformation (Manchester 2008; Maydell 1997). Although the reform pedagogues stood in a fraught relationship to Bolshevism and many were persecuted as "bourgeois specialists" under Stalin (Fitzpatrick 1970; Plaggenborg 1996), we will find echoes of their approaches and concerns in the work of postwar methodicians (Kerr 2005).

In post-Soviet Russia, the complex heritage of Soviet didacticism encounters a global trend toward theologizing approaches to personal change. Books I encountered on the shelves of Soviet-born evangelicals included translations from secular self-help literature as well as avowedly Christian titles instructing their readers on how to lead a "purpose-driven life" (Warren 2002) or find happiness in marriage. Many religious activists also readily admitted how useful experiences with Soviet cultural work had been.

The entanglement of these three sources of inspiration for didactic approaches—Soviet atheist, secular Western, and transnational religious—will occupy us for most of this book. But the secular-religious affinity is not unique to Russia. Ethnographies from other parts of the world have noted a lively back-and-forth between religious and secular approaches to solving social problems by means of personal transformation. Courses in

Islamic spirituality for the employees of a privatizing Indonesian enterprise (Rudnyckyj 2009), an evangelical Christian rehabilitation program for prison inmates in Iowa (Sullivan 2009), and a residential program of the conservative Protestant "ex-gay" movement in California (Erzen 2006) all position themselves as alternatives to nonsectarian, publicly funded ways of addressing issues of workplace morale, criminal recidivism, and sexuality in marriage. They are postsecular in the sense that they take the methods and values of secular institutions and apply them to quests for spiritual salvation, while claiming that the secular institutions themselves have failed to deliver on their promises or are too costly to maintain. What is happening in post-Soviet Russia is thus part of a more general shift of transformational hopes toward religious institutions after the end of the Cold War, as socialism is perceived to have failed and secularist welfare states are on the retreat in many parts of the world.

If religious life proves to be one of the areas where Soviet methodical training finds a ready application, the reason is thus neither that Soviet culture was just religion in disguise, nor that secular modernity has destroyed a previously existing authentic religiosity. As the reflections of Soviet atheists on their work teach us, religious and secular forms do not simply replace and supersede one another, nor do they exist in incommensurable universes. Max Weber's term *elective affinity* most effectively highlights the constant back-and-forth between the dynamics of secularization and theologization.

Although it is often used to mean little more than a vague resemblance whose causes are unknown, elective affinity has a more strictly defined meaning in the source from which Weber borrowed it, Johann Wolfgang von Goethe's novel of the same title. Goethe chose his title with reference to eighteenth-century chemistry, where an elective affinity meant an inherent attraction between chemical elements that forces them to leave their existing association and reamalgamate with another element. The new amalgamation then seems completely natural and indivisible, brought together "as if by higher providence" (Goethe 1956 [1809]: 37; see also Adler 1987).

When Weber uses the term to describe the relationship between religious practice and economic development in *The Protestant Ethic*, he introduces it as an alternative to Marxist or idealist causal explanations in which one side precedes and lays the foundation for the other. He also emphasizes that it is a provisional label that awaits the detailed historical analysis that follows (Weber 1922: 85). In an investigation of Weber's use of the concept, the sociologist Michael Löwy concludes that at its strongest, elective affinity means an ongoing relationship of "attraction and mutual influence" between two cultural forms "on the basis of certain significant analogies, inherent or meaningful affinities" (Löwy 2004: 100).

As a description of how things come to resemble each other over time without ever being essentially the same, elective affinity offers an attractive third option to the alternatives of either equating the sacred and the secular or seeing them as fundamentally opposed to each other. If didactic elements of religious and secular traditions stand in a relationship of elective affinity, this means that resemblances between them unfold in the course of a sometimes shared, sometimes separate history. Mutual influences may be so manifold that the causal question of what came first or which side is a reflection of the other is less important than insights into the shifting balance of power between secular and religious institutions and the contribution of each side to helping people live through wider historical changes. If the same people once found empowerment through participation in the didactic networks of Soviet culture, but now claim that only God can grant this sense of expanding horizons, a quite radical shift of sociopolitical context is accompanied by a reorientation of hope.

With its roots in alchemistic musings about the mysterious transformative possibilities of inorganic matter, elective affinity presents a riddle more than an answer. Part of this riddle is a question that concerns atheist and postsecular methodicians alike: the scope of human freedom and loyalty in times of transformation. The characters in Goethe's novel—two couples whose romantic attractions switch in the course of the narrative—grapple with this question when they debate whether the laws of irresistible affinity apply only to inanimate matter, or to human relationships as well. For the methodicians in charge of catching the attention of others in order to make them affirm or switch allegiances, the boundaries between persuasion and manipulation were also points of reflection and mutual critique. In religious and secular contexts, the ethics of promoting social change were intricately bound up with competing views of human autonomy and dependence.

Researching Controversial Convictions

This book is based on a total of almost two years of residence in Marij El, first as an instructor of German at Mari State University in 2000–2001, then as a researcher returning for month-long visits in 2003 and 2008 and a year-long stay in 2005–2006. Though quite centrally located by Russian standards—just one night's train ride away from Moscow—Marij El is a small republic in terms of both size and population. In an area approximately a hundred miles across from west to east and north to south, the

2002 census of the Russian Federation counted 730,000 people, more than one-third of them living in the capital city, Joshkar-Ola. Forty-two percent of the total population declared themselves to be Mari, a nationality recognized as indigenous to the area and historically speaking a Finno-Ugric language, although many urban families switched to using Russian over the decades of Soviet rule. Six percent were Tatars, the Turkic-speaking titular nationality of neighboring Tatarstan, while the remaining half consisted mainly of Russians, Ukrainians, and other eastern Slavs (Lalukka 1997; Rossiiskaia Federatsiia 2004: 73).

Lacking oil and other natural resources, Marij El is one of the poorest areas of the Russian Federation, with high unemployment since the arms factories that formed the backbone of the Soviet era economy ceased production in the early 1990s. Nonetheless, there are several barriers to migration that keep people in the republic. Brezhnev era policies had encouraged provincial youth to study in their ethnic republics and return to their home towns and villages afterward. In the post-Soviet period, the lack of effective housing and labor markets still made it difficult to move between cities in Russia for anything but seasonal, low-skill employment (White 2000). With the exception of some army personnel and evangelical missionaries, many of the members of the provincial intelligentsia who made up the main pool of atheist and religious activists had spent most of their lives in the republic.

In this environment, the former allegiances of many contemporary religious activists were common knowledge. Sociological surveys show that the number of declared religious believers in the republic rose from 13.5 percent in 1985 to 43 percent in 1994 and 68.2 percent in 2004, while declared atheists decreased from 32.2 percent in 1985 (to which can be added the 37.8 percent of respondents who declared themselves to be indifferent toward religion) to 18.4 percent in 1994 and 16.6 percent in 2004 (Shabykov et al. 2005: 10, 346; Solov'ev 1987: 118).[10] While the figures for both the Soviet and post-Soviet eras say little about actual convictions or observances, they do indicate that a good number of people who formerly sought to project an atheist persona now present themselves as religious. The few remaining avowed atheists were quick to interpret such turns as opportunism, making fun of people who used to predict the imminent demise of religion and now helped to organize theological conferences.

For those people who did make the switch to religious observance, choosing a particular denomination presented another point of division. For example, two middle-aged men had attended the same elite school for Mari students and later pursued careers in Soviet education and youth work. Now, one was a Lutheran deacon, the other trained catechists for the Orthodox diocese, and each suspected the other of wanting nothing but money and power.

Indeed, in postsecular Russia the choice of religious affiliation is often more politically sensitive than the decision whether or not to be a believer. In surveys, people can easily deny any religious belief and still claim to be Orthodox, Muslim, or Buddhist, depending on the religion commonly associated with their ethnicity (Filatov and Lunkin 2006). But trends that challenge the equation between ethnicity and religion meet with suspicion. The preamble to Russia's 1997 Law on Freedom of Conscience and Religious Associations infamously singles out Christianity, Islam, Buddhism, Judaism, "and other religions" as "an integral part of the historical patrimony of the peoples of Russia." Apparently to safeguard this patrimony, the body of the text distinguishes between religious *groups* and religious *organizations*. Only the latter have the right to be a legal person, own property, maintain educational institutions, and issue invitations to foreign nationals for teaching or missionary work. In order to register as a religious organization, a religious group of at least ten citizens has to demonstrate that it either has existed locally for at least fifteen years, or is part of a centralized, Russia-wide denomination. Since its adoption by the Russian parliament, this law has drawn much criticism from international Protestant organizations that see it as an attempt to shelter the Orthodox Church and other historically established confessions from competition (Elliott and Corrado 1999; Gunn 1999; Shterin and Richardson 1998).

In Marij El, similar ideals of a correspondence between religion and ethnicity coexist uneasily with historical reality. The government of the republic recognizes three "traditional religions"—Russian Orthodoxy, Mari Paganism, and Sunni Islam—which correspond to the main ethnic groups of the republic. At public events and special sessions of parliament, the archbishop, the mufti, and the Chimarij[11] high priest (a position created in the 1990s specifically for this purpose) sit together to represent a tradition of tolerance and peaceful coexistence. These three denominations are also the only ones to sit on the republic's advisory council on religious affairs. The argument that every ethnic group should pray in its own way predates the Soviet period; it can be found in the petitions of nineteenth-century Mari and Udmurt villagers asking for permission to leave the Orthodox Church and return to the sacrificial rituals of their ancestors (Werth 2001). But the present practice of recognizing selected religions as attributes of ethnic groups also recalls Soviet strategies of simultaneously celebrating and neutralizing ethnic diversity (Khalid 2007; Luehrmann 2005; Pelkmans 2006). Forms of religiosity that fit into this ideal order of ethnic coexistence are no longer denounced as antisocial, but officials and citizens still express concern over the disruptive potential of religious revival. Post-Soviet religious policy thus to some degree echoes the ambivalence of Soviet understandings of religion: on the one hand, it recognizes and seeks to exploit the potential of religious ritual to strengthen human solidarity; on the other hand, it remains wary of religious groups that seem to promote alternative social orders.

Challenges to the equation of religion and ethnicity are manifold: for example, many Mari families have included baptized Christians for generations, and most Russian villages of the republic were first established by Christian dissenters known as Old Believers (Iarygin 2004: 39–40; Werth 2002: 110–111). In the wake of the relocations of the Second World War, Protestant communities, including Baptists, Seventh-day Adventists, Pentecostals, and, since the 1990s, Lutherans and neo-Charismatics, further added to the mix. All of these groups were able to register under the 1997 law, while the Pagan organization Oshmarij-Chimarij was denied registration because there had been no registered Soviet era Chimarij organization with which it might claim continuity. But the boost from American and Finnish missions that the Protestant congregations received in the early 1990s had left them with the image of being "foreign" churches, although many of them met in the most familiar spaces—houses of culture—and were making efforts to indigenize their leadership. In a context where the public role of religious diversity was still uncertain, a research project that took me back and forth between people of various religious and nonreligious persuasions struck at the heart of my interlocutors' own worries.

One of the features that united different denominations was that the spatial dynamics of religious life bore palpable traces of Soviet didactic networks. Basing myself in Joshkar-Ola, I was close to the archives as well as to most formalized endeavors of religious teaching. With the exception of the Lutherans and one Pentecostal group that conducted Mari-language rural missions, most Protestant congregations were limited to the capital city, where each had between 50 and 250 members. In the evenings and on weekends, when the archives were closed, I attended services and leadership trainings and interviewed clergy and lay leaders at as many congregations as I could keep regular contact with, in particular the largest of the three Baptist groups; the Lutheran, Mari-language Pentecostal, and Charismatic churches; and the Orthodox cathedral. The Orthodox diocese of Joshkar-Ola and Marij El (created as an offshoot of the Kazan' diocese in 1993) operated a cultural and training center offering child care, courses for medically trained "Sisters of Mercy," and Bible study led by the archbishop. Chimarij activists had a more tenuous foothold in the capital through the Mari Cultural Center, housed at the culture palace of the Road Construction Authority.

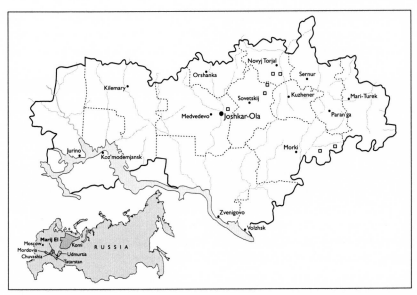

The Republic of Marij El within the Russian Federation, with the Volga River to the south. The named towns are district centers; the squares indicate villages where the author visited Chimarij ceremonies. [Map by Bill Nelson]

Most of their worship activities happened in groves of oak, birch, and fir near villages throughout the republic, where priests (known as *onaeng* in Mari or by the Tatar loanword *kart,* "old man") led prayers and sacrificial feasts at important points in the agricultural year. Orthodox churches were also spread throughout the republic, as were sacred springs visited by people of all religions, leading to a lively traffic in city people traveling in search of divine help or the advice of respected clerics.

Following invitations from students, schoolteachers, or religious activists whom I met in Joshkar-Ola, I established connections with several villages in the eastern and southeastern districts of the republic, paying repeated visits for Chimarij ceremonies or Orthodox holidays. While not allowing for the deeper insights that longer stays in one village would have provided, this approach helped me see the role of rural sites in the wider networks of didacticized religion, as organizers traveled from Joshkar-Ola to rural Marij El, but also exchanged visits and materials with more remote centers in Moscow, Ukraine, Finland, or the United States.

When I announced my interest in atheism and religion, the first question was usually: "And what is your faith?" My response, that I was a Lutheran from Germany, made sense to people in terms of the dominant equation between ethnicity and religion, and gave me a place of more or less peripheral participation in the religious observances I witnessed. Nonetheless, my project also raised concerns. Christians of all denominations were often shocked that I attended Mari ceremonies and ate sacrificial meat; Orthodox clergy and laypeople wondered if I were an American spy; the mufti seemed worried that I might be on the lookout for terrorists in his mosque; and old Mari women asked when I would start behaving as a proper ethnographer and record a specific genre of tales or songs.

Exhausting as it sometimes was to anticipate and conform to expectations of dress, behavior, and speech in the different religious and secular contexts, I never regretted the decision to focus on the Mari republic as a region, rather than on a particular religious community. While helping to see secularism as a strategy for managing religious diversity, an inter-confessional view of the Volga region also offers a corrective to studies of Soviet and post-Soviet religious policies that treat "religious pluralism" and "religious freedom" as new challenges that have arisen primarily in relation to Protestant groups (Bourdeaux 1995; P. Froese 2008; Uzzell 1997). Reminding me that Soviet atheists faced not generic religiosity, but long-established patterns of religious coexistence, research across denominational boundaries uncovered a dual meaning of affinity: between religions as well as across secular-religious divides, people and approaches tended to resemble one another more than most activists liked to admit. Rather than setting up contrasts between "religious" and "secular" ways of learning or being, the challenge of studying secularism in a multireligious setting is to do justice to the ways in which spheres of life that seem separate and mutually exclusive are also so intertwined that one would not exist without the other.

Starting from this double meaning of affinity as a mode of regional coexistence between neighbors *and* a historical relationship between secular and religious spheres, this book seeks to uncover the aims of Soviet secularism and its afterlife in the post-Soviet religious landscape. The two chapters of the first part, "Affinities," set the stage by introducing the dual challenge of secularist interventions in this multireligious periphery: reordering patterns of neighborly coexistence and mobilizing participants into didactic networks. Part 2, "Promises," focuses on the methods of standardized change that unite such networks across secular and religious spheres. Part 3, "Fissures," explores the tensions between didactic hopes, the realities of late Soviet society, and the techniques of human transformation offered by religious traditions. In part 4, "Rhythms," the single chapter brings the interweaving of secular and religious spheres back to the level of individual lives, discussing the movement between human and more-than-human aspirations in the biographies of methodicians.

In looking at Soviet atheism and post-Soviet religion through the lens of didactic methods, I may seem to impose a secular paradigm on religious life. Certainly the search for affinities across Soviet secular and post-Soviet religious spheres has led me to concentrate on practices that were central to the Knowledge Society and reform-oriented religious groups, while they remained more marginal to rural religiosity, for example. But pressures to theologize attention and persuasion affect all groups as they navigate Soviet era ideas about culture and religion, and the post-Soviet hopes and needs of their constituencies. My aim is to suggest a secularist history for these pressures, in order to show that atheist critiques of religion do not always miss their marks, but also risk shaping their adversary in their own image. Events designed to catch public attention by virtue of being interesting, entertaining, and useful are commonplace in the experience of North American readers, including those who practice a religion. The crisscrossing atheist-religious debates described in this book extol the virtues, but also count the costs, of staking future hopes on the promises of didactic methods.

I. Affinities

На горе стоит береза,
под горою стоит дуб.
Раньше мы ходили в церковь
А теперь мы ходим в клуб.

On the hilltop stands a birch tree,
At the bottom stands an oak.
We used to go to church
But now we go to the club.

—*Chastushka* from "Evening of Miracles without Miracles," April 1972

1

Neighbors and Comrades: Secularizing the Mari Country

If it seemed that atheist methodicians had no qualms about interfering in the private lives of citizens to eradicate religious attachments, they did so in the name of a particular vision of public social relations. Comparable to secularist critics elsewhere, the builders of Soviet socialism often blamed religion for upholding the distinctions of ethnicity, gender, age, and locality that threatened to hamper a vision of statewide solidarity.[1] Like other modernizers, Soviet activists failed to fully grasp the complexity of the social relations they set out to transform. But their critique of religion as a force of strife and division also emerged out of encounters between ideological expectations and this on-the-ground complexity, creating a set of constraints that remain effective in post-Soviet religious policy.

Particularly in multireligious regions such as the Middle Volga, atheist activists confronted religious solidarity and religious fragmentation as part of the forces shaping a tangle of neighborly relations among households and between villages. These relations ranged from cooperation to distrust or indifference, but were always at odds with the universal solidarity that Soviet modernization called for. The assumption that penetrating and transforming this tangle necessarily involved anti-religious struggle owed much of its persistence to the unassailable status of the writings of Marx and Engels, including their critiques of religion's role in obscuring social relations and preserving patriarchal power.[2] But Soviet atheist scholarship also elaborated its own changing answers to the question of where exactly the harm of religion lay, answers which over time came to home in on religion's potential to strengthen social boundaries and increase individual isolation. These ideas evolved in part out of encounters with historical patterns of neighborliness that ordered the coexistence between social groups at a local level—patterns that, like religion itself, seemed at once too fragmenting and too solid for the Soviet state to tolerate.

By the term *neighborliness,* I am referring to the ambivalent set of relations between households and villages that evolved in this region, whose inhabitants had lived with religious and linguistic diversity for centuries and where religious affiliation had served as a marker for legal and political distinctions up until the Bolshevik Revolution. Comparable to the Muslims, Christians, and Jews of Ottoman Salonica/Thessaloniki described by Mark Mazower (2004), villagers in the Volga region, as elsewhere in the Russian Empire, lived in a world that was simultaneously segregated by religious and linguistic boundaries and characterized by intense connections across these "painfully proximate borders" (Grant 2009: xv). In this contested zone where Finno-Ugric populations had alternately paid tribute to the Tatar Khans of Kazan' and to the Muscovite princes and tsars, largely monoreligious and monoethnic villages often lay in close proximity to other such villages whose inhabitants spoke a different language, prayed to different gods according to different calendars, ate different food, and wore different clothes. Neighbors were aware of one another's practices and recognized affinities with their own, as is attested by a wealth of linguistic, ritual, and technological parallelisms, as well as by shared uses of religious sites.[3]

More precisely than the notoriously broad term *syncretism* (Stewart and Shaw 1994), the idea of recognized affinities among neighbors captures a situation where, although fusion and mutual inspiration does occur, residents still consider different practices appropriate for different people. In the Volga region, a person whose family prayed in a sacred grove would not normally go to the mosque of the neighboring village, but would recognize activities in both places as "praying." Because of their history of partial conversion before the revolution and the uneven availability of ritual specialists in the post-Soviet era, Mari families did often worship alternately in sacred groves and in Orthodox churches, but distinguished between the offerings appropriate to each site (Luehrmann 2010; Popov 1987). Rather than creating an unproblematic mixture of religious traditions, people maintained a form of separation-in-proximity that recalls other parts of the world with histories of incorporation into multireligious empires, such as the Balkans and North India (Bowman 2010; Hayden 2002; van der Veer 1992).

Against this background, the project of Soviet secularization involved the attempt to replace the ambivalent play of intimacy and distance involved in neighborly relations (Sorabji 2008; Žižek, Santner, and Reinhard 2005) with a more predictable, transparent, and universal allegiance to an imagined community centered on Moscow and propelled forward by the plans of the Communist Party (cf. Anderson 1983). To adopt a pair of terms from Kenneth Reinhard (2005), the Soviet struggle against religion was part of wider efforts to replace a "political theology of the neighbor" with a "political theology of the sovereign," in which the rules and maxims of political life received their meaning in relation to a single master signifier—the interest of the Soviet toilers as articulated by the party. Never quite resolved, this struggle between alternative points of reference continues to shape the terms in which local residents and politicians discuss the place of religion in community life after the end of the socialist project.

Religion and Neighborliness in Post-Soviet Marij El

In the summer of 2005, a fledgling Lutheran congregation proposed to build a church in the Mari village of Ljupersola in the Sovetskij district, a thirty-minute bus ride from Joshkar-Ola. Lutheranism had made its first converts in Marij El in 1993, brought by a Finnish-Estonian couple working through the Saint Petersburg–based Evangelical Lutheran Church of Ingria. Whereas the original congregation in Joshkar-Ola was largely Russian-speaking, a Mari writer and deacon set out to conduct Mari-language services in Ljupersola, a village of 450 people where he had contacts in the collective farm administration. After several years of weekly visits during which the living room of a Brezhnev era concrete duplex served as a makeshift place of worship, a group of approximately fifty members successfully registered as a religious organization with the district administration in the spring of 2005. Having acquired a plot of land on the village's main street and secured promises from Finnish volunteers to help build a wooden church, the congregation applied for a building permit. In late August, the district administration convened a village assembly without publicly announcing the agenda. Two Orthodox priests had been invited; Lutheran clergy were only present because they had heard about the meeting from a sympathetic employee of the village administration. Addressing the assembly in Russian, the head of the district administration (a Mari) announced that the purpose of the meeting was to vote on the building application, and he immediately launched into a list of concerns:

> In connection with this question of construction, it seems to me that today, probably, the fate of your village is being decided, and of your population, of our Mari population most of all. I briefly made myself familiar with the beginning of this movement, this Lutheran [movement], yes? The recruitment of people [*Vovlechenie ljudej*]. They started very small. They helped with clothing, yes, somewhere perhaps with food provisions, somewhere still other things. Here, it seems to me, our poverty was played on. Unfortunately, this is how it is today, there's no denying it. And, after all, this isn't done for nothing [*ne prosto tak*], I ask that all understand that. Behind all this hides some sort of objective, right? Let's say, these Finns help today to do this, they're not

doing it for nothing. It seems to me, let them do this work in their own country, everything is permitted over there, they live in prosperity there, let them do their work there.[4]

The district head was making the connection between the religious choice of some villagers and the fate of "our Mari population" by identifying Lutheranism as a foreign movement, brought by Finns with suspicious motives. Having acknowledged the material attractions of foreign missions, he went on to make a plea for the region's spiritual self-sufficiency:

We have here the Orthodox Church, that is, religion, and also our traditional religion, the Pagan religion, and I think that this is exactly the religion which, probably, we have and should have. This movement, it probably has a goal, it seems to me, a bad one. To destroy the foundation of Russia, as a whole. Concretely, it seems to me that in Marij El they are doing this. After all, going over to a different faith [vera], it seems to me that grown-up people who went over to a different faith, after all, probably if a person accepted a faith once, probably in betraying his faith, switching to another, in the interest of some goal, it seems to me that this is no longer the faith to which he is, let's say, faithful [veren]. That is, he can switch again. When a better offer comes along, why not switch again.

These rhetorical links between faithfulness to one's religion and faithfulness to one's country will seem familiar to students of post-Soviet religious politics, as will the general suspicion of the motives of foreign missionaries. Like the 1997 law that distinguishes between religions with demonstrated historical roots in Russia and those that have none, this provincial official's arguments refer to the broader ideal of a correspondence between religious adherence and ethnic identity. The challenge presented by the evangelical Protestant organizations that have become increasingly active in Russia since perestroika (many of them at least initially supported by Western funds and/ or personnel) is in the way they missionize across ethnic lines, giving no credence to religious affiliations that are not based on conscious individual commitment (Pelkmans 2009; Wanner 2007).

"You don't go to a strange monastery with your own rule," said an official in charge of religious affairs in the presidential administration of Marij El, quoting a Russian proverb to argue that Protestant missionaries deserve respect for their faith, but should not propagate it among people to whom it is historically alien.[5] This self-identified Chimarij woman also thought that Protestant converts must be either very greedy or very gullible, echoing suspicions elsewhere in the world where evangelical Protestantism is making inroads against religious groups with expectations of hereditary membership (D. Martin 1990, 2002).

Several authors have argued that assumptions about religion as a corollary of ethnicity solidified during the Soviet era, when ethnicity gained primacy as a public form of collective identification, codified by census lists of officially recognized nationalities and an obligatory entry in every citizen's passport (Dragadze 1993; Khalid 2007; Pelkmans 2006; Urazmanova 2009). The idea that Finns are out to destroy the foundations of Russia also suggests the longevity of Cold War distinctions between friend and enemy. On the level of federal law and its regional applications, post-Soviet religious policy thus seems to follow the logic that cultural theorist Kenneth Reinhard calls "the political theology of the sovereign." In his critical dialogue with Carl Schmitt's ideas, the sovereign stands for Schmitt's claim that all politics begins with a distinction between friend and enemy. The figure of the neighbor, by contrast, calls this distinction into question, because it "materializes the uncertain division between the friend/family/self and the enemy/stranger/other" (Reinhard 2005: 18; cf. Schmitt 2002 [1932]).

To return to a more Weberian terminology, the political challenge of neighborliness lies in working with the interplay of intimacy and alterity that constitutes elective affinity, thereby resisting the urge to disambiguate it into clear divisions between those who are part of a social covenant and those who stand outside. Soviet citizens, by contrast, were supposed to relate with unquestioned solidarity to those within the state, and with unmitigated hostility to the "enemies of the people" or Cold War adversaries. When atheists criticized religion for upholding the wrong social divisions, this was part of a larger discomfort with the shifting scales of neighborly political allegiances, which they sought to replace with a state-centered vision of "closed sovereignty" (Grant 2009; see also Yang 2004). But while some theorists of secularism have argued that the concern with religion as a divisive force was an outgrowth of the interdenominational warfare that shook early modern Western Europe (Asad 2003: 174; Asad 2006; Madan 1998), there seems to be more going on here than an uncritical transfer of Western historical narratives. In the way villagers and local politicians deal with ambiguous religious affiliations in post-Soviet Marij El, after decades of Soviet attempts to impose their own "political theology," we see the enduring problems created by neighborly relations for Moscow-centric notions of the Russian nation. Having seen how the possibilities and limitations of neighborliness in the Volga region remain connected to religious diversity, it will be easier to understand the struggles of earlier generations of atheists.

It is certainly possible to describe federal religious policy under the presidencies of Boris Yeltsin and Vladimir Putin as a politics of sovereign distinctions between those who belong and those who do not. The law of 1997, which reserved the status of registered religious organization to those who could demonstrate a fifteen-year presence in Russia, came during a decade of nods to the cultural significance of the Russian Orthodox Church, even as some of the church's larger political ambitions remained unrealized. There was no blanket return of church property, and Orthodox religious instruction in schools remained limited to regional experiments, but Patriarch Aleksij II (Ridiger, 1990–2008) was treated as an authority on issues of public morality and Russia's historical identity (Garrard and Garrard 2008; Papkova 2007).

This moral and cultural weight could also be felt in Marij El, where the "historical reconstruction" of the capital often seemed synonymous with the building of Orthodox churches, and Orthodox clergy were the only religious specialists to have regular access to army barracks and prisons. But nationwide trends were filtered through regional understandings of religious diversity as a historical reality, sometimes producing unexpected results. The local effects of the 1997 law are one example. While registration was granted to all Protestant groups who applied, Chimarij were unable to document an institutionalized existence that went back to the period before perestroika, since their outdoor rituals were counter to Soviet law. Bound to federal legislation, the republic's administration denied registration, but sacrificial ceremonies continued without hindrance in many parts of the republic. Even though there is a Russia-wide discourse about the special legitimacy of "traditional" religions, different groups can be included under that umbrella in different places.[6]

In the same vein, national boundaries were not necessarily foremost on people's minds when they drew lines of inclusion and exclusion. According to the Lutheran deacon, the statement that made the deepest impression on those listening to the district head's speech at the Ljupersola meeting was the closing warning that Lutheran converts would not be buried in the village graveyard:

> Even if let's say the association [obshchestvo] exists here now, which, well, believes—we should not blame the person, let's say he likes it, and he doesn't understand maybe all of this, well, this person can't even be buried in our graveyard, do you understand? Simply stated, this is already a different faith, and they must have a different graveyard and all the rest. For this reason I am simply asking all of you to make the right decision. We cannot command, insist on something; each one must approach this matter conscientiously.

As the deacon recalled, the district head previously had made a similar statement on local radio, and it had caused great fear among the members of the congregation, many of whom were elderly, so that death and burial were part of their not-so-distant future. Whether made in good faith or as a deliberate misrepresentation, the threat had no backing in Russian law, which treats public graveyards as secular spaces to which no religious organization can grant or limit access. But because it reveals much about the scale of communal life at which political rhetoric about religion acquires emotional force, the claim that a Lutheran convert would forfeit the right to be buried in the village graveyard is worth dwelling on for a moment.

Though contradicting the law, the threat had some degree of resonance with local custom, giving it a ring of possibility. Some villages in the republic did have separate graveyards exclusively for Chimarij or Muslims, although most graveyards seemed to incorporate a variety of religious and secular traditions. In all the regular village graveyards I visited, Christian crosses stood interspersed with the wooden slabs or poles which marked Chimarij graves and the metal cones with red stars on top which were popularized during the Soviet era as atheist burial markers. In settlements with mixed Mari-Russian-Tatar populations, there was often a corner reserved for Tatars, with headstones carved in Arabic script.

In the face of these alternatives, it was definitely an exaggeration that only a new graveyard could accommodate the new addition to the religious mix. And later that same month, I was present at the burial of a Lutheran woman in Ljupersola's village graveyard. But the evocation of graveyards must have reminded listeners that the place where a family buries its dead forges a tangible connection to other families, shaping communal obligations of care and commemoration. For example, whole villages went out on certain days of the year for commemorative feasts at their relatives' graves (Bouchard 2004). Being buried in the village graveyard meant being part of an ongoing ritual connection between living and deceased villagers. Tatar families in Mari villages might not participate in these feasts, but they were known to have their own cycles of commemorating the dead (Urazmanova 2009: 19).[7] Lutheranism, as two villagers who spoke at the meeting pointed out, remained largely unknown, making it hard to gauge what the consequences of its arrival would be.

Whether or not villagers knew this, Protestants in Marij El did strongly oppose the local ways of commemorating the dead. In his sermon at the old woman's funeral a few weeks later, the deacon made the common Protestant reference to the parable of the rich man and poor Lazarus (Luke 16:19–31), where the rich man's pleas for relief from his pains after death are countered by father Abraham's answer that he was receiving his reward for the wealth he had selfishly enjoyed during his lifetime. The deacon interpreted this to mean that nothing could be done to change God's judgment on the dead, so the living should focus on following the commandments and ensuring their own salvation rather than trying to ritually intervene on behalf of a deceased person.[8]

Given the importance of burial places for community life, and the fact that it is obvious from the district head's speech that he was not used to making public statements on religious matters,[9] it seems quite possible that his threat that there would have to be a separate Lutheran graveyard was not a deliberate lie. Rather, it may have been an attempt to impress on converts the distance they were putting between themselves and the village community, and to frighten them out of persisting in this choice.

Collusive Unity

The warning about graveyards shows that village life in the republic can accommodate a degree of religious diversity, but this accommodation depends on each religious group's willingness to engage in mutually comprehensible practices. Residents often pointed with pride to their republic's tradition of interreligious neighborliness—for instance, the highest official in charge of religious affairs pointed out that the construction of the Orthodox church in the district center of Medvedevo was made possible by the support of that district's head of administration, who was a Tatar Muslim. Neighborliness involved an inclusive blurring of distinctions in some situations and the insistence on rigid boundaries in others, both of which were obvious in the way speakers at the meeting addressed the relationship between religious adherence and community affiliation. Many were quite vague in identifying legitimate religious faiths and scales of communal loyalty, while casting the arrival of a religious group from Finland as something unheard of. Most crucially, references to the ancestral faith of the village were usually undetermined as to what exactly that faith was, even as all speakers agreed that it needed to be preserved. Another speaker from the district administration addressed the assembly in Mari:

> You have been living in this land for a long time, and before you, your fathers and grandfathers, mothers and grandmothers lived in this land. Every one of them had his own place in this world, and in the other world everyone will also find his own place.[10] Everyone had his own faith, everyone believed in one God. I ask you, in the future too, to maintain the connection with your own faith, the faith

of your fathers, mothers, and grandfathers. You should not wander around here and there.

He was saddened, he added, to hear that there were now "two faiths" among the villagers, and quarrels between them. The district head had already made a slide from mentioning two religions—Orthodox Christianity and Chimarij Paganism—to saying that there was one religion "we have and should have." This speaker assumed only a single "faith of your fathers, mothers, and grandfathers," speaking as if only the advent of Lutheranism had led to a multireligious situation in the village.

This ambiguity had something to do with the specific situation in this district, an area where the influence of the Russian Orthodox Church had been relatively strong since the nineteenth century and where Chimarij ritual activity was weaker than in more remote parts of the republic. In spite of this, there were no prerevolutionary movements here that embraced Christianity as part of a Mari identity, as was the case on the right bank of the Volga (Popov 1987; Werth 2002: 200–222). In the early twenty-first century, Ljupersola had a sacred grove that was remembered and avoided as a past site of Chimarij ceremonies, although members of the younger generation had no memory of ritual activity there. The village was also located a mere half hour by bus from the Russian Orthodox church of Semënovka, one of the few churches in the republic to remain open throughout the Soviet period (with a short interruption between 1940 and 1944). As one of the speakers at the assembly pointed out, many of those who were now converting to Lutheranism had originally been baptized there. The monastery of Ezhovo, which had been closed during the Soviet era, but whose healing spring had remained a pilgrimage site, was even closer. Some villagers visited these Orthodox holy sites occasionally, for rituals addressing specific life events (baptisms, weddings, funerals) or illnesses. Sporadic religious activity at circumscribed sacred sites thus united the forms of worship familiar to villagers. Adding to the Lutherans' transnational proselytizing efforts and rejection of commemorative rituals, their insistence on holding weekly services right in the village was another feature that set Lutherans apart from the range of recognized religious practices.

By maintaining ambiguity about "the ancestral faith of the village," speakers deemphasized differences between Orthodox and Chimarij sympathies while stressing the outsider status of Lutheranism. The district head seemed to give preference to Paganism by calling it "our traditional religion," and another speaker from outside the village described the religion of their ancestors as *toshto mari jumyn jüla*, "the old Mari god customs," using the Mari-language neologism for "religion" favored by High Priest Tanygin and other activists working for a republic-wide Chimarij revival. A villager, making the same case for religious unity, explicitly named Orthodox Christianity as the religion of the village. As with other speakers, treating the religious unity of the village as a given also made it easier for him to deemphasize differences between the situation of Ljupersola and that of Russia as a whole. Participants often left open whether the community threatened by the Lutheran presence was the village or the nation.

Switching back and forth between Russian and Mari (represented by italics in the quote), this villager started out on the national level: "V tom-to i delo, chto my v Rossii *ilena*, a oni zhivut v Finljandii. *Tyge* prosto zhe *iktezhe ushanen ona kert*" ("The thing is, we *live* in Russia, and they live in Finland. *So* simply *for this reason we cannot unite*"). Before switching into pure Russian for an interpretation of world politics, the man used the combined resources of Mari and Russian grammar to underscore the threat of the "global plan" to destroy religious unity:

> *Tide* global'nyj plan, chtoby *Rossijym* razrushit' *pytarash*. . . . Ved' u nikh tam nichego netu, eto u nas v Rossii tak; Sibir' eshche bogataja u nas, neft', gaz, vse, vse est', u nikh netu vot, i idet bor'ba za eto, eta problema mirovaja problema, ne nasha! Nas tuda prosto podtalkivajut. Vot tak, tovarishchi. Tak chto, u nas, my odna vera, da, nu eto pravoslavie, znachit, dolzhny byt' vsegda. Znachit, otdelis', i dolzhen verit' etoj veroj. U nas zdes' dve very ne dolzhno byt' i ne mozhet byt'.

> Th*is* is a global plan to destroy *Russia completely*. . . . After all they don't have anything over there, it is here in Russia; our Siberia is still wealthy, oil, gas, everything, everything is there, and they don't have it, and there is a struggle going on over it, this problem is a worldwide problem, not ours! We are just being pushed into it. This is how it is, comrades. So that here, we are one faith, yes, well that is Orthodoxy, so this means that is what we should always be. This means, if you separate yourself off, you have to believe according to that faith. Here among us there must not be two faiths and cannot be.

The Russian-Mari compound "razrushit' *pytarash*," which I translate as "to destroy completely," gives the neighborly affinities on the Middle Volga a linguistic face. Russian, like many Slavic languages, has a system of verb aspects where most actions can be expressed by a perfective or imperfective form, emphasizing either the result of an action or its ongoing nature. *Razrushit'* (to destroy) is the perfective form, corresponding to the imperfective *razrushat'*. The Finno-Ugric languages of the Volga region lack such an aspect system and, more generally, the mechanisms for modifying verbs with prefixes and suffixes that constitute an important part of Russian morphology. Instead, they contain a number of verbs that can double as modal verbs. Combinations between modal and full verbs take on some of the functions of Russian aspects. The Mari verb *pytarash,* meaning "to finish, to end, to eliminate," can be combined with the gerund of another verb to give the action the nuance of completeness and fulfillment, comparable to the perfective aspect in Russian. For example, *tülash* means "to pay," *tülen pytarash* "to pay off completely, to settle a debt." The form "razrushit' *pytarash*" combines Russian and Mari ways of constructing a perfective aspect (the Russian verb with a perfective ending and the Mari modal verb). In this man's speech, "the mutual and internalized equivalence of value" (Jakobson and Pomorska 1983 [1980]: 86) between a regional and a national language corresponded to equivalences between different scales of communal identification. His repeated use of *u nas* (Russian for "here among us") sometimes clearly stood for Russia as a whole, sometimes ambiguously either for the village or for Russia. The opposing *u nikh* ("among those people there") was more clearly located outside of Russian national borders, in Finland or in a generalized abroad. In the political rhetoric of neighborliness, internalized equivalences found their limit in internalized incommensurabilities.[11]

The Russian address "comrades" (*tovarishchi*) also helped the speaker align his village audience with a Russia-wide public. In post-Soviet Marij El, *tovarishchi* was a common form of address in all manner of official speeches, without connoting particular communist sympathies or nostalgia for the Soviet Union. For addressing an audience of Mari speakers, however, *tovarishchi* and its translation, *joltash-vlak* (lit. "friends"), competed with the pair *rodo-tukym, poshkudo-vlak* (Mari: "relatives, neighbors"), a greeting from village rituals that seemed the preferred choice for political figures who wanted to appeal explicitly to an ethnic Mari community. Compared to the more locally and personally specific "relatives and neighbors," addressing a Mari audience in Russian and as "comrades" created an opening to larger scales of community, be they the worldwide proletariat or the Russian nation.

There was certainly room for friction between all these levels, and the meeting itself was an example of the kinds of manipulation of democratic procedure which many of my interlocutors in Marij El routinely expected of politicians. But political differences aside, all speakers colluded in maintaining ambiguities in some areas while making clear distinctions in others. The boundaries between Orthodoxy and Paganism were left unclear, while both stood in opposition to Lutheranism. Likewise, there was a sliding scale of loyalties between the village and the nation, and between Mari and Russian speech communities, whereas international aid was cast as definitely coming from hostile, greedy outsiders.

When I say that participants in the meeting colluded, I do not mean that they were intentionally covering up preexisting religious and political differences. Rather, the term *collusion* is intended to draw attention to the rhetorically produced and potentially fragile nature of such unity. As linguistic anthropologists have understood it, collusion means the collaboration of interlocutors in a given social interaction, which they are "holding together for each other" through a "marriage of indefiniteness and precision in utterance interpretation" (McDermott and Tylbor 1995: 219–220). At this meeting, district administrators and residents colluded in constructing indisputable connections between an unspecified ancestral faith and local, district-level, and national solidarity. But the situation might have been different if the villagers had been asked to contribute to the financing of a Russian Orthodox Church in the district center. It is this fragility of collusive links that made rural neighborliness seem suspicious to successive Soviet and post-Soviet administrators interested in stable political loyalties.

Religious Friction

Even during the assembly, the fragile nature of collusion emerged. What was at play there was not a common front of Russian nationalism against the religious diversity coming from abroad. Subtle differences between speakers pointed to the fissures between religious and communal loyalties. The contributions of the two Orthodox priests at the meeting, for instance, showed the strategic importance that the ambiguity of the "one faith" has for the church, but also its reluctance to participate in the collusion. One priest, rector of the church in the nearby village of Orsha, spoke on the familiar nationalist theme of Orthodoxy as a guarantor of Russian national unity going back to the conversion of the Kievan Rus', whereas "divide and conquer" had always been the strategy of enemy outsiders, from the Golden Horde to the German fascists. The other priest, from the church in Semënovka, showed his greater sense of diplomacy and higher theological education by offering a more careful substantiation of Orthodoxy's claim to special status. Acknowledging that the state as well as the church was interested in a unified society, he presented Orthodoxy's claim to providing such unity as based not so much in its support of national sovereignty, but in historical manifestations of divine will:

> Orthodoxy is one of the traditional faiths in the Mari country. At the time when Lutheranism first appeared in Russia, in the sixteenth century, . . . Ivan the Terrible conquered Kazan', and Orthodoxy already

spread here on Mari land. Among the special signs that the will of God was for the spread of Orthodoxy, we see them in the history of the miracle-working icon of the myrrh-bearing women in whose honor the monastery was built [at Ezhovo], and in the life of the great man St. Gurij of Kazan', who did much to enlighten the Maris with the light of the faith in Christ and to teach them learning; he did much for this, as the first bishop of Kazan'. And many more sacred objects [svjatynii] which can be found on Mari land bear witness to the will of God, because God visited this land and helped people gain salvation in it.

Even as he explicitly directed his comments against Lutheranism by emphasizing the centuries of Orthodox presence in the region, this priest indirectly challenged the district head, who had referred to Paganism as "our traditional religion." In closing, the priest insisted that there were "categorical differences" between Lutheranism and Orthodoxy, and stressed that each villager had to make a "spiritual choice" (dukhovnyj vybor) on how to live from now on. From his standpoint, to allow or not allow Lutheranism to take root in the village was a choice between paths of development that had consequences beyond questions of community integration. By treating religious observance as more than a sign of trustworthiness and belonging, the priest subtly departed from the opinions voiced by the political leaders, without openly breaking the framework of consensus.

Although they had clearly been invited to represent the legitimacy of the "faith of the grandfathers and grandmothers," the priests at this meeting were in a difficult position vis-à-vis the villagers as well as the officials. Nationally, the Russian Orthodox Church has been one of the principal proponents of the discourse on the primacy of "traditional religions."[12] But this rhetoric presents risks in regions where Orthodox expansion is only a few centuries old and the church faces criticism from populations trained with Soviet history books that portrayed prerevolutionary missions as instruments of tsarist colonialism (e.g., Korobov 1957). The Lutherans have repeated similar criticisms in their own publications, in order to portray their own branch of Christianity as more benign and compatible with Finno-Ugric traditions (Uvarov 2000). So while the Orthodox diocese in Marij El generally goes along with the collusive production of unity between traditional faiths,[13] the priests' attempt to anchor the special status of Orthodoxy in divine will shows their awareness that human tradition alone may be too ambiguous a basis for legitimation.

The frictions between discourses of traditional unity and theological claims to primacy show why religious commitments can present a dilemma to a secular state-building project: while the state may try to appropriate the moral authority of religion, borrowing from divine forces can ultimately undermine the claim of government agents to act on behalf of all citizens and uphold universal standards of moral right (see also Sullivan 2009).

In contrast to their Soviet predecessors, politicians in post-Soviet Marij El do not attempt to eliminate all religion from public life. But they still treat it as a potentially divisive force which they seek to neutralize by giving preference to those religious groups that can be identified with the cultural traditions of one of the ethnic groups of the region. These traditions are understood to be diverse but ultimately infused by the common moral sensibilities of long-term neighbors. In the case of Ljupersola, the neighborly construction of unity-in-diversity turned out to be expansive enough to include the Lutherans after some struggles. Although the village assembly rejected the application for a building permit, this decision was successfully challenged by the Lutheran deacon, who wrote a letter to the district head listing the violations of Russian law that had occurred at the meeting and threatening to take the matter to court.[14] Without waiting for the congregation to act on its threat, the district head gave permission to construct a parsonage, not a church, on the plot of land.

The Lutherans had been prepared for this outcome; indeed, the pastor had suggested it at the village council meeting. With help from the Finnish volunteers, they proceeded to build a wooden structure according to the original plan, simply omitting the steeple. By the time the building was consecrated three years later, in September 2008, the congregation had received permission to call it a "prayer house" (*molitvennyj dom*), and the head of the village administration was present for the service of consecration. According to the catechist in charge of the congregation, this village official had accepted the invitation, saying, "There is one God, but many organizations" (*Bog odin, organizatsii raznye*). He thus extended the collusive discourse about the "oneness" of all religions to this new group that had come to the village and stayed.

From this discussion of the post-Soviet religious landscape, two things are worth retaining for understanding the stakes faced by Soviet atheists (and secularists elsewhere) in disentangling religion from community. First, "our faith" was named as important by speakers with a vague or fluid sense of its dogmatic or institutional content. As we will see, Soviet atheists already had encountered this fluidity, which presented a challenge to their understanding of religion as a system of dogmatically determined truth claims. As a result of confronting religion as an aspect of communal adherence rather than as dogmatic conviction, atheist workers in the Volga region added new facets to their critique. While retaining the focus on religion as false epistemology, which they inherited from Marx, Engels, and other nineteenth-century authors, they more and more came to emphasize its socially divisive character. Since this second angle of anti-religious critique was only fully elaborated during the last decades of the Soviet Union, it shows how atheist thought evolved in response to the local politics of neighborliness.

A second noteworthy aspect of post-Soviet religion is that the ambiguously defined religious solidarity is thought to exist with reference to various scales of communal belonging. Some of these scales were among those which Soviet activists tried hard to eradicate for several decades, foremost among them the village as a ritual community of "relatives and neighbors" in which outsiders could never fully participate. The idea of a nation whose resources were coveted by Western enemies, by contrast, was something that became real for rural residents during the Soviet period, as did the potentially dangerous, but also desirable, world of international ties (Grant 1995; Yurchak 2006: 190–195). In Soviet and post-Soviet times, state-centered "political theologies of the sovereign" were always destabilized by sliding scales of alternative communal identifications.

In that sense, the blurred boundaries of neighborliness have remained a political reality. But the example of micro-politics in Marij El also shows that there is no reason to idealize neighborly politics: while its mechanisms of inclusion and exclusion may be flexible and open to expansion, a hardening and contracting of communal boundaries is equally possible. The threat of not burying Lutheran converts in the village graveyard was realistic enough to have rhetorical force, even though in this case it remained unrealized. Far from being community members simply by virtue of living somewhere, as Kenneth Reinhard claims is characteristic of neighbors (2005: 66–67), neighbors in Marij El are measured against standards of social conformity and authority that may ultimately be less flexible than the number of groups that can be included. Faced with the ambivalent character of neighborly politics, Soviet atheists saw religion as a force that at once divided communities and made them more resistant to change induced from outside. Far from merely wanting to endow the state with a sacred authority stolen from religion, they distrusted the fracturing potential of the religious sacred and saw its elimination as a necessary condition for a society of citizens to transcend neighborhoods and regions.

Before Atheism

Readers familiar with the latent or acute violence that can accompany religious divisions in other parts of the former Soviet Union and elsewhere in the world may be struck by the harmlessness of bureaucratic haggling about building permits and burial places.[15] It is true that even the sharpest critic of religion would hardly claim that the Volga region has historically been plagued by religious strife. To understand why Soviet atheists nonetheless came to identify religion with intercommunal divisions, recall that this is a part of the world where religion has long served as a marker of communal identification.

When Maris were paying tribute to the Khanate of Kazan', religious distinctions already served as dividing lines between different kinds of tax and labor obligations, a practice which continued after Kazan' fell to Ivan IV in 1552.[16] Despite efforts to convert Tatar and Mari elites and, later, commoners to Russian Orthodoxy, the area retained significant Muslim populations into the nineteenth and twentieth centuries, while many baptized Maris continued to sacrifice ducks, sheep, and sometimes horses in prayer ceremonies led by hereditary *onaeng,* in addition to attending church services (Popov 1987; Werth 2002).

In the century preceding the Bolshevik Revolution, religious and ethnolinguistic categories were the primary contenders for social identities on the regional scale. A series of reconversion movements among Christianized Tatars and Maris, culminating in 1866, challenged imperial laws against apostasy from Orthodoxy with the argument that God had given different ways of worshiping to different peoples. As part of the state's reaction to these movements, training courses for non-Russian clergy and teachers began in the 1860s and '70s under the auspices of Nikolaj Il'minskij, a professor at the Kazan' Theological Academy. These courses contributed to the formation of indigenous Christian elites who went on to promote literacy in their native languages while maintaining links with each other and an orientation toward Kazan' as a regional center (Geraci 2001; Werth 2000, 2001, 2002).

While these regional identities evolved, the village retained its importance as a unit of communal affiliation. Villages in the Volga region were often inhabited by people of a single linguistic and religious affiliation, although in some places Mari, Tatar, and Russian villages were close neighbors. Each village was an important ritual unit, both among unbaptized Maris, where the households of a village or a cluster of villages carried out sacrifices in a common sacred grove (Popov 2005), and among Christian converts. Nineteenth-century Christian Maris exerted pressure on their fellow villagers to give up Chimarij practices, which they saw as a threat to the purity of their own Christian life, while some Kräshens (Christian Tatars) who petitioned to re-register as Muslims argued that they could not be Christian in a Muslim village (Werth 2000: 500; Werth 2002: 212). This sense of mutual dependence was underscored by the tax laws of imperial Russia, where the village community (*mir*) held collective responsibility for paying taxes and providing the required number of army recruits.

Tensions could emerge between neighboring villages of different faiths and languages, as shown by the accusations of ritual murder which Russian peasants leveled against a community of Pagan Udmurts in 1892, resulting in a lengthy court case (Geraci 2001: 195–207).[17] While this incident shows that neighborly relations could be characterized by "antagonistic tolerance" (Hayden 2002) rather than harmonious respect, there were no significant outbreaks of intercommunal or interreligious violence in the Volga region in the nineteenth century. Rather than being divided by deep-seated enmities, the region which Soviet officials came to govern was fractured by a diversity of religious and emerging ethno-linguistic identities, reinforced by the enduring importance of the village as a unit of ritual, economic, and political life.

The Soviet government came in with a commitment to foster the ethnic distinctiveness of those groups which it understood to have suffered under tsarist colonialism, but also with the determination to keep the empire it inherited from breaking apart (T. Martin 2001). During the decades before the Second World War, the struggle to disentangle ethnic identities from religious affiliations focused on determining which groups deserved recognition as legitimate Soviet nationalities. Groups such as the Kräshens, who were religiously distinct while sharing the language of Muslim Tatars, were dropped from census lists in the late 1930s, at the same time that clergy and religious leaders suffered intense persecution and the Kugu Sorta reform movement among Mari Pagans was completely wiped out (Hirsch 2005; Sanukov 2000; Werth 2000; Y. Wichmann 1932). Starting a process of ethnic consolidation whose incomplete results can be seen in post-Soviet Marij El, recognized ethnic groups were given cultural and economic resources, while religion was deprived of any independent institutional base (Slezkine 1994). The assault on religious institutions did not remain the sole focus of Soviet atheist policy, however. In the postwar era, a new emphasis on the bureaucratic supervision of the surviving religious groups emerged, along with new efforts to turn the population away from them through education. This also required new rationales for why religion remained harmful.

Transforming Festivals

While the link between religion and social identity had been a principle of governance in the Russian Empire, it became a problem for Soviet activists. Representing a revolutionary state claiming to liberate its inhabitants from the fetters of the old regime, they identified religious authority as one of the ways in which magistrates and gentry had secured the obedience of peasants and workers. The more discerning among them also recognized how deeply ritual practices permeated rural labor and community relations, in ways that simple critiques of exploitative and wasteful religion failed to capture. One set of dilemmas that many scholars have noted arose from Soviet attempts to separate potentially progressive ethnic "culture" from harmful and backward "religion" (Hirsch 2005; Humphrey 1998; Sadomskaya 1990). But atheist activists struggled not only with connections between religion and ethnic custom, but with the relationship between religion and social boundaries more generally. As they attempted to transform life in the Volga region, officials contrasted the boundedness and chaos of religiously infused neighborliness with the barrier-free, ordered secular public opened up by atheism. Starting as a frustrated response to the lack of identifiable religious communities with clearly delimited functions, this critique took on sharper contours in the 1960s and '70s as a result of a wave of empirical research on religion.

The attempt to contrast religious boundedness with the desired new secular community goes back to the 1920s, when activists created ethnic festivals in order to develop progressive models of ethnic diversity while combating religious influences. As part of a wave of measures for the "demonstrative recognition" (T. Martin 2001: 183) of the folklore of peoples of the USSR, *joshkar peledysh pajrem* (Festival of Red Flowers) was instituted among the Mari. First organized in 1920 in the district center of Sernur by students and instructors from the teachers college, it was timed to coincide with the end of spring sowing and with *semyk*, a ritual commemoration of the dead during the seventh week after Easter.[18] Comparing the fate of this festival to its Tatar equivalent, *sabantuj*, shows that choices about new Soviet celebrations were determined not only by a concern with demonstrative ethnic equality, but also by a particular vision of secular society.

Throughout the 1920s, pledges were collected from village councils and collective farms to forgo *semyk*, Easter, or Pentecost, and instead to celebrate *joshkar peledysh pajrem* after spring sowing, with performances of song and dance and recognition of exemplary workers (Solov'ev 1966: 9–13). Among the Tatars, *sabantuj*, previously a ritual held at the time of first plowing, was also transformed into a post facto celebration of the sowing campaign, and thus purged of its connotation of invoking divine blessing on agricultural work. In some Mari villages, *peledysh pajrem* was held in the sacred grove, a gesture of substitution typical of prewar anti-religious strategies.

Like other new festivals elsewhere in the Soviet Union, these were also occasions to denounce traditional forms of inequality between men and women. Organizers in the Volga region showcased modernized versions of embroidered women's costumes, omitting the regionally and ethnically distinctive forms of headdress for married women, which were becoming targets of campaigns comparable to those against veiling among Muslim women in Central Asia (Molotova 1992: 87; cf. Massell 1974; Northrop 2004). Although they did not cover a woman's face, the Mari *shymaksh* and *soroka* were attacked for being unhygienic and "diminishing a woman's dignity."[19] Since the embroidery on these headdresses was intended to protect against the evil eye and dangerous spirits (J. Wichmann 1913), asking women to give them up when entering a sacred grove also sent potent messages about the self-reliant courage required of a Soviet person.

Official promotion of *peledysh pajrem* and *sabantuj* stopped in 1931, at the beginning of the Stalinist crackdown on "bourgeois nationalists" (Sanukov 2000: 36), and it is hard to ascertain from published sources how widely they were observed before that. As long as they lasted, the festivals offered a demonstrative occasion to experience the kind of communal life promised by Soviet secularity: an opening up of spaces that were formerly marked off by ritual precautions, and an elimination of social distinctions of gender, age, or marital status. The framework of equivalence in which cultural distinctiveness was celebrated was not unfamiliar to residents of the Mari countryside: Maris had their festival, Tatars theirs; Maris, Russians, and Tatars all had their own music and forms of national dress. What the Soviet version of this framework ignored were the sub-ethnic divisions between villages; even a fellow Mari would have little reason to visit another village's sacred grove for a celebration dedicated to village concerns. In the vision of the festival planners, groves were to be turned into symbols of a generalized attachment to the beautiful Mari countryside, places for people to enjoy each other's company unperturbed by fear of nonhuman forces and by human distinctions. But postwar discussions about reviving ethnic festivals among the Maris and Tatars show that such reconfigurations were neither easily achieved nor easily verified.

As has been pointed out by many historians of Soviet religious policy, the Second World War brought fundamental changes to the relationship between the state and religious organizations (Chumachenko 2002; Shkarovskii 1995). After spending decades destroying the power of religious institutions, the government realized that it needed their moral support in the war effort. Toward the end of the war, a specialized bureaucracy dealing with religious affairs was put in place, reflecting a change in orientation from efforts to quickly eradicate religion to the realization that it would be part of Soviet life for the foreseeable future. The Council for Russian Orthodox Church Affairs (Sovet po delam Russkoj pravoslavnoj tserkvi) was created by decree on October 7, 1943. In May 1944 it was complemented by the Council for Religious Cult Affairs (Sovet po delam religioznykh kul'tov), in charge of relations with all other officially recognized religious groups in the Soviet Union. Each council began to establish a network of commissioners (*upol-nomochennye*) in regions and republics, who would report to the council on local religious life, receive and verify petitions for registration, and handle the registration documents for clergy, cult buildings, and religious organizations (Chumachenko 2002: 17–27). In 1965, the two organizations merged into the Council for Religious Affairs (Sovet po delam religii).

The first commissioner for religious cult affairs in the Mari ASSR was Aleksandr Kharitonovich Nabatov, who served from 1945 until 1952. He took special interest in those forms of local popular religion which did not seem to fit the institutionalized model foreseen by the registration requirements, among them village festivals. He also noted important differences in the official treatment of Mari and Tatar festivals, revealing some of the conditions for the successful secularization of folk customs.

Reporting to Moscow from a region struggling under the high work obligations of postwar agriculture, Nabatov noted the importance of agricultural celebrations to villagers and collective farm authorities. According to him, the Tatar festival *sabantuj* had achieved widespread recognition as a secular village festival by the early 1950s. Local administrative bodies often organized it as a reward for those collective farms that completed spring plowing and sowing on time. In 1951, the executive committee and party committee of the Paran'ga district, one of the areas of the Mari ASSR with significant concentrations of Tatars, staged a celebration of *sabantuj* in honor of the thirtieth anniversary of Mari autonomy.[20] Nabatov's superiors marked this part of his report with a question mark, and Nabatov himself noted a year later that although *sabantuj* had become "an ordinary civic festival," it still involved city residents giving gifts to mullahs in their home villages.[21]

In spite of the misgivings of administrators higher up in the hierarchy, local officials were apparently convinced enough of *sabantuj*'s success in motivating rural laborers that they were searching for a Mari equivalent. *Peledysh pajrem* appears to have been forgotten by that time, so the candidate became *agavajrem*, a meatless food offering and prayer for successful sowing conducted in special groves at the edges of the village fields (Kalinina 2003: 43–77). Its secular adaptation had first been suggested in a regional party committee decision of 1936, to mitigate the perceived negative effects of abolishing *peledysh pajrem*. This decision was apparently never put into practice, probably owing to the political atmosphere of suspicion about anything that might be perceived as nationalism (Sanukov 2000: 37). After the war, Nabatov repeatedly reported that *agavajrem* was indeed taking on secular forms as it became integrated into collective farm life, and that it would be helpful to further develop such tendencies. While previously, he wrote in one report, "the leading and decisive role was played by the Mari *kart*—a religious minister, . . . now the leading role in the organization of the festival is taken by the collective farm administration." In 1949 this "communal feasting without killing of animals and sacrifices" was "obligatory for collective farm workers and had the character of communal merrymaking [*obshchestvennogo uveselenija*]."[22] Only in some places, he had noted the year before, were there such "religious formalities" as special gifts and food offerings to the *kart* in exchange for prayers and petitions to the gods.[23]

Nabatov observed that many collective farms in the late 1940s and early 1950s organized celebrations of *agavajrem*. But promotion of the holiday was never made official policy, although Maris remarked on the injustice of the Tatars being allowed their festival, while Maris lacked theirs.[24] Much later, the search for a secular Mari festival led to the official revival of *peledysh pajrem* during a union-wide wave of renewed atheist campaigns in 1965.[25] By that time, *sabantuj* was well established as a Soviet festival honoring exemplary collective farm workers and celebrating Tatar culture with athletic competitions, music, and dance (Aleksandrova 1978: 93–98).

Compared to *sabantuj*, *agavajrem* had two features that seem to have disqualified it from secular adaptation. First, official promotion of *sabantuj* relied on a narrative of folk custom versus clerical religion. According to an atheist propaganda lecture on Soviet festivals, Islamic mullahs had long tried to eliminate the festival "because the folk customs were incompatible with the dogmas of Muslim religion." Unable to abolish *sabantuj*, the mullahs had deprived it of its original joyous character by forbidding music and excluding women from participation. Only the Bolshevik Revolution returned the festival to its true form (Anonymous 1963: 22–23). Similar strategies of playing off a purported Pagan past against presently professed world religions are evident in Soviet adaptations of the seasonal celebrations of other Muslim and Christian populations.[26] But in the case of Mari food offerings, there was no Christian layer under which to excavate the folk traditions, and Paganism was too much alive to be regarded as the harmless vestige of a more democratic past. For Nabatov and the readers of his reports, it seemed too difficult to determine whether or not the need to propitiate divinities was still lurking behind the sense that this kind of feasting was "obligatory" for the communal life of a collective farm.

Besides being seen as an active occasion of worship rather than a cultural vestige, *agavajrem* had another disadvantage. The Mari festival mainly involved the offering, sharing, and consumption of food, followed by rather homely games, such as egg-throwing competitions. It thus lacked the spectacular elements of athletic competition that Soviet organizers most emphasized about *sabantuj*. Competitive wrestling and horse racing, whose functions as rituals linked to the fertility of the fields were ignored in official descriptions, attracted the mass audiences that best embodied the new secular public. Small clusters of villagers rolling eggs or pushing swings did not provide the same experience of strangers united by a common object of attention.

Caroline Humphrey, a British anthropologist who visited Burjat collective farms in southern Siberia in 1967 and 1975, reports that atheist activists there made a comparable distinction between *suur-kharbaan,* a summer festival with athletic competitions that had been adapted into a secular, officially organized holiday in the 1920s, and *tsagalgaan,* the lunar new year. Despite suggestions from ethnographers, the latter was not turned into a celebration of livestock breeders, but was celebrated only at the family level and met with official disapproval (Humphrey 1998: 380). The spectacular athletic components of *sabantuj* and *suur-kharbaan,* performed before the whole village and open to spectators from elsewhere, resonated with Soviet notions of the openness and visibility appropriate to public life.[27]

By contrast, the sanctification and sharing of food during *agavajrem* and *tsagalgaan* were associated not only with invoking the blessing of spirits, but also with social fragmentation. *Tsagalgaan* is an occasion to visit and share food with members of one's kin group (Humphrey 1998: 379–380), and the food blessed at *agavajrem* and other Mari sacrifices is brought back to be shared with members of one's own household. "You bring it from your home, and take it back to your home, otherwise you are giving away your family's good fortune," as a participant in one ceremony in 2005 explained the rule that food left over from the sacrificial meals should not be given away to non-kin.

If *sabantuj* and *suur-kharbaan* were judged to be less irredeemably religious, this shows that secularizing, to Soviet activists, involved breaking down what they saw as the debilitating divisions of rural life: between households, between kin groups, between villages. Secular festivals helped integrate villages into a union-wide public of strangers by directing attention to Soviet administrative centers. *Peledysh pajrem, sabantuj, suur-kharbaan,* and their equivalents among other ethnic groups were celebrated first in individual collective farms, then in the district center, and finally in the regional capital, with the more centralized celebrations featuring selected workers, athletes, or folk ensembles from the lower levels.[28]

Soviet laws that confined religious practice to liturgical worship by registered congregations in their own buildings actively prevented the development of translocal religious publics to rival the secular one. Evidence of religion's capacity to mobilize across boundaries occasionally disturbed atheist observers throughout the postwar decades, but their critique of religion as associated with isolation and division became more elaborate over this period. This reflected Marxist narratives of progress that associated religion with an outdated rural past. But atheist analyses also evolved as alternatives to other ideas about the harm done by religious attachments.

From Economic Harm to Selfish Particularity: The Problem of the Mari Cult

The reports Nabatov wrote as the commissioner for religious cult affairs in the Mari ASSR speak of his efforts to apply received models of antireligious critique, even though he recognized all too well when they did not fit. Apparently a native or long-time resident of the republic, he furnished detailed descriptions that often frustrated his Moscow superiors.[29] His correspondence reveals much about the creativity required of provincial officials if they wanted to apply staple Marxist tenets to the intricacies of rural life (cf. Humphrey 1998: ch. 2).

The first problem to which Nabatov alerted his superiors was that the most widespread religious practice outside of Russian Orthodoxy was not included on the list of religious institutions with which he should concern himself. In his first preserved report in 1946, Nabatov called this religion the "Mari cult" (*marijskij kul't*), rites carried out by Maris "in prayer groves" under the leadership of priests known as *karty* or *muzhany*, who "officiate at prayer ceremonies, slaughter the sacrificial animals, give names to newborns, conclude marriages and funerals."[30] The prayer ceremonies "sometimes constitute a mass gathering" (*byvajut massovymi*). For instance, at a ceremony in the Kozhsola rural council of Sernur district, offerings amounting to 12,000 rubles, three wagonloads of linen, and significant amounts of leather and wool were collected and given over to the national defense fund.[31]

Pointing to the significant numbers of worshipers at these gatherings, Nabatov raised the question of their legalization, asking if communities of adherents of the "Mari cult" could be registered as religious organizations. He gave noticeably shorter treatment to the Old Believers, Muslims, Baptists, Seventh-day Adventists, and Jews who also were part of his responsibility, noting simply that he was beginning to receive petitions for the registration of religious organizations from some of these groups.

The council apparently gave some consideration to Nabatov's argument that the "Mari cult" deserved its attention. Council member Fil'chenkov was sent to inspect the Mari ASSR in February 1946. He reported that, although the Maris were for the most part considered "baptized in the orthodox faith," a substantial part of the population was "under the influence of the Mari cult," as shown by the thousands of people who had attended the region-wide "world prayer ceremonies" (*mirovye molenija*) up to 1924 and again in 1945, when ten such ceremonies, involving the sacrifice of sheep, geese, and ducks, were held.[32] Local officials and party members not only did little to stop these ceremonies, but sometimes actively supported them. The current chairman of the presidium of the supreme soviet of the Mari ASSR, when he was secretary of the party committee of a rural district, had permitted a Mari priest to hold a harvest ceremony at night, as long as the collective farm workers reported for work in the morning. Petitions by villagers to conduct ceremonies were sometimes accompanied by declarations from collective farm or rural council chairmen that they had no objections.[33]

Noting the history of tsarist persecutions of Mari ceremonies, Fil'chenkov reported that members of the Mari intelligentsia and state and party officials often participated in ceremonies, "commenting on them with enthusiasm, without seeing anything compromising in them." Christian rituals, by contrast, were carried out by Maris "extremely pro forma," and before the closing of the churches in the late 1930s many Maris preferred to lock the doors of their houses rather than receive an Orthodox priest.[34]

The "Mari cult" and other local religious practices posed several challenges to Soviet understandings of religion and the harm it did. First, adherents did not form stable communities with set times and places of worship, thus defying registration. The phrase "spontaneous appearance" (*javochnyj porjadok*, the same term one might use about an unscheduled public demonstration) occurs again and again in Nabatov's reports, referring to Mari sacrifices, but also to prayer gatherings near Tatar graveyards for Muslim holidays and to pilgrimages to sacred springs in which Russian Old Believers, baptized and unbaptized Maris, and Muslim Tatars participated. In addition to the worrisome support of such activities by the local intelligentsia, the scale of some of these gatherings and their capacity to draw people from long distances made them hard to ignore, since they rivaled Soviet attempts to determine the rhythms and foci of public life.

Eventually, the council took the position that "like other pagan cults, the Mari one does not constitute an object of the Council for Religious Cult Affairs"[35] and that it was "inexpedient to pose the question in terms of any kind of legalization of the actually occurring rituals, prayer meetings and the like."[36] Justifying its decision to the Central Committee, the council stated that Mari ceremonies caused "considerable harm to agriculture" and were "usually carried out during the height of agricultural work"[37]—probably a generalization from Fil'chenkov's story about the nighttime ceremony at harvest time. Nabatov's own reports show how difficult it was to sustain this narrative of economic harm, motivating his search for alternative ways to understand the meaning of rural religiosity.

In general, Nabatov's observations do not confirm that Mari ceremonies always occurred "during the height of agricultural work." In a draft circular to the district executive committees of the republic, Nabatov notes the following times for ceremonies: "in the spring before the beginning of the spring sowing campaign—*agapajrem* (*aga*—plowing, *pajrem*—holiday), in the interim after spring sowing—*semik*, and in the fall after bringing in the harvest and sowing winter grains."[38] As might be expected of the ritual cycle of a peasant population, these festivals seemed to fall into times of relative quiet preceding or following the major work tasks of the year.

Although the sacrifice of much-needed farm animals could itself be construed as economic harm, Fil'chenkov reported that since collectivization, there had been no instances of the sacrifice of animals owned by collective farms (which would have been a criminal act); all sacrificed animals had been privately purchased. Nor were the priests enriching themselves through the ceremonies: the meat was consumed on the spot, and other offerings were handed over to the union-wide defense fund.[39]

Even when his stated purpose was to prove that religion was harmful, Nabatov's observations often pointed him toward its usefulness to rural economic managers struggling to meet the strenuous demands placed on Soviet agricultural producers in the postwar years (Nove 1982 [1969]: 298–304). Evidently answering a list of questions in a 1947 report, Nabatov used the heading "harm to the population" to enumerate the animals sacrificed and notes that "hundreds of horses" were used by thousands of participants from all over the republic to travel to the site of a "world prayer ceremony" in the fall of 1946, implying that this caused disruption of agricultural work.[40] But he also stated that collective farm administrations themselves were sending petitions for permission to conduct prayer ceremonies and that these came from successful farms which fulfilled their requirements for grain requisitions.[41] A year later, having attended a ceremony, Nabatov noted that a number of collective farm chairmen told him that "these sacrifices bring people closer together; . . . afterwards the population works more willingly."[42] In cautious and circumspect wording, Nabatov concluded that there was, "I would say, a dependence of the collective farms on the observance of religious cults," a dependence "almost being promoted by local councils."[43]

There was a material side to this dependence that had little to do with belief in ritual efficacy. At the 1948 ceremony, offerings were sold and the proceeds were divided between savings toward the cost of next year's ceremony and the collective farm's budget. A few years later, offerings made by pilgrims at the Shabashi healing spring on the feast day of the Kazan' icon of the Mother of God became the object of a dispute between the collective farm and the rural council.[44] Nabatov's readers understood these cases as instances of "accommodationalism,"[45] where people in leadership positions made concessions to the ideological immaturity of their workers when it fit the short-term interests of the collective. These reports revealed the troubling attraction of religious rituals, but at least they could be explained away as strategic, if misguided, steps by local leaders.

More disturbing was the case of the collective farm Samolët, where the managers showed their own commitment to religious thinking. In the summer of 1948, the farm leadership presided over the sacrifice in a sacred grove of an old horse and its subsequent ritual consumption in the stables. They explained that their hope was to remedy their "insufficient number of horses" by killing one of them and then feasting on it "in the horses' stalls, at the immediate spot where the collective farm experiences, by their explanation, misfortune, a lack of horses."[46] Although this was a successful farm and the horse was no longer able to work, the district executive committee fined the workers collectively for the damage. Punishment was necessary because the actions challenged the logic of mutual benefit that underlay the planned economy. By seeking to increase its own productivity by means that ran counter to union-wide visions of scientific progress, this collective farm exemplified the parochial selfishness associated with religion.

Discussions about the effects of opening houses of worship also show that ritual practice was perceived to give too much of a boost to local self-sufficiency and self-interest. When Nabatov considered recommending the reopening of a mosque in the Paran'ga district, an area with a large Tatar population lacking any legal opportunity to worship, the district executive committee spoke out against it. Far from serving the whole district, the opening of a mosque in one village would cause a flood of petitions from others. "By established custom, Tatar muslims don't go, don't visit the mosque of their neighboring village," the district chairman explained, showing his awareness of the fragmenting potential of neighborly religion.[47]

The case of the republic's only legally registered mosque, which was in the Tatar village of Kul'bash (Morki district), aroused similar misgivings about the mutual entanglement of religion and local pride. After the opening of the mosque, the local collective farm, Kzyl bajrak, "began to excel in its work" and was repeatedly held up as an example by the district radio station. "As if as a service in exchange for the opening of the mosque," the collective farm had built a bridge and a fire shed and was currently building a communal bathhouse. It had also constructed a minaret for the mosque.[48] A few months later, Nabatov reported that the mosque was also serving as a place for public announcements, such as appeals to buy government bonds.[49] This provoked severe reproaches from his superiors for having allowed the mosque to be transformed into a "communal-political organization."[50]

Though more in line with local realities than was the attempt to link religion to economic harm, the critique of religion as parochial also distorted the image of its adversary. In 1950, collective farms in the republic were consolidated, and Nabatov found that Mari ritual communities adapted, now gathering for sacrifices at the scale of the enlarged farms.[51] But Soviet laws sought to hamper such initiatives to integrate religion with the new economic and political realities, by prohibiting publicly visible processions and pilgrimages as well as religious charity work (Kolymagin 2004: 51). It has even been argued that Soviet restrictions were a major factor in forcing religion into the parochial, domestic frames denounced by atheist propaganda (Dragadze 1993; Kormina 2006: 141–142). Indeed, the lack of evidence for further interregional Mari sacrifices after the immediate postwar years may confirm that atheist policies, whose vigor picked up again from the mid-1950s onward, caused ritual activities to become more locally constricted.

At the same time, polemics against the fragmenting force of rural religiosity were not just a product of the atheist imagination, but a response to the elusiveness of neighborly politics. Each of the interregional gatherings at sacred springs or groves had a host village on whose territory the site was located. Local authorities felt entitled to the offerings made at "their" sacred spring, suggesting a sense of ownership where nonresidents could be guests, but remained to some degree outsiders. Villages and collective farms petitioned for and defended "their" houses of worship. As Nabatov put it in one of his characteristic musings, what troubled officials like him was that religious customs, though normatively "alien to our Soviet person," often seemed to "enter into communion with communal life [*vstupajut v obshchenie s obshchestvennoj zhizn'ju*],"[52] at once strengthening communities and steering them away from their task of becoming interchangeable parts of a secular nation. What remains an inchoate sense of discomfort in Nabatov's writing would become a theory of the link between religious belief and social fragmentation in the sociological work of later decades.

Religious Isolation and Statistical Proof

Nabatov was relieved of his post as commissioner for religious cult affairs at the end of 1952, apparently as a cost-saving measure. Even before the official merger of both councils in 1965, successive commissioners for Russian Orthodox Church affairs seem to have carried out the functions of the commissioner for religious cults.[53] While time constraints forced these officials to limit themselves to monitoring the officially recognized religious groups and their compliance with Soviet law, a budding empirical sociology applied itself to the study of religious life more generally.

Over the course of the 1960s and '70s, sociologists in the Volga region and other multiethnic areas of the Soviet Union refined statistical criteria to depict the harmful effects of religion and the benefits of atheism. The answers they came up with involved ideas about religion and rural segmentation that recall the concerns of Nabatov's generation. But the sociologists were more explicit in their rejection of alternative explanations, arguing that religious believers were neither deliberate wreckers of the Soviet economy nor ignorant people deceived by malicious priests. In published studies, attempts to demonstrate the link between social isolation and religious practice often turned into calls for more resources to be devoted to social and cultural services for underserved segments of the population, such as rural residents, housewives, and pensioners. In the words of one scholar involved in the atheist section of the Mari division of the Knowledge Society, a religious person was someone "whose links to society for some reason or other are insufficient in some places (low level of education, underdeveloped spiritual needs) or are even completely lacking (self-isolation from the social-political life of the collective, separation from the work collective)" (Sofronov 1973: 8).

Part of this critique focused on the impact of religiosity on interethnic relations, but this was only one among several factors. Viktor Stepanovich Solov'ev, a sociologist trained at the Academy of Social Sciences in Moscow (an institution directly subordinate to the Central Committee of the Communist Party), carried out surveys of popular beliefs and traditions in his native Mari ASSR in 1972 and 1985. Modeling his surveys on a study first conducted by his Moscow teacher, Viktor Pivovarov, in the Chechen-Ingush ASSR (Pivovarov 1971; Smolkin 2009), Solov'ev combined questions about religious belief with wide-ranging inquiries about gender, ethnicity, language skills, attitude toward ethnic traditions, participation in Soviet cultural practices, access to commodities and services, and degrees of social engagement.

The study concluded that compared to atheists, Tatar and Mari believers were less likely to speak Russian at home, cutting themselves off from this "important medium of active communion with social practice, with the achievements of science, technology, and Soviet and world culture" (Solov'ev 1987: 144). Believers of all nationalities were more critical of interethnic marriage (10.5 percent of believers objected to them compared to 3.2 percent of atheists; ibid.: 145). And commenting on the separation of Tatar and Mari graveyards, Solov'ev argued that this was proof that "customary orders set up by religion, even after losing their religious content and religious basis to a considerable degree, have become national traditions of far from positive character" (147–148).

Solov'ev's ideal of an atheist society was one in which people would transcend ethnic or local selfishness and recognize "the indivisible unity of national [i.e., ethnic] interests with the interests of the Soviet people as a whole" (Solov'ev 1987: 145). Success was measured not only in views about interethnic relations, but also in participation in modern Soviet culture. In 1972, the percentage of religious believers participating in voluntary social and trade union work was less than a fifth of that of atheists (Solov'ev 1977: 100). In 1985, when figures were adjusted for differences in age, education, and rural or urban residence, atheists were still found to be more engaged with Soviet cultural life. People who had never held religious beliefs reportedly read an average of 2.3 books per month, people who had abandoned religion 2, and religious believers and people wavering between belief and nonbelief less than 1. For attendance at public film showings, lifelong atheists averaged 1.5 per month, believers and waverers 0.4 (Solov'ev 1987: 116).

In his interpretation, Solov'ev never clarifies if he thinks of religion as the cause of this withdrawal from modern social life, or as the consolation sought by those who are already isolated. What appears to interest him is not so much the causal role of *religion,* but the causal role of atheism in overcoming divisions within local communities and connecting residents to larger Soviet and world contexts. The 1972 study was programmatically entitled "How's it going, comrade?" (Russian: *Kak zhivesh', tovarishch?*), addressing respondents in the casual tone common among familiars, but also as members of the larger Soviet public. The published results portrayed atheism as the solution to the tangle of religious, economic, and communal structures in rural neighborliness that so frustrated Nabatov. Like attempts to divert animals from the national productive cycle for the benefit of local collective farms, separate graveyards and disinterest in secular literature were symptoms of a vicious circle between religion and the limited horizons of rural life that atheism would break apart.

In practice, the struggle to completely dissolve rural communities into a union-wide sovereign domain was never taken up in earnest in the postwar

Mari ASSR. Often of local origin and always trained in the rhetoric about the value of ethnic cultures, Soviet officials tended to treat rural religion as relatively harmless. Residents of several Mari villages recalled that prayer ceremonies continued throughout the Soviet era, especially in the more remote districts, often with the tacit knowledge of local party and collective farm officials. Even atheists eventually began to find redeeming features in religion's capacity to sustain the traditional communities whose demise was increasingly lamented during the final decades of Soviet socialism (Solov'ev 1987). With the onset of perestroika and the disintegration of the Soviet Union, Solov'ev reinvented himself as a scholar of nationalities questions. In a 1991 brochure entitled "Ethnic diversity is our wealth," he presented religion as a tool for preserving "national" culture, praising Paganism in particular as "the deepest and most natural merging of the religious and national elements of spiritual culture" (Solov'ev 1991: 116).

This softening of atheist positions paralleled intellectual trends toward a greater valuing of prerevolutionary and folk heritage, which began during the Brezhnev era (Arutiunian et al. 1992: 324–331; Garrard and Garrard 2008: 93–97). But even as religion found a more and more comfortable niche as an integral component of ethnic traditions, the steadfast atheist Solov'ev retained his sense that strengthening communal bonds was not its only effect. When I interviewed him (then vice dean of the faculty of law of Mari State University) in 2005, he first acknowledged that atheists had underestimated the link between religion and ethnic solidarity. But then he added another thought, which pointed in the direction of religion as radically asocial, suggesting a different reason that it proved difficult to eradicate. Citing Marx, Solov'ev said that he had always understood that some people still needed the "opium" of religion, even if he himself did not. For instance, a war widow could find in religion "what society cannot give her"—the joy of a relationship with God to compensate for her loneliness (never mind that it is an imaginary relationship, he was quick to add).

Solov'ev refers to what scholars of religion have described as the "double movement" of religion, horizontally connecting people and (for lack of a more multidimensional spatial imagination) vertically connecting them to something other-than-human (Lincoln 1994: 2–3). More keenly perhaps than many disengaged theorists of religion, atheist activists felt the tension between these two movements, because their attempts to replace and reorient the horizontal bonds between humans were threatened by the claims of the extrasocial dimension. In the dilemmas of officials and empirical scholars, we see the struggle between the sociocentric humanism of secularizing projects and religion's capacity to infuse life with considerations beyond human sociality. This tension is in play when secularizers in different places worry about the divisive effects of religion, making their apprehensions more than just figments of the enlightenment imagination.

Political Theologies?

Coming full circle to the official correlation between recognized ethnicities and "traditional" religions in post-Soviet Marij El, the once-secular festivals of *sabantuj* and *peledysh pajrem* have comfortably included religion since the early 1990s. When the festivals are celebrated in Joshkar-Ola on Russian Independence Day (June 12), each in a separate park, Chimarij and Muslim dignitaries bless their respective festival grounds. Only the Russian celebration, *berëzka*,[54] lacks the presence of an Orthodox priest. The Orthodox diocese is wary of equating itself with Russian folklore and, unlike other groups, has the institutional resources to maintain a public presence almost on its own terms. Religious events not subsumed under the label of ethnic culture are carefully excluded by the city administration: in 2001, an application by the Charismatic Protestant Joshkar-Ola Christian Center to put on an evangelizing concert for the June holiday was denied.

From the perspective of the Volga region, the Soviet secularization process involved the construction of a public sphere in which there was no place for religion either as an instrument of social cohesion or as a means to open human society to nonhuman forces. Since the collapse of the Soviet Union, politicians have been seeking the benefits of religion-as-cohesion while remaining suspicious of the destabilizing potential of extrasocial commitments. The sense that religious commitments can foster and reinforce social divisions has thus outlived the official promotion of atheism.

Soviet approaches to atheism drew on Marxist ideological dicta, but also evolved as the transformative promises of this ideology came up against the tenacity of religion in social life. As Christopher Brittain has argued in a thoughtful critique of Talal Asad's genealogical approach to the secular, it is just such "contextual tensions" within religious and cultural politics that get overlooked when scholars understand the secular "as primarily an ideological myth, rather than a concept with deep material and social roots" (2005: 158, 162–163; see also Das 2006). Taking the analysis beyond an identification of broad intellectual continuities with enlightenment discourse, a detailed view of the Soviet secularizing project helps us see the complex adjustments made by political actors as their understandings of ideological aims encountered their interpretations of social reality. In particular, the tribulations of secularist thought in the face of a religiously diverse region such as the Middle

Volga suggest that it is no accident that secularist solutions emerged in the twentieth century in several successor states of multiethnic empires, notably Turkey, India, and the Soviet Union. The ideologies espoused by political reformers in these diverse parts of the world may well contain echoes of the trauma of the European wars of religion. But it also seems worth considering how each movement diagnosed local religious differences and affinities, the tensions among neighboring populations, and the degree to which these threatened national integration.[55]

The processes of expulsion and violence by which modernist secularizers established themselves are warning enough against any idealization of secular imaginaries (Aktar 2003; Husband 2000; Mueggler 2001; Pandey 2003). Even in the comparatively benign times that are the focus of this book, attempts to pressure the Soviet population into adopting a "scientific world view" remained above all a way to buttress the Communist Party's sovereign right to define the qualities required of comrades within the Soviet polity. This recalls a basic question that underlies much of the recent interest in Carl Schmitt's notion of political theology (de Vries 2006), and that also provides the critical impetus for Asad's genealogies of the secular: is it possible to construct a political vision that does not have "theology" lurking within it as some form of mystified authority that eludes collective human agency and reason?

Atheist activists were occasionally troubled by this question in their efforts to construct an exclusively human society. Although remaining within the confines of official Soviet discourse, their debates about legitimate and illegitimate methods can illuminate dilemmas of transformative authority in other settings as well.

2
"Go Teach": Methods of Change

[M]атериальная сила должна быть опрокинута материальной же силой; но и теория становится материальной силой, когда она овладевает массами.

[M]aterial force must be overthrown by material force; but theory, too, becomes a material force when it takes hold of the masses.

—Karl Marx, "Contribution to the Critique of Hegel's Philosophy of Right: Introduction"

Задача методиста—связать теорию с практикой.

The task of the methodician is to link theory with practice.

—A. V. Fomina, methodician at the Center for Folk Creativity, Ministry of Culture of the Republic of Marij El, April 2005

Итак идите, научите все народы, крестя их во имя Отца и Сына и Святаго Духа.

And so go, teach all peoples, baptizing them in the name of the Father and the Son and the Holy Spirit.

—Matthew 28:19 (Russian Synodal Bible translation)

Political decision makers in Moscow were anxious to have life on the Middle Volga conform to a vision of union-wide social solidarity, but they were not always interested in the intricacies of local religious life as reported by Commissioner Nabatov. In the academic world, the empirical sociologists of the 1960s and '70s were also often criticized for burrowing too deeply into accidental facts instead of finding ready-made answers in Marxist-Leninist philosophy.[1] Both Nabatov and the sociologists found a more responsive audience among a particular group of applied intellectuals: instructors whose task was to assimilate knowledge about religion for the purpose of promoting an atheist society. In 1950, Nabatov was invited to join first the

Mari division of the All-Union Society for the Dissemination of Political and Scientific Knowledge, then its newly founded atheist section. Although the Council for Religious Cult Affairs prohibited its commissioners from openly engaging in atheist propaganda, he prepared the texts of several lectures on Mari religious life for the society and for the lecturers deployed by the regional party committee, materials which were then used by other activists.[2] The sociologist Viktor Solov'ev, born in 1934 in a Mari village in a northeastern district, started his public career as a teacher and lecturer for the regional party committee. After obtaining his academic degrees, he served for a long time as the liaison between the party lecturers and the Knowledge Society. Both men thus combined political ambitions with an interest in understanding the social implications of religious traditions, and both found receptive partners among propagandists of atheism.

Charged with closing the gap between the fragmented present of religious neighborliness and the union-wide comradehood that the Soviet Union proclaimed as its ideal, atheist propagandists needed information about religious life in order to convince others of its harmfulness. These specialists, who turned expert knowledge into teachable information with practical effects on people's lives, represent a type that has reappeared in post-Soviet religious life. In both contexts, the tasks of ideological transmission promoted a concern with methodology as the crucial link between recognizable facts and changing ways of life, between knowledge and behavior, theory and practice. The organizations these methodicians served, whether secularist or religious, took didactic interactions as a structuring principle, assigning an intrinsic value to teaching as a transformative and mobilizing experience not only for those taught, but also for the teachers themselves. In Marx's terms, they saw pedagogical method as the path to making theory "take hold of the masses," and considered the grip to be firmest when teaching itself became a mass activity. The preoccupation with didactic methods is thus a key affinity between Soviet atheist and post-Soviet religious practice, and has had an effect on the "ecclesiology" of some secularist and religious groups: their doctrine about the nature of their community and the mechanisms that hold it together. In particular, the network of teacher-student relationships, held together by methodical instructions, was a Soviet way of organizing social relations that had a curious afterlife in religious practice.

Affinities between Soviet and post-Soviet methods of mobilization are not limited to religious life, but have also been noted in civic activism and political movements (Hemment 2009; Kurilla 2002; Phillips 2008). But because of the irony of seeing religious activists benefit from skills they gained in working to build a militantly secularist culture, the interplay between atheism and religion brings the many meanings of affinity into sharpest focus: a long shared history has brought distinct cultural forms to resemble one another, but has also equipped each side to oppose and deny the other more effectively.

Planned Learning

In the Soviet Union, the task of turning theory into practice through pedagogical methods was so ubiquitous that a separate profession was devoted to this problem. The *metodist* was an expert in designing, organizing, and moderating didactic events, who might be employed by the Ministry of Culture, the party or Komsomol department for propaganda and agitation, a library, a museum, a culture club, or a public park. Although the equivalent in U.S. terminology would be a director of programming or an events manager, *methodician* best preserves the connotation of someone whose expertise is in applying, developing, and disseminating ways of engaging others in self-transformative behavior. These were the people who wrote and consumed books and brochures with titles such as "The forms and methods of scientific-atheist propaganda" and "Forms and methods of visuality in propaganda," a genre of Soviet advice literature that proliferated in the postwar decades.

While I have found no explicit discussions of the history of the profession of methodician, historians have dated to the 1920s the emergence of the "festival expert," in charge of organizing mass celebrations and smaller-scale events (Rolf 2006: 72). These experts drew on the influence of various strands of prerevolutionary reformist cultural practice, from Wagnerians (Clark 1995) to movements for workers' education (Plaggenborg 1996), as well as on more recent developments in Soviet psychological and pedagogical research. Organizations of "science popularizers" (Andrews 2003), whose activities also had prerevolutionary precedents, likewise carved out an important niche in Soviet society for specialists in public pedagogy.

But the concern with method was not limited to people whose official job was methodician, nor to professional pedagogues in schools and universities. From the literacy campaigns of the 1920s to Komsomol groups and the party study circles of the Brezhnev era, Soviet society presented numerous occasions where people of all walks of life passed on acquired knowledge to others. This could happen among peers—for instance, when a member of a workplace study circle on political economy was asked to summarize the week's topic in a presentation (*doklad* or *referat*; see Kelly 2001: 274) or when the workers of a factory were encouraged to design and contribute to a wall newspaper (Kelly 2002). Or the setting could be more stratified, when someone considered to be of higher political consciousness or higher expertise was sent to work with a less enlightened audience. Examples include a teacher or university instructor lecturing at an enterprise, university students or factory workers going to the countryside to talk about the importance of upcoming elections, city women modeling modern standards of dress and hygiene to female collective farm workers, and village teachers helping the local collective farm organize a festival.

Many authors have noted the ubiquity of didactic elements in as seemingly diverse areas of Soviet life as the theater, courtrooms, and public demonstrations, indicating the amount of institutional energy that was devoted to creating, expanding, and evaluating networks of instructors and peer facilitators (Benn 1989; Bloch 2004; Northrop 2004: 154–160; Wood 2005). Just as the commitment to secularism links the Soviet Union with a number of twentieth-century regimes that sought modernization by constructing exclusively human societies, this pervasive didacticism presents an instance of what Francis Cody, writing about India, calls the "pedagogical function of development" (2009: 354): an institutionalized effort to bring the actual abilities and self-understandings of citizens into alignment with the characteristics that will be required of them as inhabitants of the promised future. In the postwar Soviet Union, networks of instructors were treated as tools of development, but also as indications of its successes: one measure of the effectiveness of an instructor often cited in methodical literature was how many students became instructors themselves (Chernykh 1967: 24; Gorokhov 1974; Moiseevskaia 1961; Vershlovskii and Lesokhina 1968). The advice literature encouraged methodicians to think of themselves as both instruments for developing the population and ideal end points of such development.

Because of the association of religion with "backward" and "isolating" forms of sociality, atheist propaganda was an integral part of developmental pedagogy. But regardless of the disciplinary content of the methodicians' teaching, seemingly technical questions of method—*how* to transmit knowledge in such a way that it would affect behavior—dominated the self-reflections and mutual interactions of amateur as well as professional methodicians. The Knowledge Society, with its broad mandate of disseminating politically useful knowledge, was also a major source of methodical awareness among the population.

The Content of Method

After the Knowledge Society replaced the prewar League of the Militant Godless as the primary agent of atheist propaganda, disseminating atheism became a small part of the broader aim to popularize knowledge on topics as diverse as Communist Party history, foreign policy, scientific innovation, and literature.[3] By denouncing the anticlerical tactics of the league as counterproductive, the new organization politicized methodological choices. But the quest for better methods also came from the society's own membership. Though officially voluntary, participation in the Knowledge Society could open up career and travel opportunities for teachers, university instructors, and physicians who joined, and could also be imposed as an assignment on members of the intelligentsia who were Communist Party members.[4] Since not all of them had experience presenting scientific discoveries and political developments to audiences whose educational level widely diverged from their own, many lecturers needed practical guidance.

In some ways, the circulation of methodical directives helped Soviet mass organizations bridge the gap between local neighborly concerns and the centralizing claims of state sovereignty. Annelise Riles (2000: 90–91) remarks that commitment to a common aesthetics of rule-bound process and form enables United Nations NGO consultations to bridge several levels of geographic scale without foregrounding contradictions between "local" and "global" concerns. But the UN networks describe their main purpose as "sharing" information, whereas participants in Soviet didactic networks seemed more interested in how those higher up wanted them to use the knowledge they already had. At a 1956 seminar of the Knowledge Society, for which atheist propagandists from various parts of the Soviet Union had gathered in Moscow, a representative from the Tatar ASSR stated that methodical directions from Moscow were needed more than finished lecture texts, because members of the regional sections had sufficient expertise to furnish the content of lectures themselves.[5] Eight years later, a lecturer from a state farm in the Moscow region made the same point at a seminar for rural propaganda workers. What rural lecturers needed was not information of the kind they could find in newspapers, but "such literature that would help people give up their belief in religions once and for all [*okonchatel'no razuverit' v religii*]. . . . I say [to believers]—god does not exist, and they say to me—prove it, and I don't have any proof [*mne nechem dokazat'*]."[6] By asking how to operationalize his knowledge, the lecturer shifted responsibility for the success of his efforts to faraway Moscow, while affirming his own theoretical expertise.

Methodical directives thus gave a sense of central direction to the task of transforming vastly different locales. Local propaganda workers did much of the day-to-day work of planning and putting on events on required topics. What they demanded from the center was, above all, prompts that would make their own efforts produce the desired effects—the argument that would shatter all belief in religion, the proof of God's nonexistence that would end all counterquestions.

From the point of view of the center, method was a way to assert control by prescribing aims and giving general instructions for attaining them, without having to provide all the resources or overseeing all the steps. From the point of view of the lecturer, the concern with method arose in part out of the peculiar position of popularizers: they had to disseminate information without being able to change it. Printed lecture texts from Moscow were helpful, a natural scientist from Chita in the Russian Far East said at the 1956 seminar, but they did not answer such basic questions as how to explain to a person with an elementary school education or less "that protein, just through its chemical potentialities, could become the primary carrier of life."[7] He recounted the plight of a lecturer who attempts to deliver a lecture with a standard narrative of the progress of science, but runs into unanticipated queries:

> These questions, after all, are in need of a particular methodical format [nuzhdajutsja v opredelennoj metodicheskoj razrabotke] and it is here that the lecturer runs into particular problems. From Aristotle to our days the lecturer tells his story and everything works out fine, works out splendidly, here it is quite possible to bring in a certain atheist element, but the moment they start to ask you questions—but what is protein, that is where the searching starts. Some consider it possible to say that protein consists of small particles formed by amino acids, but we have no serious methodical points of orientation.[8]

The dilemma of the lecturer consisted in having to answer for the contradictions of official doctrine without being in a position to reshape it. The question about proteins arose because of the official materialist definition of life as "the form of the existence of protein bodies," which Soviet scientists borrowed from Friedrich Engels's "Anti-Dühring" (Engels 1962a [1878]: 75; Graham 1972: 272–273). Note that the scientist did not challenge the definition of life with which atheist lecturers operated, but simply asked for guidance on how to make that definition meaningful to a lay audience. Some of the predicament grew from widespread uncertainty about political constraints during the post-Stalin Thaw, as indicated by the cautious formulation "Some consider it possible to say that . . . ," and an earlier speaker's inquiry about whether or not to use the works of a particular biologist.[9] In an organization whose charter treated political *and* scientific knowledge as part of a single mandate, asking for help in adapting scientific findings to different audiences and testing the limits of the politically permissible could be bundled into a single question about method.

The predicament of the popularizing lecturer is not restricted to societies with authoritarian regimes. More generally, the emphasis on method can be understood as part of what Theodor Adorno (1971: 75) calls "the immanent untruth of pedagogy": the fact that its task is the circulation, not the production, of knowledge. There are a number of pedagogical systems that actively seek to restrict teachers' capacity to question the underlying premises of what is being taught, including the "teacher-proof" curricula of test preparation in contemporary U.S. schools (Collins 2003: 32) and the uniform weekly Bible lessons studied in Seventh-day Adventist families and congregations worldwide (Keller 2005). As in the discussions of the Knowledge Society, method has a curious double role in these pedagogical approaches. On the one hand, it is never treated as an end in itself, but as a tool for helping didactic content reach diverse recipients. But with its promise of making content comprehensible and relevant to diverse audiences, method can so preoccupy the teachers that the underlying premises of what they are being asked to teach recede into the background.

Methods in Circulation

In order to bridge the gap between the worlds of planners and researchers and the lives they seek to transform, methods themselves have to be able to circulate. Two features of the concept of method with which the Knowledge Society operated ensured this capacity for circulation: a method had to be specific to a particular audience, but should in principle be universally applicable. Universal applicability meant first of all that the method should produce the same results no matter who applied it, provided it was applied correctly. Disappointing results could only be caused by the insufficient preparation of peripheral practitioners. This was a common way of explaining the failure of universal schemes for improvement during the Khrushchev era, as exemplified in the analogy between a badly written lecture and badly grown corn made at the 1956 seminar. Alluding to one of Khrushchev's pet projects—the promotion of maize as a food crop—one participant complained: "When we receive a lecture from the districts it is like a corn plant that is barely alive in the hands of an incompetent manager."[10]

When correctly applied, a method should not only work independently of who was using it, it should also produce the same result in any audience of comparable social and educational background. The emergent empirical sociology of religion argued that different social backgrounds required specific methodical approaches (Pivovarov 1974). But the underlying idea was that human beings were so similar to one another that they would respond in the same way when given equal access to training and information—an idea that runs counter to some of Russia's religious traditions.

A look at the actual methodical directives in printed lecture texts shows that the quest to adapt universal truths to the specifics of local life encouraged a fill-in-the-blanks approach to local realities. In 1962, the Mari division of the Knowledge Society reproduced 250 copies of a lecture by a historian from Joshkar-Ola, "The realization of the decisions of the March plenum of the Central Committee of the CPSU—The concern of the whole party, the whole people." Intended for the use of lecturers in the rural districts, the text is interspersed with pieces of "methodical advice for the lecturer," all of which ask for specific local information. Where the lecture text talks about the contribution of the Mari ASSR to the task of provisioning the USSR with agricultural products, the lecturer is advised to "provide data on the condition of agricultural production, the plans for 1962 and the coming years in the district, collective farm, or state farm in which the lecture will be read."[11] In other places, directives recommend the insertion of the names of local progressive workers and enterprises, or ask for instances of assistance to agriculture rendered by the industrial enterprise or school where the lecture is delivered.[12]

In this understanding, the point of methodology is to help a speaker adapt content to make it comprehensible and relevant to the intended audience. The performative genre of the lecture as encounter between propagandist and audience remains constant. But the 1960s and '70s also saw a renewed interest in a greater variety of genres, known as the "forms" of propaganda. Such experimentation had been a feature of Bolshevik political culture since the 1920s, when knowledge was made mobile with the help of mass spectacles, propaganda trains, mock trials, and innovative forms of classroom discussion (Clark 1995; David-Fox 1997; Kenez 1985; Petrone 2000; Plaggenborg 1996).

As a speaker at a 1959 meeting of atheist propagandists reminded the audience, forms were genres of performance common to all agitation work, while methods needed to be specific to the content they were intended to bring across.[13] While there were indeed generic forms, such as film showings or evenings of questions and answers, some named forms were used exclusively to bring across atheist content, such as the Evening of Miracles without Miracles. In practice, instructions for performative genres (forms) circulated together with directives on how to adapt content to audiences (methods). If Knowledge Society planners were reluctant to acknowledge the link between content and performance, this speaks of their ambivalence toward emotional appeals in propaganda, and preference for the text-heavy lecture as the prototype of cultural enlightenment work.

The tension between central regulation and local improvisation inherent in the circulation of forms and methods offers a key to understanding what atheist work meant to those who conducted it. While some historians have described Soviet propaganda as ossified and boring, the constant pressure to produce quantifiable and reportable results did more than just create meaningless and ill-attended events designed to impress on paper more than in reality (Peris 1998). In order to produce the infamous paper trails, methodicians had to imaginatively engage with information about the work of institutions in other parts of the Soviet Union, because by reporting on copying and adapting new performance genres they could demonstrate that they were working to increase the effectiveness of their own events. Conferences, publications, and circulars were geared toward facilitating the exchange of experiences and the circulation of new forms. Officially encouraged copying helped preserve doctrinal orthodoxy, but it also encouraged a degree of innovation by asking cultural workers to adapt approaches from elsewhere to the needs of their communities. Akin to Malagasy Seventh-day Adventists following study guides designed in North America (Keller 2005), provincial Soviet activists could find pleasure in replicating correct procedures in spite of the lack of resources and the ambiguity of directions that separated them from the center.

Method as Metadiscourse

The focus on procedural matters that comes with methodical training confirms Alexei Yurchak's observation that late Soviet authoritative discourse was organized around an interest in performative rules rather than in the referential meaning of the underlying ideology. In his work on the political subjectivities of postwar Soviet generations, Yurchak claims that this "performative turn" happened shortly before Stalin's death, and meant that there no longer was a metadiscourse in which ideological messages could be made explicit, questioned, or modified (Yurchak 2006: 74–76). The archival records of Khrushchev era atheist training sessions indeed lack any explicit debate or questioning of ideological matters. But what generated controversy during those sessions were precisely the matters of performance that, in Yurchak's view, fostered a sense of unquestionable reality. At times, debates about the match between performance rules and desired outcomes came close to constituting a metadiscourse on ideologically inspired action, bringing to the surface divergent views about the ethics, rather than the truth value, of the socialist ideology people were being trained to promote.

An example of a form that aroused controversy is the Evening of Miracles without Miracles (Russian *Vecher "Chudesa bez Chudes"*), a demonstration of chemical experiments designed to pit the wonders of science against religious miracles. The first mention of this event in the files of the Knowledge Society is in the transcript of the 1956 seminar for atheist propagandists, where section chairman Khudjakov reports on a performance in Tashkent. The audience sat "holding their breath" for three and a half hours, watching an astronomer, a biologist, a physicist, and a chemist perform experiments. Among other things, they showed "concretely and convincingly how one form of energy turns into another."[14]

The Tashkent demonstration seems to have been an attempt to show the mastery of science over the natural world without any direct reference to religious narratives. Khudjakov was impressed and recommended this form for use elsewhere. But the subtlety of propagating science without direct anti-religious polemics proved difficult to sustain. Three years later, a leading atheist from the Stavropol' region complained that audiences could fail to get the message that science and religion were incompatible and might understand the demonstration of humanly produced "miracles" as confirmation "that such miracles happened, and we, supposedly, merely demonstrate their mechanism, explaining how Jesus Christ turned wine into water [*sic*], and our Ivanov turns water into wine."[15]

Different from Tashkent, the Stavropol' performance aimed at showing how religious narratives masked the involvement of human agents: it was no miracle that Jesus Christ turned one sort of liquid into another, because "our Ivanov"[16] could do it too. This direct juxtaposition of science and religion was intended to expose the absurdity of the latter, but involved the risk that audiences would see the performance as a scientific confirmation of biblical narratives. Doubts in higher places notwithstanding, the Stavropol' variant seems to have been the one more widely used, probably because of the greater entertainment value of direct criticism and ridicule. In the Mari ASSR, Mikhail Nekhoroshkov, a biologist from the teachers college, traveled through the countryside with groups of students, giving atheist lectures followed by chemical demonstrations which showed how icons could be made to weep or bleed, why holy water did not become stale, where thunder and lightning come from, and how volcanoes erupt (Nekhoroshkov 1964).

These demonstrations were quite popular in the Mari ASSR and were carried out at least from 1961 to 1972, when recordings of a performance became the centerpiece of a radio feature.[17] But there were also local critics, who deplored the mismatch between the intended results and the methods used. In an interview, the sociologist Viktor Solov'ev called the genre "vulgar anti-religiosity," where anticlericalism and ridiculing of religious beliefs took the place of "elevating the level of the masses." For the Moscow-trained social scientist, his older colleague's approach smacked of the unrefined tactics of the League of the Militant Godless.

Defenders of the direct unmasking approach pointed to its greater emotional effect. In response to the critique of the Evening of Miracles at the 1959 seminar, a propagandist from Tambov argued that atheist methods had to be commensurable with the emotional pressures exerted by the church:

> After all, the church people used these effects as a form for emotional impact, for impact on feelings. Who wouldn't be able to see that when in the church the words "Christ is risen" appear, they affect ethnic [natsional'nye] feelings. That is why we carry out this chemical experiment with a talk where we show that the church people use some experiments for a particular goal, and others for more emotional impact. And this is how one has to approach this question.[18]

In this argument, the point of propaganda forms and methodical approaches was not simply to convey information, but also to affect audiences emotionally, and to make them aware of how emotions could be manipulated by less benign agents. There was no consensus among late Soviet atheist propagandists about the range of permissible emotional impacts, however. Recognizing that the orchestration of mass gatherings necessarily involves choices about some kind of "emotional regime" (Reddy 2001), scholarship on Soviet public events has long noted their relatively dry, intentionally rationalist character. Though encouraging a certain amount of joyful exuberance, Soviet propaganda theory avoided appeals to deep psychology (Benn 1989; Humphrey 1998: 399; Rolf 2006). Comparative work on Stalinist and National Socialist mass gatherings has interpreted the Soviet distrust of undirected emotions as an expression of the party's didactic claim to transforming mass consciousness, rather than appealing to a popular unconscious in the fashion of the Nazis (Klimó and Rolf 2006).

In the postwar discussions of Knowledge Society members, one finds no explicit comparisons to Nazi practices and only occasional references to Stalinism as a negative foil helping to justify the society's own approaches.[19] However, in the ambivalent messages lecturers received about the proper balance of emotions and intellect in propaganda, one hears echoes of Khrushchev's and Brezhnev's successive denunciations of the policies of their predecessors as "personality cults," and perhaps of an even more long-standing Soviet wavering between encouraging revolutionary "enthusiasm" and fearing its excesses (Breslauer 1982; Gorsuch 2000).

One training session on the art of oratory at a 1963 seminar summarized the authoritative view of what proper methods should accomplish by comparing the "world view" that was to be communicated to a light bulb. Only the lamp in a dark room allowed the owner to "correctly make use of [his] things, as a master of the house [po-khozjajski]."[20] This vision of cultural enlightenment work as a lamp turned on in listeners' heads, enabling them to gain instrumental mastery over their surroundings, seems to preclude any search for methods of psychological influence at other-than-rational levels. And yet, as shown by the lecturer who compared the tactics of "church people" and of the Evenings of Miracles, the assumed emotional appeal of religious liturgies remained a source of envy for Soviet methodicians. While never systematized into an explicit ethical discourse, debates about the appropriateness of particular methods did constitute a site of controversy and reflection, where participants articulated their ideas about the ends of cultural enlightenment work.

Another site where a metadiscourse of methodical didacticism emerged was in reflections on the purpose of training ever-growing numbers of people to be instructors. In retrospect, some former participants identified the performers, rather than the audience, as the real target of the desired emotional influence. One former member of Nekhoroshkov's atheist student club, now a Lutheran pastor, remembered that the traveling atheists were well received by rural audiences, probably because people found the spectacular experiments interesting (he specifically remembered the volcano eruption) and because talented students were chosen to give musical and poetry recitals between the experiments. But in hindsight, he thought that the performances were less effective in converting the believers among the audience than in confirming student propagandists in their atheist convictions—"through emotion, feelings, logic."

Analyses that pinpoint the instructors-in-training as the real objects of transformation are not restricted to post-Soviet hindsight. According to one report from Joshkar-Ola's teachers college, written in 1960, training in agitation and propaganda was supposed to encourage students in the "development of creative initiative, self-activity [samodejatel'nost'], [and] the search for new, engaging [uvlekatel'nye] forms of agitational work." Students would develop "a serious attitude toward their work" as they "systematically hold talks, readings, use works of fiction, illustrations, slide shows, magazines and other things."[21] This report mentions in one breath the ethos of responsibility for one's work and the technical mastery of a battery of propaganda forms. If religion worked through deception and manipulation, the Soviet educational system produced people whose scientific knowledge, combined with such personal qualities as creativity and self-responsibility, would keep them secure from errors and help them take responsibility for their contemporaries.

Soviet assumptions about didactic skill treat it as an embodiment of the secular ideal of exclusively human communicative action. But methodical training turns out to be detachable from its atheist content, even as the assumptions about teaching as a tool of mobilization and transformation remain. The stories of post-Soviet religious methodicians show the surprising resilience of Soviet didacticism, which is now used for quite different transformative goals.

Religious Methodicians

In post-Soviet Marij El, I encountered many people who would have been able to identify with the atheist propagandists' concern with method. Almost all religious communities had clergy or active lay members who exemplified the didactic ethos described in the report on the student agitators: taking responsibility for a social ideal through striving to shape the views and behavior of others. These religious activists also shared the worries and questions of the participants in the atheist seminars: how to find a language for doctrinal truths that people would understand and put into practice. Some of them, such as the Lutheran pastor, had conducted atheist propaganda themselves at an earlier point in their lives. Even more had trained in Soviet cultural professions, including teachers, journalists, methodicians in cultural institutions, artists, and musicians. With only a few exceptions, they had not grown up in religious households and had typically taken up religious practice in the early 1990s, after the collapse of the Soviet Union.

Some Soviet-trained methodicians readily acknowledged that the skills they had acquired in their secular training served them well in religious work. Those they instructed also recognized them as long-time teachers, and had particular expectations of them. The example of religious methodicians shows the success of Soviet efforts to inculcate teacherly qualities into large parts of the population, but also the collapse of the hope for purely human-driven transformations that had animated Soviet cultural enlightenment work. Using the resources offered by the religious traditions they had joined, converts conceptualized the relationship between the different periods of their lives in various ways.

Among those who found that their Soviet pedagogical or methodological training had served them well in religious work was another Lutheran, a woman born in 1968 who graduated from the foreign-language department of the teachers college and now served as a Sunday school teacher and translator. She claimed that "the methodology for foreign-language teaching and Sunday school are the same" and that her training for work with children helped in her new duties. Likewise, a retired instructor from the teachers college who coordinated courses for the Sisters of Mercy in the Orthodox diocese, found that it was quite easy to find physicians willing and able to teach basic medical skills to these devout laywomen. During the Soviet period all physicians had been required to "carry knowledge to the people" and give public education lectures, she explained.[22] A retired childcare worker now leading a Baptist Bible study had been the propagandist in charge of political education sessions in her work collective. She stated that this experience had helped her learn the skill of gathering information on a specific topic and adapting it to the understanding of her audience.

As I have argued elsewhere, religious work in post-Soviet Russia is one of a limited number of areas where people can recycle the didactic skills they acquired in Soviet cultural work to make a modest living, while preserving values of economic disinterestedness and service to others (Luehrmann 2005). The various religious traditions offered different ways to resolve the moral quandary created by this change of ideological allegiance. Among the centrally determined topics the Baptist Bible study leader had covered as part of her former duties as a propagandist were atheist ones; she specifically remembered making a wall newspaper entitled "Sticky spider's web," devoted to the evils of religion and sectarianism. Whenever she mentioned this aspect of her past, she asked God's forgiveness in an aside—"Forgive me, Lord, for this disgrace [bezobrazie]." But as a believer in predestined salvation, she also maintained that her previous work had been part of a divine plan to prepare her for her current church service.

The Lutheran deacon who founded the rural congregation of Ljupersola, a trained journalist and a well-known writer of Mari-language fiction, was more outspoken about the functional and moral equivalence of his work throughout his life. It was difficult, he admitted, to travel to schools now and speak about Lutheranism when people knew that he "used to speak about other things" (first as a Komsomol official, then as the editor of the youth newspaper of the republic, also under Komsomol control). But really, he added, he was still speaking about the same thing, about goodness, except that earlier he had been "without God." But he felt "as if he, the Lord, had prepared me all my life—that may be putting it too grandly—for this work.

Because now I feel at ease before an audience, I have all the skills, I know how to communicate, and people see me, understand me, accept me, listen to me." For example, as the graduate of a boarding school for artistically gifted children, he was a good singer and skilled at designing hand-painted posters. "What God gave, that's what I'm using now, only now, so late, but God knows when it is time. Back then, maybe, I didn't have the life experience to talk to people. God knows better after all." When I later told this man about my archival research with the records of the Knowledge Society, he said that, although it was certainly bad that the society conducted atheist propaganda, in principle its lecturers did good work by "carrying knowledge to the people," and that it was a pity that no one was visiting the villages with lectures any more.

The Tatar woman teaching courses in Quranic reading to women in Joshkar-Ola's mosque had a somewhat different biography from these retired professionals, but like them, she had once done cultural work within a Soviet bureaucracy. Born in 1942, she was the daughter of a war widow who could not afford to keep her in school beyond sixth grade, which forced her to give up her dream of becoming a teacher and work in a factory instead. Though refusing to join the Communist Party, she became active in the trade union and was put in charge of organizing *samodejatel'nost'*—literally, self-activity, meaning amateur concerts and recitals put together by collectives of workers to entertain colleagues or to enter into competitions with other enterprises. This places her among the amateur methodicians into whose training and supervision late Soviet organizations invested such efforts and resources.

Quite in line with the ideal of elevation through self-activity, this factory worker had acquired an authoritative demeanor which people in the mosque community recognized as the habitus of a teacher. One of her students and the woman who ran the mosque store both told me that she had been a teacher all her life. She also shared with a Soviet era teacher a high esteem for knowledge, but did not place it in contrast to blind religious faith, as a lecturer of the Knowledge Society might have done. For this Quran teacher, the transition between her secular and religious careers was marked by the acquisition of knowledge about Islam—she had had "faith" all her life, she said, but no "knowledge"—and it was only the time spent at a *medrese* in Kazan' after retirement that enabled her to acquire whatever authority she now had to teach others.

Not everyone saw a moral break between cultural and religious work. The director of the culture club in the village of Shin'sha, who was also the chairwoman of the local chapter of Mari Ushem, a Mari cultural association with a mildly nationalist agenda, had taken the initiative to revive Mari sacrificial ceremonies in her village. These had not been publicly conducted since the sacred grove was appropriated for use in the secular festival *peledysh pajrem*. Tellingly, the club director used the language of Soviet cultural administration when talking about the revival of religious ceremonies in the grove: "I asked the administration not to hold these mass events there, but, so to speak, to renew the work which was carried out before [*kotoraja provodilas' ran'she*], to clean the prayer grove." By using the verb *provodit'* (to carry out), whose subject is typically a bureaucratic agency, the director assimilated ceremonies to such other forms of cultural work as mass festivals, classes offered in the club, or youth discos. Using another expression from the Soviet centralized networks of continuing education, she recalled identifying potential priests and sending them to the capital to study with the high priest of the republic "through the line of Mari Ushem" (*po linii Mari Ushem*).

Although she attempted to defer to the expertise of the "grandmothers" whose memories of past ceremonies she collected, the club director found that the villagers accepted the ceremony as one more kind of event which it was her job to organize. After having organized a ceremony on St. Peter's Day[23] (July 12) for the first time in 2001, she had expected that next year the grandmothers would take the initiative. But as July approached, people started asking why there weren't any posters with announcements similar to those she had put up the previous year—"So there'll be no St. Peter's Day this year?" Again in the style of Soviet festival planners, the director stated that the ceremony on St. Peter's Day was still in the process of "entering into tradition" (*vkhodit v traditsiju*).

If culture and religion seemed to merge easily for the club director, this may not have been the case for all residents. One of the old women of the village (to whom I was introduced by younger relatives who considered her an expert on Mari traditional religion) told me that if I wanted to know about the sacrificial ceremonies, I should ask the club director. If old women accepted the much younger club director's role as organizer of the ceremony, this may indicate either that cultural work and religion were not opposed for them, or that the association with cultural institutions had so changed the event that they did not recognize it as the same ceremony that was conducted in their youth. Other Shin'sha residents told me that some old people refused to attend the ceremonies because they thought that the grove had been irredeemably desecrated by the Soviet secular holidays.

While such reservations may also have existed in other places, I encountered the staff of culture clubs and schools at work on village ceremonies in various parts of the republic: as assistants of the priest or as organizers who talked the collective farm chairmen into donating sacrificial animals and mobilized villagers into cleaning up the sacred grove before the ceremony in a *subbotnik,* the Soviet era term for a voluntary-compulsory community workday. If villagers expected the involvement of cultural workers in ceremonies, this indicates that they had come to accept a crucial part of the Soviet social imaginary: that of a village community in which neighborly relations were not sufficient, but that needed the mobilizing efforts of state institutions to fully constitute itself. As religious ceremonies were understood by analogy with forms of "society work" (Rogers 2009), they found a place in administrative pyramids in which all lines led to the capital, much as they did for the secular festivals.

All these methodians drew on theological resources to conceptualize the relationship between their former and current work. For the Protestants, the idea of instantaneous salvation through newfound faith made their past morally neutral, available as a source of skills that posed no threat to a convert's current standing in the church. The Quran teacher expressed more regret at not having fulfilled her obligations as a Muslim through much of her life, but cited her previous lack of knowledge and young age as attenuating factors. For those villagers who accepted the sacrificial ceremonies as a method for creating social cohesion, there was no moral problem in the transitions between sacred grove, festival ground, and back. But at least some villagers apparently thought that reviving the correct actions did not salvage the spoiled sacred place. Russian Orthodox theology presents even greater obstacles to assumptions about the primacy of methodical action over the inner qualities of people or places.

Method and Anti-Method

The Russian Orthodox Church does recognize teachers and cultural workers as keys to making religion matter in social life, but keeps them at a certain institutional distance. Since 1998, the diocese of Marij El has organized a yearly joint conference with the Ministry of Education on topics of religion and morality. The 2005 conference was held under the title "Secular education and the spiritual-moral traditions of Russia." The archbishop required all priests to attend, and each of them brought a group of teachers from their parish to Joshkar-Ola. Seeing the small buses parked around the Socio-Political Center (formerly owned by the Communist Party and known as the House of Political Enlightenment) was a reminder of the cultural power wielded by the church through such modest but significant resources. Some parishes owned their own bus, others had access to buses owned by the district or village administration, and being able to offer teachers an excursion to the capital at a time of low salaries and rising transit fees was likely to make an impression.

As during Mari ceremonies in the villages, religion at these conferences coexisted quite comfortably with cultural work and education. Unlike Chimarij Paganism, the Orthodox Church had an institutional structure of its own and was able to partially set the agenda in its relationship with state institutions. Although the church hierarchy sought to collaborate with the state on issues of moral education, conversations with Orthodox clergy showed that their ideas about learning, personhood, and community were quite far removed from the Soviet understanding of method. It was from these clergymen that I heard the most pronounced skepticism against the transfer of methodical approaches to religious practice, helping me understand some of the assumptions built into the enthusiasm about methods I encountered elsewhere.

This skepticism existed even among clergy whose backgrounds also made them religious methodicians. The parish priest of one of the district centers had formerly been an instructor at the College for Cultural Enlightenment (Kul'tprosvetuchilishche, renamed the College of Culture—Kolledzh Kul'tury—in the 1990s). Several of his parishioners made a positive link between the fact that he was "a former cultural worker" and his qualities as a priest: he was well educated and "articulate" (*gramotnyj*), and he had a good voice and clear diction, making his services impressive and easy to follow. The priest also used a very didactic—and Soviet—simile in his Easter sermon, saying, "We should come to church as to a school, but instead we treat it as a House of Everyday Life." The House of Everyday Life (Dom byta) in a Soviet city was a center for services such as hairdressing, watchmaking, repairs of household appliances, and other everyday needs of the population, and it often mutated into a department store in post-Soviet times. Although the exhortation not to treat the house of worship as a place of commerce has New Testament roots, the positive counterpoint in the biblical passage is not a school but a "house of prayer."[24] In his sermon, this priest thus accorded a moral dignity to the school that was reminiscent of Soviet didactic discourse. But when I interviewed him, he decisively denied that his training in the cultural education sector was useful for what counted most about church service:

Q: Some of your parishioners told me, our *batjushka*[25] is a former cultural worker, that is why his diction is good, everything is easy to understand. Do you think that your worldly education has given you anything for church work, or are those totally different things?

A: I think it hinders me. Because spiritual education[26] is different. The foundation, take the one I received—I after all received a Marxist-Leninist foundation. Philosophy, economics, political economy, scientific communism, and atheism, scientific atheism. But it is a surprising thing, it strengthens me still more in my faith in God. Knowing all that, knowing these things, knowing psychology, social psychology, that strengthens me still more in my faith. In this sense, yes, it helps. But for the service, it only hinders me.

Q: And for the service in the church in your view, what is the most necessary quality in a person?

A: To be without sin yourself. If I were totally without sin, if I never sinned, if I were pure of heart, that is, everything would be a hundred times better. A hundred times better. The most important thing is not the word, the most important thing is personal example, personal life, everything, everything. People feel this from far away. A saint can be felt from far away. And my goal, as of all Orthodox people, is to draw close to saintliness, draw close to God, that is the goal.

Another Orthodox parish priest, this one a former instructor of agricultural engineering, gave an equally anti-methodical answer when I asked how he would explain to a person who worshiped in both Mari prayer groves and Christian churches that these are not the same thing. There is no way to explain it, he said. If someone does not see in the heart what stands behind the outwardly similar practices, that person cannot be made to see it.

In both cases, the priests evaded my attempt to speak about the methodical skills of diction and persuasive argumentation by directing the conversation to the inner qualities of teachers and learners. Instead of assuming universal applicability, they insisted that the most ingenious methods would fail if the person applying them or the person on whom they were used lacked the requisite traits and dispositions. In reverse, if these were present, the specific methods applied were secondary. The qualities in question were not necessarily innate, but could be acquired through patient exercise, similar to the virtues of humility and submission to God which Muslim women in the Egyptian piety movement studied by Saba Mahmood (2005) sought to cultivate through prayer and dress. The cultural-worker-turned-priest speaks of life as a process of "drawing close to saintliness"; the other priest alludes to the notion of freedom of will in Orthodox theology, according to which one can become receptive to spiritual truth through deliberate work on oneself (Zigon 2011). Transformation here does not come from quickly following the steps outlined in a set of methodical instructions. Rather, it

requires a process of self-fashioning through discipline and liturgical observance that potentially takes a lifetime, and the goal is to become a new kind
of person rather than a bearer of skills. This is why the cultural-worker-
turned-priest laments the wrong "foundation" he received in his personal
development, and the time he lost pursuing other goals, and why he says
that his secular education "hinders" him in his church service.

The swift conviction with which these priests repudiated my attempts to
engage in the conversations on method that worked well with members of
other denominations brought into focus some of the ideas underlying Soviet
and post-Soviet didactic discourse. The notion of the learning process as a
stimulus to which everyone responds in a similar way relies on assumptions about the essentially similar makeup of each human being, assumptions Louis Dumont has identified as a feature of modern individualism.
The contrasting idea that people are qualitatively different from each other,
whether by birth or by long, disciplined development (and for that reason
complement each other in different tasks), is among the features of Dumont's
(1966) depiction of hierarchical society that make it so alien to modern
social imaginaries. The priestly ideal that several Orthodox clergymen and
laypeople described—a saintly hermit in a remote rural location endowed
with powers of prophecy and second sight, by whose prayers any miracle
was possible—had as little in common with the equalizing impulse of the
Knowledge Society's quest to make as many people as possible into teachers as it had with the Protestant notion of the priesthood of all believers.[27]

Involved here are different visions of personhood, but also different
visions of the foundation and dynamics of a community, each bringing certain values of temporality and scale. Soviet methods, like the ones used by
churches oriented toward growth through evangelizing, were designed to
be transmissible in short training sessions in order to produce the many
lecturers, study circle leaders, and methodicians needed to quickly integrate
a population to follow a centrally defined vision. Even where the actual
audience for the events organized by these specialists was small, their spatial, visual, and auditory layout treated spectators as an open-ended mass
of strangers. Such audiences exist through being mobilized, a feature that
unites modern publics and voluntaristic denominations (Warner 2002) and
distinguishes them from the hierarchical imaginary, where the community
precedes any of its parts. In light of this distinction, it is understandable
why the club director in Shin'sha contrasted the Soviet era "mass festivals"
(*massovye prazdniki*) with "religious festivals" (*religioznye prazdniki*). Religious rituals in a village might draw as many people as a Soviet mass festival,
but they do not constitute their public through the number of individuals

they attract—one member of a family might attend, for instance, and fulfill duties for relatives.

The same principle of hierarchical complementarity applies to Orthodox Christianity, as it was understood by lay believers in Marij El and explained in church doctrine. Different from the interchangeability of individuals gathered in a mass public, Orthodox ecclesiology contains a strong emphasis on the church as a hierarchy, where people are endowed with different capacities for attaining divine truths and have distinctive roles to play in order to obtain common salvation (Headley 2010). In the words of Hermann Goltz, interpreting the Corpus Areopagiticum, the anonymous but influential body of work of a sixth-century theologian, hierarchy is an "interlocking celestial and terrestrial order" representing "the ideal (final) condition that divine philanthropy has instituted for the salvation of fallen human *physis*." In this social order, the capacity to see divine truths is "deflected" through the descending ranks, which are "adapted to the respective intelligences in their greater or lesser perfection" (Goltz 1974: 148). The church as an institution offers participation in this divine order, but without the expectation that every member will be able to be a teacher and transmitter of divine truths.

In the post-Soviet Russian Orthodox Church, this view of the primacy of the institution over its individual members helps make sense of the tribulations of clergy and believers under socialism. One history of Russian Orthodoxy in early Soviet Russia argues that the compromises made by the Moscow Patriarchate with the Bolsheviks starting in 1923 were a sacrifice on the part of the bishops of that time for the sake of preserving the institutionalized ritual life of the church, at the cost of compromising their own integrity. In the view of the author, a professional historian and ordained priest, what mattered was to preserve the church as a transhistorical entity "for the children, for the grandchildren, the great-grandchildren of those who had now abandoned the church hierarchy" (Mitrofanov 2002: 295). The value of the institution lies in the tradition of worship and spiritual experience it embodies (Florovsky 2003 [1963]), not in its ability to mobilize and train members at any given point in time.

But however eternal the church is imagined to be, it must still be animated by its living members. In Marij El, people became active as Orthodox Christians by performing and receiving what Goltz calls "hierarchical actions": blessings (which are given by someone of higher status to someone lower down, for instance by a priest to a layperson or a mother to her children), mutual intercessory prayer, and virtuous acts that people performed for someone else's benefit. When, after mass one Sunday, I joined a group of predominantly elderly women who helped clean the floor of Joshkar-Ola's

Russian Orthodox cathedral (a pious act said to procure the forgiveness of sins), one of the women said that she would be doing this for her grandchildren as long as she could, and then at some point they would have to do it for her. These acts constitute community not by asking people to go beyond their intimate relationships and address a public of strangers and potential recruits, but by transforming the meaning of these intimate connections. Mobilization through pyramids of teacher-student relationships attempts to reorganize neighborliness into universal comradeship. Instead, Orthodox hierarchical actions leave the apparent chaos of neighborly and kin relations intact, but superimpose the biblical understanding of the "neighbor" as one who gives and receives care.

Of course, it is hard for contemporary Orthodox clergy to completely ignore the promises of didactic method for revitalizing community life, and pedagogical conferences are only one way in which the diocese cultivates allies among cultural and educational workers. As far as the priests are concerned, we might consider their reticence about the very idea of methods as an outsiders' version of the insiders' tribulations about *appropriate* methods that we saw among the Soviet propagandists. By comparison, some of the didactic models that come to post-Soviet religiosity from abroad ask few questions about permissible means in transformative efforts, treating increases in membership as ends in themselves.

Cells of Growth

One of the Protestant churches that sprang up in Joshkar-Ola in the first half of the 1990s is the Christian Center, founded as a mission project of a Charismatic church in Beaumont, Texas. A missionary from Texas conducted services and Bible studies in a rented auditorium space from 1993 onward, and donations from his home congregation eventually helped buy the building of the disused cinema Mir (Peace) in the eastern part of the city. Although its membership was small (less than fifty people attended Sunday services on average during the time of my fieldwork), the Christian Center epitomized everything that seemed wrong with Protestantism to city officials and Orthodox clergy. Its evangelizing strategies were aggressive and loud, without respect for preexisting Christian traditions or established religious-ethnic boundaries. Its worship style included speaking in tongues and dancing to rock music, which seemed to mark it as just as foreign as its initial funding sources. But the popular appellation "the American Center" notwithstanding, by the end of the 1990s the church maintained only loose connections to its American founders. The last American pastor had paid only infrequent visits due to visa problems, and had finally found a permanent replacement in 2004 in a young Russian man from Joshkar-Ola who had joined the church as a teenager. Now in his late twenties, the young pastor had spent a few years in Moscow, where he received no formal theological training but had served and studied at a church named Triumphant Zion, a mission of the Embassy of God in Kiev, a Charismatic megachurch founded by the Nigerian Sunday Adelaja (Wanner 2007). After returning to Joshkar-Ola, the pastor maintained spiritual and educational bonds with Pastor Aleksandr Dzjuba of Triumphant Zion, and through him with Adelaja, and sought to reorganize his church according to their model.

Much of this model was concerned with making relationships of spiritual learning and teaching into structural principles of church growth. In the tradition of Pentecostal Protestantism,[28] the members of the Christian Center believed that publicly asking Jesus to forgive one's sins was sufficient for salvation, but that a Christian would reap even greater earthly and heavenly rewards for a life of service to God's kingdom. In order to become fit for service, two things were necessary: receiving the baptism of the Holy Spirit (which manifested itself in the gift of praying in tongues) and improving oneself through study and spiritual discipline. As a precondition for successful evangelization, the Embassy of God and its affiliate churches emphasized the need to obtain God's blessing through human intermediaries endowed with spiritual and social authority. According to one of its junior pastors, the mission of Triumphant Zion in Moscow was to offer the "apostolic protection" of Pastor Sunday to the many churches in Russia that, like the Christian Center, had been founded by Western missionaries and then left to their own devices. "It is good when a church has one apostolic protection, and this protection constantly watches over [*bljudet*] the growth of the church, the development of the church. That makes for healthy growth of the church." Western missionaries had not inculcated the same respect for spiritual authority: "They deserve thanks for planting churches, but they didn't give them moral training [*ne vospitali*]."

In order to institutionalize spiritual protection at all levels, Triumphant Zion promoted a model for church growth that all involved considered to be a Western import, although again the claim was that its American popularizers did not grasp its full spiritual significance. Under the G-12, or "cell church," principle, twelve church leaders (known in Russian by the Anglicism *lidery*) receive teachings directly from the pastor and pass them on to members of small prayer groups with which each leader meets once a week. Each member of such a "cell group" (*jachejka*) or "house group" (*domashnjaja gruppa*) is in turn encouraged to find his or her own "disciples" (*ucheniki*) either among less experienced church members or among the unconverted, drawing them into the church. Ideally, groups should split once they reach more than twelve members—the number of Jesus's disciples and, as the young pastor at the Christian Center explained, the maximum number of students to which any teacher could realistically transmit his or her knowledge. As the links between the Christian Center and Triumphant Zion strengthened, the church in Joshkar-Ola struggled to move to the G-12 principle from a less strictly ordered set of house groups that met on Tuesday nights in various parts of the city.

Cell groups at the Christian Center were in many ways reminiscent of Soviet study circles, but the complex network of international circulation through which the form had come to Joshkar-Ola shows how deceptive such resemblances can be. During my year-long stay in 2005, I was invited to attend the house group that met in the church building itself, which was attended by approximately eight long-standing members who lived close by. Based on experiences with small groups in other Protestant churches, I had expected the group to be engaged primarily in Bible study. But at the first meeting the group members, after an opening prayer and some chatting over tea and cookies, all took out the notes they had taken on the previous Sunday's sermon on the topic "The foundation of your victory," and proceeded to discuss what the pastor had tried to tell them. They studied the Bible verses mentioned in the sermon, which ranged from the story of King David's adultery with Bathsheba (2 Samuel 11) to a verse from the epistles saying that God judges without reference to the person, but by the deeds of each (1 Peter 1:17). The focus was on understanding the pastor's intention in grouping the passages together, and on making decisions about applying the sermon's message to one's life. When the discussion veered too far, the group leader (a woman in her forties who taught English at the technical university) injected quotes from the sermon to draw attention to the pastor's core points about vigilance against sin: "he [the pastor] pronounced the following phrase several times: When Jesus died, God did not take off the robe of the judge," and "[the pastor] said several times: flies don't land on a hot skillet."

The group referred to this activity as *razbirat' propoved'* (taking apart the sermon), using terminology familiar from Soviet and post-Soviet education. There, *razbirat' temu* (taking apart or going over the topic) meant a presentation and discussion of the day's lesson as prescribed in the curriculum. The participatory structure of such a lesson—based on student presentations and joint discussion rather than lecture and rote learning—was akin to the study circles (*kruzhki*) and seminars that Russian socialists had developed in exile in the late nineteenth and early twentieth centuries and brought with them into the Soviet educational institutions founded in the 1920s (David-Fox 1997: 122, 170). Workplace-based study circles expanded during the Khrushchev era, guided by a centrally determined curriculum and textbooks (Benn 1989). The following excerpt from an evaluation, conducted in 1960, of the study circle on political economy attended by staff and faculty of what was then the Polytechnic Institute gives a taste of the method:

> Left over from the last class meeting was the question: "the role of banks in socialist society." They took apart that question [*Razobrali etot vopros*], but without bringing in new material. They started a new topic: "Socialist reproduction and national income." They took apart the questions: 1) The essence of socialist reproduction. 2) The gross social product. The participants were prepared for the lesson within the bounds of the textbook on polit-economy. . . . The passivity of the leader manifested itself in the fact that he underestimates the significance of introductory words, [simply] asking the participants "what question is left from the last class?" and "please present" [*pozhalujsta vystupajte*].[29]

Though set in the apparently open-ended form of a discussion, the aim of "taking apart" a textbook topic or a sermon is less to question, alter, or expand its content than to fully understand it and apply it to contexts of everyday life, a process whose appeal Eva Keller (2005: 129) aptly compares to that of completing a jigsaw puzzle and seeing the pieces come together in a predetermined design. In line with the role of methodicians as popularizers of received knowledge, the leader in the above quote is criticized for "passivity" because he does not provide proper guidance to the students, neglecting to steer the discussion and summarize key points. A similar concern with stimulating grassroots engagement while maintaining central control was seen in the sermon study groups at the Christian Center. This is how the young pastor explained the practice:

> It's about the thoughts that, for example, I think that God wishes that they would start working in the church. For example, I see that God moves the pastor to lead in a certain direction. And in order to lead, a word is necessary [*neobkhodimo slovo*], that is, we need to know where we are going, are we going in the right direction or not. For that reason, we take a particular topic, each month is distinguished by a particular topic. Every sermon has its topic within the framework of this big given topic. And to make sure that the people can also

move in that direction, for that reason they take apart the sermon. But there is nothing so strict about this that all would have to subscribe to the thoughts that *I* say. . . . The foundation in any case for all discussions is the Bible; it is the priority, the authority. The pastor can err, that's for sure. So sometimes even people can give advice, say that something is wrong. That is normal. That is what the Protestant movement consists of, that everyone has an opinion. But some kind of order needs to exist, and some kind of basic direction has to be given by the pastor, and discipleship needs to be maintained, I think, on all levels. But again, there should be freedom, only there shouldn't be any extremes in either direction.

With its similarity to Soviet study circles, the authoritarian didacticism of this church might appear to be a compromise between the Protestant principle that "everyone has an opinion" and a post-Soviet, or even Russian, reluctance to give up order and common direction. Going further into the history of Soviet study circles, political scientist Oleg Kharkhordin traces their way of deploying collective authority back to Russian Orthodox traditions. He argues that the Soviet collective, as theorized by Stalin era pedagogue Anton Makarenko, with its "relations of responsible dependency" and practices of mutual evaluation (Kharkhordin 1999: 91), represents a distinctive Russian-Soviet path to self-fashioning, different from the introspective practices of Western Europe. Drawing on Foucault's work on the importance of the private confession common in Catholic Europe for the formation of the Western European subject, Kharkhordin argues that Orthodox monastic practices of public penance and collective "unmasking" (*oblichenie*) created Russian and Soviet selves less concerned with psychological depth than with defining themselves in relation to others (228). In his argument, party cells are secularized versions of Orthodox monastic communities. Thus, Russian Protestant church cells might appear as newly theologized outcomes of a local tradition of collective control.

One problem with this idea is that many Bolshevik methodologies of collective study were pioneered before 1917 among exiled Russian social democrats in Western Europe. The traditions of the European Left and reform pedagogy constitute more obvious influences than Russian Orthodoxy (David-Fox 1997: 26–37; Scherrer 1978). Post-Soviet cell churches also find their inspiration outside of Russia: all the features of collective responsibility and mutual surveillance that might seem reminiscent of communist and perhaps even Orthodox collectivism are already part of the model that has reached Russia from Western Christendom and its extensions in the global south. The young pastor himself named two inspirations for cell groups in his church, the church of Yonggi Cho in South Korea and Brazilian churches organized along the G-12 principle. Some of the literature on church organization sold in the Christian Center and in related Moscow churches was written by U.S.-based authors such as Larry Stockstill, whose *The Cell Church* (2001 [1998]) was translated and published by Word of Life, a Charismatic church in Moscow.

Stockstill, the pastor of a megachurch in Colorado, describes cell groups as an ideal structure for a large, growth-oriented church because they serve several crucial functions simultaneously. As small groups meeting according to a centrally coordinated timetable and with leaders who report back to the pastor, they make possible a personal "ministry to each member of the body of Christ," as the subtitle of Stockstill's book proclaims, while realizing the principle of "flexibility and accountability" (Stockstill 2001 [1998]: 136; see also Hornsby 2000; Hurston 2001). As places where members can invite their unconverted friends and to which newly converted church members are referred, they serve as tools for evangelizing and retaining new members, and thus as instruments for church growth. Because of the expectation that members of a group will eventually become leaders of their own cell when the existing group grows and splits, the cells also serve the "formation of leaders" (110). Reminiscent of Kharkhordin's analysis of individuation through collective evaluation, it is the cell's responsibility to "analyze the spiritual gifts of its members, to help them take their place in the church" (34). For the content of the weekly meetings, Stockstill recommends the same mix of socializing, prayer for individual needs, discussion of the week's sermon, and development of service projects that was practiced in Joshkar-Ola, justifying the focus on the pastor's ideas by the need to keep cell group leaders from trying to elaborate their own teachings (154).

Stockstill's book and descriptions of discussion groups in Latin America and South Korea (D. Martin 1990: 143–144; D. Martin 2002: 13; O'Neill 2010: 26) show that there is nothing particularly "post-Soviet" about the cell group's aim to steer the circulation of knowledge while developing personal responsibility through collective accountability. In a variety of secular and religious contexts, such didactic structures are a way to put the benefits of face-to-face community to the service of a fast-growing organization. In the eyes of the members of Triumphant Zion and the Christian Center, what distinguished their cell groups from Soviet predecessors was the spiritual potency of a deferential teacher-student relationship that tied students not to a tradition of human knowledge, but to the leader's divine inspiration.

Although they credited American mentors with teaching these organizational principles, Russian Charismatics felt that the Americans missed part of their significance—another sign perhaps of the divine origin of ideas that could circulate even without human understanding.

The critique of lax American interpretations of teacher-student relationships was a major theme of Aleksandr Dzjuba's visit to the Christian Center in September 2005, on the occasion of the church's twelfth anniversary. The American legacies he singled out for criticism included first-name address and use of the familiar *ty* (you). The young pastor should be addressed with the formal *vy,* and church leaders and administrators by first name and patronymic in the usual Russian way of expressing respect. Leaders visiting from Moscow to hold workshops had to be thanked properly, so that they would come back. "I know that the Americans did not teach that, but we are in Russia now, it is time to return to natural life."

One of Dzjuba's aides went so far as to compare the young pastor to a prophet, whose teachings church members had to accept in the interests of their spiritual and material future. In search of a deeper understanding of deference and discipline, the Embassy of God and its affiliate churches often looked to guest preachers from an array of developing and Asian Tiger countries, such as the Jamaican Myles Munroe, the Korean Yonggi Cho, and the Singaporean Kong Hee. On one of his sermon tapes, Sunday Adelaja recommends such preachers as representing the future directions of God's work in the world, while dismissing the books of well-known American Charismatics such as Kenneth Hagin, which deal with how to receive health and prosperity through faith, as good for the first steps of the newly converted, but too simple for mature leaders.[30] The secrets of effective church growth, he argues, should be learned from places where churches are attracting new members against great odds, among people who live in economic or political hardship.

The Embassy of God and its affiliated churches could afford to be eclectic in their inspiration because the origin of an organizational principle mattered less to them than the fact that it had proven successful elsewhere. The young pastor described the search for appropriate methods as a process of abstracting basic principles from foreign models and biblical texts, looking for secrets of divine inspiration:

> There are principles, certain biblical principles. I think there are biblical principles that stand behind leadership, for example the principles of Jesus' success. In any case, behind any success there is a secret, there has to be a secret of some kind. Just by itself it doesn't happen. So when we discover these secrets, they begin to work in our lives.

But the main source of success is God. Success comes when a person listens to God and follows Him.

The implication of this characteristic mix of scientific positivism and biblical universalism (see also Sullivan 2009) was that it did not matter who designed a method and for what purpose, because the fact that it worked meant that it had God's approval. Somewhat ironically then, the idea of divine inspiration precluded ethical reflection on methods in this group.

Questions of Inspiration

While lines of actual historical influence are complex, with multiple crossings from West to East and back, one of the reasons that cell groups work in Russia is doubtlessly that there are many people who honed their discussion-leading skills in Soviet study circles. Unlike Marshall Sahlins's "structure of the conjuncture" (1985), where actors interact with elements of a foreign cultural system *as if* they were functional equivalents of something familiar, the affinity between study circles and cell groups presents a case where misrecognizing the equivalences allows people to continue acting in familiar ways.

A significant difference between postwar Soviet study circles and cell churches is that the former never theologized the teacher into a "prophet," something that would have been easily criticized as a Stalin-type "cult of personality" after the Twentieth Party Congress. Where Charismatic gatherings eagerly used elements of music, coordinated movement, and the mind-altering effects of fasting and sleepless nights to make the audience receptive to their messages, attempts to stir up mass exuberance met with suspicion among Soviet methodicians. If there is a point in identifying the elective affinities between Soviet and post-Soviet uses of method, it is not to establish a causal connection in which one element is the original and the other its copy or descendant. Rather, it is to see different axes along which method-talk can be compared: faith in standardized approaches to social transformation with rapid, predictable results animates Soviet atheist and Protestant mobilizations, but runs counter to Orthodox conceptions of hierarchical tradition. However, Soviet thought resembles Russian Orthodox and other regional religious traditions in another respect: they all offer resources for the ethical distinction between appropriate and inappropriate methods, while those branches of Protestantism that attempt to discern God's will from the success or failure of human endeavors can ultimately encourage an instrumental ethics that equates what works with what is good (Weber 1922).

Beyond these axes of difference, what unites methodicians of all stripes is that their work forces them to pay close attention to the reality that they set out to change. To borrow terms from Stefan Plaggenborg, methodicians have to concern themselves with the "transformation and transformability of mental and physical constitutions," rather than assuming the "interchange-ability" of dispensable people and circumstances (Plaggenborg 1996: 40). Working at a nodal point between centralized institutions and neighborly politics requires artful compromises, a constraint that may help reconcile Adorno's perception of the subservient powerlessness of pedagogues with the widespread suspicions about their manipulative power.

"Godless *chastushki* for all occasions," 1962. Part of a series published by the Artists Union of the USSR, this poster uses the genre of popular teasing verses to portray deception and ignorance as causes of religious beliefs. "Miraculous" renewals of icons are actually caused by chemical solutions; a seemingly devout woman uses icons to hide her moonshine distillery; and a flight through the heavens is sufficient to convince even an old woman that God does not exist. [Courtesy of State Museum of the History of Religion, Saint Petersburg, SM 441/1]

A Mari family in the Morki district, 1945. The older woman in the back is wearing the pointed *shymaksh* headdress that Soviet campaigns in the 1920s had targeted for elimination. [Private collection]

Peledysh pajrem in the former sacred grove, Shin'sha village, early 1970s. The headscarves worn by the women may be part of festive attire, but they may also indicate the women's awareness of entering into a sacred space. [Private collection]

На развилке дорог

В летнее время проводится много религиозных праздников, пропадают рабочие дни.

— Куда же податься?

Рис. И. Бакланова

"At the crossroads." In this cartoon from the campaign against religious holidays, an accordion player—an indispensable fixture at rural celebrations—tries to decide whether to go to a village with a church or to one with a sacred grove. The text above the drawing reads "In the summertime many religious holidays are celebrated, work days wasted." The text below literally translates as "Where should I wander?" But the verb, *podat'sja*, also evokes *poddat'sja*, to get drunk. [Drawing by I. Baklanov, *Marijskaja Pravda*, June 25, 1960]

The grain-grower's pledge, a secular coming-of-age celebration for collective farm youth, Sernur district, 1967. The sign in the back reads "Glory to those whose minds and hands forge the greatness of the motherland." [Courtesy of State Museum of the History of Religion, Saint Petersburg, SM 2349/1]

The jury at the harvest festival of a collective farm in the Sernur district, 1967. Judging competitions was an intricate part of Soviet festivals. [Courtesy of State Museum of the History of Religion, Saint Petersburg, SM 2350/1]

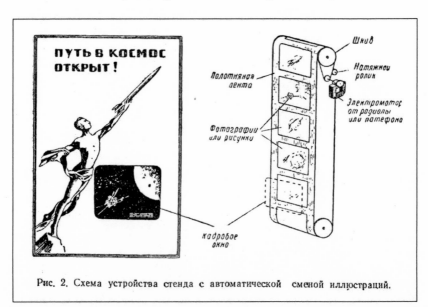

"The way to space is open!" Instructions for setting up a poster wall with a rotating inset to showcase Soviet space exploration. Soviet cultural workers were skilled at creating this kind of self-made display. [From Bazykin and Komarov 1961]

II. Promises

Комсомольца полюбила,
Сразу изменилася.
Крест на шее не носила,
Богу не молилася.

I fell in love with a Komsomol guy,
And changed at once.
I wore no more cross around my neck,
No longer prayed to god.

—*Chastushka* from "Evening of Miracles without Miracles," April 1972

3

Church Closings and Sermon Circuits

Between August 15 and 18, 1960, 110 enterprises and medical, educational, and cultural institutions across the city of Joshkar-Ola held assemblies of their workforces. On the agenda everywhere was a lecture on the topic "The communist education of the toilers and the overcoming of religious prejudices at the present stage," followed by discussion and a resolution on the closing of the last functioning Orthodox church of the city, the Church of the Resurrection. The result was not surprising, given the mounting pressure to close houses of worship all over the Soviet Union in 1960 and 1961 (Chumachenko 2002; Shkarovskii 1995): all of the assemblies, representing 17,000 workers and white-collar employees, passed resolutions demanding the church be closed, many of them unanimously.[1] At the request of the republic's Council of Ministers, the USSR Council for Russian Orthodox Church Affairs confirmed the closing of the church on November 19, forcing the congregation to merge with that of the village of Semënovka, approximately five miles outside of town.[2] The church building was demolished a few months later.

Although the result was predictable, the process of this church closing is perhaps more remarkable than it seems at first. Perfunctory as these assemblies may have been, it was no small feat to bring together thousands of workers at over a hundred locations in the city within a space of four days to listen to lectures on an identical topic, delivered not by radio, film, or television, but by dozens of human individuals, and to secure voices from among the employees formulating support of the resolution in a dogmatically acceptable but not uniform way. For this task of mass mobilization to succeed, local lecturers had to be able to understand the message behind the prescribed lecture theme and generate variations of it. Because of the risks of human error and misunderstanding in the reproduction of doctrinary truths, the success of attempts to make theory take hold of the masses could never be taken for granted.

Taking the workers assemblies of 1960 as a starting point, one can see how didactic networks create their own internal dynamics. Through a peculiar combination of flexibility and central direction, they seem to embody the change they are promising. Although didacticism is most powerful when the promise of future change has some resonance with present experience, it also transforms people's perspectives on present reality in ways that those designing the curricula can never fully control. Through the rhetoric of reports and methodical trainings, didactic networks salvaged some of the commitment to transformation from the Khrushchev era and brought it into the Brezhnev era and beyond, preserving it as a value for religious revivalists to appeal to.

Didacticism and the Power of the Future

In order to understand the mechanisms by which didactic interactions draw participants into ideological projects, it helps to take seriously their promise of making both teachers and students into something they currently are not—more proficient, more skillful, more informed, more responsible. The forward momentum of pedagogical mobilization calls into question common views of Soviet society and modern educational systems, both of which are associated more often with stasis than with transformative movement. But especially in peripheral locales, networks of ideological instruction were one way in which people experienced their society as being in an ongoing process of transformation.

Scholarship on Soviet propaganda and cultural work often emphasizes the repetitive and normative aspects of this work, arguing that its main concern was to generate required paperwork (Peris 1998) or perform the subject position of the normal Soviet person (Yurchak 2006). This approach hinges on the assumptions that the official discourse was generally known and accessible, and that cultural and political activists had a certain bored mastery over it. But how did people learn what was expected of them? Deep into the postwar decades, documents from provincial archives paint a picture of ill-prepared methodicians only partially proficient in the discourse they were transmitting to the masses, and of overburdened training networks beset with misunderstandings. Participants at events such as the workers assemblies were not simply reiterating normative speech and behavior, they were also learning what a normal Soviet person was and how she should act.

While early research in the ethnography of education drew attention to the way in which schools reproduce preexisting social inequalities (Bourdieu and Passeron 1970; Philips 1982; Willis 1981; Wortham 1994), Soviet history shows that the opposite effect deserves equally critical scrutiny. Sheila Fitzpatrick's (1979) work on the link between education, purges, and social mobility under Stalin reminds us that the capacity of mass schooling to propel people into new social positions can have even deadlier consequences than the conservative tendencies that worry analysts in other contexts. During the mass mobilizations of the Khrushchev era, the issue was no longer to create a new generation of elites that would be loyal to the Soviet government, but rather to train enough transmitters to help align popular activity with the ambitious plans proclaimed by the party. This was a time when young people were roused to participate in the virgin land campaigns to claim steppe lands for agriculture (McCawley 1976) and comrades courts and people's patrols involved citizens in promoting communist morality at workplaces and residences (Field 2007).

Such initiatives set the tone for an increased expectation of change that peaked at the time of the 1961 Party Congress, which declared the construction of communism as being within the reach of living generations. Both expectations of radically different futures and didactic strategies of popular mobilization would be scaled back under the more bureaucratic style of Leonid Brezhnev, who succeeded Khrushchev in 1964 (Breslauer 1982; Taubman 2003). By 1970, it would not have been as important to generate evidence of popular demand for the closing of a church as it was in 1960.

But even as a toned-down claim, the commitment to education as a force of change survived into the era of stagnation. The numbers of students in the party and Komsomol systems of education, which had expanded dramatically under Khrushchev, were at first reduced, but then started to grow again under more strictly regulated curricular guidelines (Benn 1989: 135–138). A renewed campaign for secular festivals that started in 1965 still heralded "new revolutionary traditions," although many had first been introduced in the 1920s (Smolkin 2009). Methodicians still had to report on using "new methods" and "new forms" of propaganda, and to portray didactic approaches to atheist propaganda as innovations over prewar *popoedstvo* (anticlerical "parson eating"), although most of the softer alternatives had precedents in the experimentation of the first decade of Soviet power (Andrews 2003: 110; Solomonik 1977: 3).

The rhetorical homage to newness was tamed by what Yurchak terms a "citational temporality," where "all types of information, new and old, were presented as knowledge previously asserted and commonly known" (2006: 61). To solve the apparent contradiction, one might think of citation and newness as two aspects of a teaching interaction. Social interactions in training networks have a necessary openness toward the future, because part of their "felicity conditions" (Austin 1965: 14–15; Goffman 1983) is the assumption that, though at present the instructor is relatively more proficient and the students owe him or her a degree of deference, this imbalance will change through the process of learning. For example, linguistic analyses have pointed out how teachers address students as in some way already the accomplished speakers or professionals they are training them to become (Jaffe 2003; Mertz 2007). At the same time, classroom interactions are "anchored" to wider social and political frameworks (Goffman 1986 [1974]: 247). In the Soviet case, the institutional anchoring gives teachers as well as learners pressing reasons to pay attention to the content and form of official discourse: within pyramidal networks of training and supervision, "getting things right" could become an important measure of progress toward becoming a new kind of person. Just how much change was considered possible or desirable at a personal or social level differed at different times in Soviet history.

Lessons of a Church Closing

The anti-religious campaigns of the Khrushchev era were part of a general climate of anticipation of imminent social transformation (Paert 2004; Stone 2008), and show how didactic elements helped stir this anticipation while keeping it within disciplined bounds. When a 1954 Central Committee resolution unleashed verbal and physical assaults by members of the Komsomol against religious congregations, they were quickly criticized in a second resolution. A second campaign, which began in 1958 and lasted until 1961, emphasized "communist legality" in official interactions with religious organizations. Local administrations were urged to apply Soviet laws on religious affairs more stringently than had been the case since the war, leading to the closing of many houses of worship for alleged violations (Chumachenko 2002: 131, 161). The workers assemblies that led to the closing of Joshkar-Ola's last functioning church fall into the time frame of the second campaign, and show the enduring importance of a didactically staged popular will for legitimizing administrative decisions.

Popular mobilization and legalistic discipline came together in the emphasis on "[moral] education" (*vospitanie*) as a purpose of all official initiatives (Field 2007). It is thus no coincidence that each workers assembly began with a lecture on "the communist education of the toilers [*kommunisticheskoe vospitanie trudjashchikhsja*]." Propagandists in the Mari ASSR were encouraged to lecture on this topic in response to the Central Committee resolution "On the tasks of party propaganda under present conditions" (January 9, 1960), which declared that the "moral education of the masses" was "the basic method for the regulation of the vital activity of Soviet society" during the transition from socialism to communism.[3] Under Khrushchev's ambitious program of governing through didactic measures, a morally trained populace was expected to be able to participate in political life vigorously and in politically desirable ways.

The minutes of the workers assemblies show the difficulty faced by such educational efforts, but also suggest that the emphasis on imminent change hit a nerve among the population. The lecturers anchored their calls to transformation to such elements from outside the assembly hall as city architecture and newspaper articles (Reid 2004). Speakers often referred to these materials when drawing contrasts between the church as a thing of the past and Soviet society as moving into a shining future. Mass-mediatized information and the new built environments were thus among the "teaching aids" that made didactic messages compelling for Khrushchev era citizens.

In Joshkar-Ola, the changing topography of the socialist city had placed the Resurrection Cathedral in an increasingly alienated and marginal position. The church was first closed between 1928 and 1944, when the eighteenth-century brick building housed first the cinema October and then one of the factories evacuated from Moscow to the Volga region at the outbreak of war in 1941.[4] It was the only church in the city to be reopened after the war. Two other large churches had once stood on the same street on the banks of the Kokshaga River, but the Church of the Holy Trinity had been destroyed in 1939, and the Cathedral of the Ascension of Our Lord had been turned into a beer brewery (Starikov and Levenshtein 2001: 17, 24).

Demoted from a cathedral into a church and having lost its formerly imposing bell tower in 1928, the reopened Resurrection Church had an uneasy existence in the center of a Sovietizing Joshkar-Ola. The prerevolutionary market square which it once dominated was now a park with a statue of Lenin at its center, and the street on which it stood, formerly known as Ascension Street, had been renamed Karl Marx Street in 1919.[5] When official documents referred to the church as located in "the building of the former cinema 'October,'"[6] this further underlined its status as a tolerated but alien institution, whose roots in the city were erased.

The campaign to close the church in 1960 occurred during a time of rapidly changing cityscapes. Earlier that year, following a Central Committee resolution, the Mari regional party committee had ordered construction firms in Joshkar-Ola to adopt the new technique of constructing multistoried apartment blocks out of prefabricated concrete panels, one of Khrushchev's projects that continues to shape the face of cities across the former Soviet Union to this day.[7] As construction began on the housing projects, a new central square named after Vladimir Il'ich Lenin was almost completed near the western end of Karl Marx Street, farthest from the church and the former market square. The new Lenin Square was framed by a neoclassical theater, a hotel, and the building of the Technical Institute. Soon to follow were government offices in the modernist style along nearby Lenin Avenue (Sanukov et al. 2004: 85–86).

The efforts to modernize Soviet cities in the late 1950s and early 1960s had many goals—from offsetting wartime destruction and accommodating growing urban populations to promoting a modernist aesthetic of functionality, rationality, and control (Buchli 1999; Ruble 1990). Statements recorded at the assemblies show that an additional—and probably not unintended—effect was to make such prerevolutionary buildings as the church appear anachronistic and out of place (see also Stronski 2010). Speakers frequently drew a contrast between the church and its surroundings and expressed indignation or embarrassment about its presence in the middle of the city. A member of the committee for radio and television was quoted as saying that he avoided walking along Karl Marx Street with his children, because he preferred that they did not even know the word "church."[8] In the minutes of the assembly at the repair factory, a similar concern about children came up: "In the center of town there is a church and when you pass it by with children one gets an uncomfortable feeling [stanovitsja ne po sebe], and children are curious and ask 'What is that there?' Against your will you have to lie to them and give them false explanations."[9]

The proximity of the church to the small park, a place of modern, cultured rest in Soviet rhetoric, was often remarked upon as particularly inappropriate. One employee of the Mari publishing house was quoted as complaining that the church formed the backdrop to the Lenin monument when viewed from the park's main entrance.[10] This potential leakage between church space and public space was also treated as worrisome by the authorities: the charge that members of the congregation solicited money from people in the park was one of the arguments for closing the church in the official conclusion by the commissioner for church affairs.[11] As a place to spend free time, the church should be replaced by the other offerings of a modern city: "People used to think it was a holiday to go to church. But now we have many places where you can relax and have fun," a storage worker was quoted as saying.[12]

Such statements show that the attempt to frame the church as a scandal and an anachronism was intelligible enough to be reflected in documents from all over the city. Even the members of the congregation who wrote a letter of protest to Nikita Khrushchev acknowledged this sense of incompatibility by insisting that the church was not in the center of the city ("no longer" might have been a more accurate expression), implying that this made it less necessary to remove it.[13]

In addition to showing people's interpretations of long-term trends in urban topography, the documents also bear witness to more immediate preparations for the closing of this particular church. A series of newspaper articles across the spring and summer of 1960 had initiated the gathering storm. Assembly minutes indicate that lecturers read from or referred to these articles in their speeches, and participants in the discussion drew on them for formulating their arguments. A separate assembly of pensioners was held in the Park of Culture and Rest on August 12, framed not as a lecture, but as a discussion of the article that most immediately preceded the meetings: "A brawl in the 'divine' temple," published that day in *Marijskaja Pravda*, the republic's main Russian-language daily.[14]

The article described a fight between parishioners that had erupted after the evening service on August 1, the eve of St. Elijah's Day, a popular Orthodox holiday in Russia on which church attendance was likely higher than average. The fight, which allegedly started in the church and spilled into the street, was between supporters of the rector of the parish and those of a younger priest, whose impending removal to another parish had been announced at the end of the service. The author traced the falling-out between the two priests to competition over church funds, and accused the supporters of each priest of merely wanting to lay their hands on a larger share of the church's income. Tellingly for the effects of such caricatures of greed-driven churchmen, speakers at some assemblies referred to "fights" between the two priests over the division of church funds, although the article only described parishioners physically fighting.[15] Others cited the newspaper as evidence that the church was creating a "disturbance of the public order" or encouraging "hooliganism."[16] These phrases came directly from the article itself, which anticipated the conclusion which the assemblies were supposed to draw: "Therefore the workers in enterprises, having learned of the systematic debauchery in the church, of the disturbance of public order by the churchmen, are saying with indignation:—Isn't it time to close down this breeding ground of hooliganism?"[17]

Two earlier articles that same year had a less explicit message, but were also used during the discussions. On January 16, *Marijskaja Pravda* had already reported on disagreements between the two priests in "Preachings and deeds of the spiritual fathers."[18] On May 11, both *Marijskaja Pravda* and its Mari-language equivalent, *Marij Kommuna*, reprinted versions of an article from a newspaper in the Tatar ASSR, which denounced the greed, debauchery, and warmongering of Iov, who was subsequently deposed as the archbishop of Kazan' (the diocese to which the Mari ASSR belonged) under accusations of tax evasion and a past as a Nazi collaborator.[19] Although the case had no direct connection to Joshkar-Ola, this article was frequently mentioned in the discussions about closing Resurrection Church. Lecturers and audience members referred to Iov's alleged ties to the Germans in occupied Ukraine, his illicit self-enrichment in Kazan', and the threat he posed to peace both within the Soviet Union and internationally.[20] In addition to the charge of welcoming the Germans to Ukraine, the article accused him of making priests in the Kazan' diocese use "long-forgotten *akathistoi* [hymns in praise of a saint or an icon] calling for ethnic enmity between Russians and Tatars."[21]

These are stereotypical charges that may have no factual foundation, although it is not entirely unlikely that a church dignitary in occupied Ukraine at least initially welcomed the German forces, who cast themselves as liberators from "godless" Bolshevism (Berkhoff 2004; Peris 2000). The objectionable *akathistos* could have been the hymn to the Kazan' icon of the Mother of God, which was revered throughout Russia but of special local significance in the Volga region. The icon's discovery in the sixteenth century was during a time when the conquest of Kazan' by Muscovite forces was still challenged by Tatar resistance, and the *akathistos* (written in the nineteenth century by a professor of the Kazan' Theological Academy) addresses Mary as "exposure of unbelief," "confirmation of the Christian faith," and "deliverance from the invasion of foreign tribes" (Sretenskii monastyr' 2004). The icon repeatedly played a role in the defense of Moscow from European foes: Polish armies in the seventeenth century, Napoleon in the nineteenth, and Hitler's armies in the twentieth (Shevzov 2007; Sretenskii monastyr' 2004: 30–32). So its veneration in Kazan' in the 1950s may have been intended as an expression of Soviet patriotism rather than a call to interethnic strife, but it still would have fit into the image of religion as a bulwark of ancient hatred.

Although the articles about the archbishop and those about the fights in the church made no explicit references to one another, speakers at the assemblies made connections between them, and contrasted their stories with positive themes that were prominent in press coverage. The front page of the same August 12 issue of *Marijskaja Pravda* that carried the article about the fight in the church featured a report on Khrushchev's speech at the UN General Assembly, reprinted from Moscow's central party organ, *Pravda*. A female worker connected both themes to demand drastic measures against Archbishop Iov and others, who she had concluded were making money from preaching "the inevitability of war":

What horrors and suffering war brings! I would now travel around the whole world together with Khrushchev in order to preserve peace for eternity. In my opinion, the church in Joshkar-Ola must be liquidated, all the property confiscated, the buildings handed over to state services, and the clergy themselves should be sent to build roads in the North.[22]

The use of newspaper articles in lectures and discussions indicates the didactic function of information in Khrushchev's populism (Wolfe 2005). Since *Marijskaja Pravda* was the organ of the Mari regional party committee and had to coordinate its content with the party bureau, the timing of articles about the church was certainly no coincidence. What is more, the files of the commissioner for religious affairs suggest that, although state organs may not have been wholly responsible for the discord between the two priests and the factionalism in the congregation, the commissioner and the KGB had monitored it through reports and complaints from parishioners over several months.[23] So discussions about the church closing took place in a carefully controlled context. There is also evidence that the lists of speakers at the assemblies were culled to reflect a vision of what public opinion should be, rather than the diversity of views that actually existed. In a letter sent simultaneously to Khrushchev and to the offices of the Patriarchate in Moscow, elderly believers from Joshkar-Ola claimed that the pensioners assembly which sanctioned the closing of the church was attended not only by pensioners, but by "many young people," and that only the preselected speakers were in favor of the closing, "and the others were all unanimously against the destruction of the temple, but they weren't even allowed to say a single word."[24]

The thick file of minutes thus speaks volumes about the didactic intentions of the city's party leadership and networks of methodicians. Whether we can say that their efforts had public resonance hinges to some degree on the question of whose voices are recorded in these documents. In addition to culling the lists of speakers, it is possible that invented quotes were inserted into the minutes or that some of them were written without ever holding an actual meeting, a well-documented practice from Soviet cultural and political work (Humphrey 1998; Yurchak 2006: 100–102). Especially those minutes that record neither the names of the speakers nor summaries of what they said, but simply give the text of the resolution passed, cast into doubt whether anyone actually met to vote.[25]

While the minutes thus tell us little about the degree of atheist conviction among the working population of the city, they do show the inevitable engagement of large parts of the population with propaganda messages, anchored as they were in wider processes of change. In the 1960s as in the 1920s, documenting didactic efforts was always on the border of becoming an end in itself. But the resulting paper trail suggests something important about the dependence of ideological mobilization on people's capacity to learn. Whether they record the voices of actual workers or the imagination of trade union activists entrusted with writing minutes, the documents connected to the church closing show the particular urgency that ideological discourse takes on when its users are not (or not yet) fully proficient in it.

Risky Transmission

Regardless of whether these minutes record the actual statements of participants or the fabrications of note takers, they present evidence of the kind of learning that needs to occur for ideological messages to spread, in the Soviet Union and elsewhere. First, even if some of the assemblies did not take place, writing fictive minutes would still require at least one person in each enterprise to be capable of making ideologically correct statements about the incompatibility of the church with current developments in the Soviet Union. The wide range of graphic styles (typed or handwritten, in various hands and colors of ink, with varying degrees of orthographic correctness) indicates that the minutes come from diverse sources and are unlikely to have all been composed in the office of the commissioner of religious affairs. The resolutions, too, are predictable in their general thrust, but differ in their wording and in the concrete recommendations for what to do with the church building.[26] And although the content of the initial lecture is not always recorded, where the minutes do include a summary, these are quite different in each case (see table 1).

Far from just disseminating a pregiven text, organizing the assemblies involved training an adequate number of people to prepare and deliver lectures on the topic "The communist education of the toilers and the overcoming of religious prejudices at the present stage." Earlier in the same year, the plans of Joshkar-Ola's city committee for fulfilling a recent Central Committee resolution "On the tasks of party propaganda under present conditions" contained a list of training seminars for atheist propagandists to be held at the house of political enlightenment, the first of which had the same title as the lecture.[27] This was one probable source of preparation for a number of lecturers.

Responsible for the training seminars was G. N. Chistjakov, a staff member of the city committee's department of propaganda and agitation who also participated in the work of the Knowledge Society.[28] He himself delivered the lecture at a number of enterprises. At other places, this task was performed by lecturers from the party or the Knowledge Society or,

Automatic Telephone Exchange, August 16, 1960

Heard: A presentation of the head of the telephone exchange [name], who noted in his presentation that besides suffering and deceit religious prejudices do not bring any good to the working masses. Religious ideology makes people into slaves to all kinds of imaginations of divinity, causes laziness, stinginess, and deceit. In some cases it takes away the last hard-earned penny from the toilers, and even promotes anti-Soviet preaching, provoking Soviet people—those people who overthrew the power of capitalism, built socialism, opened the era of Soviet satellites, the era of rockets, and are moving successfully toward the bright future of communism. For their part, the religious obscurantists are slowing down the building of communist society to some degree, and for this reason the only correct decision for us can be to uproot this religious evil in the city of Joshkar-Ola, to ask the superior organs to end the existence of the church of Joshkar-Ola, that is to say the Resurrection Cathedral. Not to allow in the future the breeding ground of deceit, stinginess, and hooligan "fights" for the benefit of the clergy.

[Source: GARME, f. R-836, op. I, d. IIa, I. 5.]

Workshop No. 6 at the Arms Factory, August 16, 1960

Presentation of the candidate of historical sciences, Comrade [last name]:

In our country religious prejudices and survivals have largely been liquidated, but they still occur among elderly people and especially among old Maris. The youth of our country is being brought up in a communist spirit and knows neither church nor gods. Among the backward milieus there are still believers in christ and other gods, there are various sects, which pull weak-willed people into their milieu even from among young people and the adult population. Religious confession is not prohibited by law in our country, from the earliest days of Soviet power the church is separated from the state and the fulfillment of religious rites is not prohibited, but nonetheless we know that religion leads to no good, it spiritually poisons our Soviet people.

[Source: GARME, f. R-836, op. I, d. IIa, II. 116–117.]

Table 1. Two Sample Lecture Summaries on "The Communist Education of the Toilers and the Overcoming of Religious Prejudices at the Present Stage"

occasionally, a leading member of the enterprise or educational institution. Working with materials from the seminar and from newspaper coverage, each speaker had to come up with an ideologically acceptable version, part of the art of putting together new products from pregiven elements that was a crucial aspect of the methodician's work.

Mistakes in the minutes are perhaps the clearest indication that they document the efforts of people relatively unfamiliar with official discourse. In a produce store, either the lecturer had misunderstood information from higher sources, or the person who was taking the minutes did not fully understand what the lecturer said. In the words of the handwritten minutes: "Professor Bogoslov wrote the latest publishing house of the bible, but he renunced [sic] religion."[29] Either the lecturer or the minutes taker must have heard the Russian word *bogoslov* (theologian) as a family name, failing to understand *professor-bogoslov* as a professional designation, a "professor of theology." Likewise, somewhere along the chain of transmission *izdanie* (edition) turned into *izdatel'stvo* (publishing house); the more likely fact that this theologian published an edition of the Bible was understood to mean that he wrote it; and the irregular past tense *otrëksja* (he renounced) was heard and then spelled as *otrësja*.

Such semantic and grammatical mistakes show that the organizers of atheist campaigns could never take the availability of capable lecturers and comprehending audiences for granted, especially in regions such as the Mari ASSR, where Russian, the language of all official meetings, was not the first language of many participants (cf. Humphrey 1989). More evidence of the efforts required to reproduce ideological discourse comes from statements that seem unintentionally ideologically incorrect. In Stephen Kotkin's terms (1995: 222), one might say that someone tried to "speak Bolshevik," but failed. For instance, the same man who reportedly objected to the church forming a backdrop to the Lenin monument also demanded that the prison, located on the other side of park, be removed from the city center, equating the prison (a state institution, albeit one that was expected to become obsolete with the impending arrival of communism) with the church (which was considered alien to the Soviet state).[30] Elsewhere, a woman with a Tatar surname complained that Russians have a church to pray in while Tatars have no mosque in Joshkar-Ola.[31] While this statement could be useful as evidence that the presence of religious institutions incited interethnic envy, it plainly did not speak of a developed atheist consciousness. One questioner from the floor inquired if the city government could force the church to lower its fees for religious rites, suggesting an interest in enlisting the state's help in making religious practices more affordable rather than eliminating them.[32] All statements were framed as support of the general criticism of the church, and none of them elicited corrections from the lecturers or other participants. At a time when so many elements of social life appeared to be in flux, even local organizers of atheist events struggled to correctly apply the message of radical incompatibility between religious and Soviet institutions.

Some minutes also recorded comments that opposed the church closing or cautioned against its possible consequences, but those were often followed by immediate rebukes from the lecturer or other participants. For instance, a woman was quoted as saying that since the church was mainly visited by elderly people, these pensioners, rather than the working-age population, should decide whether to close it or not. Her remark was followed by a colleague's reminder about social responsibility: "At the present time people's consciousness is rising, people are taking the creation of public order into their own hands, and we cannot just walk past such a disgrace."[33]

In some minutes, such dissenting voices translated into small numbers of votes against the resolution to close the church.[34] But as we have seen, explicit opposition was just one of a number of ways to fail at the performative role of the conscientious and responsible builder of communism. Some ideologically incorrect positions were challenged by other participants; some were not. If, as Yurchak argues, voting for a resolution at an official meeting was a performative act by which participants reproduced themselves "as a 'normal' Soviet person . . . with all the constraints and possibilities that position entailed" (2006: 25), these instances of misalignment raise the question of how people knew what was expected of them. In a situation where neither activists nor their audiences were fully competent performers, spreading authoritative discourse was a learning challenge: widening circles of participants had to pick up the requisite vocabulary and performance styles. This dependence on constant processes of teaching and learning was at once a weak point of ideology and a key to its mobilizing power.

Teaching as Dissemination and Replication

Records of Khrushchev era atheist campaigns invite us to think of ideological discourse as something that is not reproduced by rote repetition but through the generative efforts of more or less competent transmitters. To help keep the transmitters themselves on track, higher authorities distributed training materials and coordinated media publications. The result was a combination of local flexibility and disciplinary rigidity that was not unique to the late Soviet Union, but is also an organizational strategy employed by transnational religious groups active in the twenty-first century, including evangelical Protestants. In both contexts, didactic relationships link centers and peripheries while allowing for expansion outward. Creative possibilities become harnessed to centrally defined goals in ways that are not always obvious, but that comparison makes easier to see.

Strikingly, while scholarship on Soviet didactic efforts often assumes a general cynicism among practitioners that makes it impossible to take records of past statements at face value, ethnographers of evangelical organizations accept the self-descriptions of church members more easily. When scholars characterize evangelical churches as "nondenominational," emphasizing "Jesus rather than creeds or doctrines" (Erzen 2006: 61, 71) and having a "no-frills, ordinary-folks approach" to worship (Luhrmann 2004: 519), they lift their terminology directly out of these organizations' self-representations as locally independent bodies whose practices grow from the personal predilections of their members more than out of any centrally defined authority. To make both types of organizations comparable as didactic networks, one has to give the words of Soviet methodicians a little more credence than is customary, and treat their evangelical counterparts with more suspicion. With this twist of perspective, some specific affinities between postsecular church-planting and Soviet strategies of building a secular public become apparent. In the mobilization of atheist lecturers to deliver nearly simultaneous performances of 110 lectures with identical themes but different texts, we can see a similarly "potent combination of external influence and radical local adaptation," as David Martin (1990: 282) has noted for global Pentecostal missions.

One affinity lies in the way that particular strategies of transmission become linked to the ideal of a particular kind of community, a nexus that Michael Warner has identified as characteristic of the modern notion of a "public." As institutions constantly reaching beyond their own membership to mobilize new partipants, Soviet networks of cultural enlightenment and evangelical missions both strive to form a public in Warner's sense of a social entity made up of strangers, who are brought together "by virtue of being addressed" (2002: 62). Constituted through the circulation of lectures, sermons, and methodical advice, these incipient publics participate in what Greg Urban calls a "metaculture of newness," a system of judgments about culture propelled by the speedy travel of things, people, and ideas, and characterized by the value placed on new creation rather than the invariable reproduction of old forms (2001: 67). Within Soviet and evangelical networks, "new approaches" and "new inspirations" are treated as preconditions for success, but both manage to restrict the range of the permissible through recourse to the "citational temporality" (Yurchak 2006) that imposes limits on the apparent infinitude of possible new creations.

In Urban's analysis, which focuses on the cultural effects of technologies of mass production, the metaculture of newness becomes possible through technical innovations in the transmission of knowledge. The mechanically reproduced mass media are freed from the constraints of cultural objects whose "dissemination" as externalized, perceptible things depends on individual reception and recreation. For a myth or a basket design to circulate, its telling or demonstration must be followed by "replication," when people internalize the skill and can recreate a performance or object that counts as similar by local standards. With the advent of mass media, dissemination is largely disconnected from replication: a film can be viewed in many places by people who will never learn how to make one themselves (Urban 2001: 42–48). Though valued more highly, "original" creations are also outcomes of dissemination because they usually recombine elements from existing models, without which "the new entity would have little prospect of future motion or future circulation. It would simply become incomprehensible" (5). So the metaculture of newness is made possible through a combination of techniques of mechanical reproduction and efficient dissemination with the availability of people skilled in reworking circulating models into products that will be recognized as new.

In their own attempts to simultaneously value and control newness, Soviet and evangelical contexts quickly encounter the limits of mechanical reproduction, and end up relying more strongly on replication by human agents through internalized skills than Urban's model would lead one to expect (Luehrmann 2011). Not unlike some instances of capitalist consumer culture, such as person-to-person marketing and interactive social media, ideological networks resort to pyramids of personal interactions as a cost-efficient way to create an expansive and motivated membership. The citational practices in which the bonds between teachers and learners are expressed make Soviet and evangelical publics more limited in their range of possible innovation than classical analyses of the liberal public sphere would allow for. But in both cases, these limits—set by state and party in the Soviet case, by denominational authorities among evangelicals—are enforced quite efficiently without recourse to rote repetition. Each public is able to extend its reach through creative combinations of mechanically disseminated didactic materials and personal interactions between teachers and learners.

Listing Titles

Titles of lectures and sermons are a common way to express citational bonds in both Soviet and evangelical networks. For organizations such as the Knowledge Society and party departments of propaganda and agitation, disseminating lists of recommended lecture titles was a tool for reaching a maximum number of lecturers with minimum expenditure.[35] While full lecture texts were also printed and circulated,[36] lists of titles were printed more systematically and in larger editions. In 1955, the All-Union Knowledge Society printed 600 copies of a three-page list of recommended topics of lectures on scientific-atheist propaganda.[37] In 1959, 25,000 copies of an expanded four-page list were printed. Number six among the seventy-one titles is "The communist education of the toilers and the overcoming of religious prejudices at the present stage,"[38] the title of the lecture delivered at the assemblies in Joshkar-Ola. Mimeographed lists circulated by the Mari division of the society were shorter, and presumably reflected those lectures that could be delivered locally.

Like the RSFSR and the all-union societies, the Mari division also mimeographed full lecture texts in editions of several hundred copies, but the very fact that this effort was duplicated on the regional level shows that texts from the center were not available for all lectures, or had to be adapted to local conditions.[39] To an important degree, then, Soviet propaganda networks entrusted the reproduction of dogmatic orthodoxy to the generative ability of local methodicians rather than relying on radio and television alone or asking lecturers to animate written texts. A former leader of Komsomol study circles whom I met during my research remembered choosing topics each term from a list of recommendations. What she did with the topic was largely up to her, and she recalled that it was welcomed when propagandists supplemented the materials provided in Komsomol brochures with additional information from journals and books.

One reason for the reliance on personal replication may have been economic shortages: lists of titles require less paper, ink, and space on postal trains than full lecture texts delivered at comparable print runs. But as we have seen, the task of reflecting on and adapting content was also thought to have a transformative influence on the transmitters. Methodical guides praised the "living word" of the lecturer as better able to forge a connection to the audience as "the speaker [*vystupajushchij*] and the listeners [*slushateli*] enrich each other with their knowledge and impressions" (Tiapkin 1970: 3). In addition to being potentially more persuasive than mass-mediated texts and performances, personal interaction with a lecturer or seminar leader was also expected to "activate the listeners" (Gorokhov 1974: 50), to encourage them to participate in the process of knowledge transmission through presentations, discussions, and research.

Lists of lecture titles promoted the ideal of an active, engaged public while allowing for control through the messages encoded in the titles themselves and through systems of evaluation of lower-level lecturers by their superiors. Although explicitly value-laden titles came under critique among postwar Soviet atheists, readers trained in the intertextual web of seminars and atheist literature could still derive important information from the lists. Activists within the Knowledge Society warned against titles such as "Religion—An enemy of science and progress," "The origin of Christianity and its reactionary role,"[40] or "Church weddings and their incompatibility with Soviet ideology"[41] as likely to deter believers from attending the lectures. It thus remained up to lecturers to decode the intentions behind the binary oppositions and rhetorical questions in approved titles. For instance, they had to understand that titles such as "Scientific predictions and religious prophecies" and "Science and religion on unusual celestial phenomena"[42] called for an argument that demonstrated the superiority of the scientific over the religious approach, rather than presenting them as complementary.

Before receiving permission to speak on a given topic, Knowledge Society lecturers had to present to a board of older colleagues from the regional presidium, which could require changes of content as well as delivery. Ad hoc evaluations of lectures by inspectors from regional centers suggest that it was not always easy for lecturers to interpret and follow the expectations encoded in a title. In addition to aspects of performance and delivery, as when lecturers read from a prepared text without taking their eyes off the page[43] or failed to answer audience questions,[44] criticism often focused on wrong or insufficient political contextualization: no connection was made between a topic and the decisions of the latest Party Congress;[45] historical or scientific facts were simply listed without critical analysis and atheist conclusions;[46] or the criticism focused on long-abandoned religious customs rather than present practices.[47]

Through evaluations and intertextual clues, lecture topics helped anchor the "living word" to centrally defined goals. Post-Soviet evangelical churches in Joshkar-Ola used citations in similar ways: to reconcile the local flexibility of independent congregations with the rigid demands of "discipleship." Though lines of authority were more discrete and sometimes more short-lived than in the Soviet party bureaucracy, they relied on a similar combination of mechanical reproduction with personal internalization and learning. Even in denominations that did not use the snowball structure of cell groups, there was an expectation that members would bring in converts by inviting relatives and neighbors to read and discuss printed literature or view videos with them. In addition to such personal acts of "incarnation" of mass-disseminated materials (S. Coleman 2000: 133), congregations also maintained relationships with popular preachers by selling and consuming their mass-produced books and recordings as well as by sending members to attend seminars taught by them in person. Similar to lectures in the Knowledge Society, sermons in evangelical churches are often identified by a title and become an entity for circulation and replication by preachers who consider themselves disciples of the pastor who originally delivered it.

As Susan Harding notes, preachers "may borrow aggressively from one another, appropriating exegeses, illustrations, stories, quotations, logics, style, tone, gestures, and even entire sermons without citation," since among them "piracy is not a vice, it is a virtue" (2000: 24). But such piracy is not random, since "whom they [preachers] choose to imitate and impersonate" matters a great deal, not only for "their audience and their reach," as Harding says, but also for the relations of discipline and authority in which preachers place themselves (Bartholomew 2006; S. Coleman 2006). The personalization of such relationships to well-known preachers through borrowings from their sermon titles and themes allows even self-declared nondenominational churches to maintain conformity even as they emphasize the joys of the personal discovery of spiritual truths through study and prayer.

The story of how the young pastor of the Joshkar-Ola Christian Center aligned his church with the Kievan Embassy of God via Moscow's Triumphant Zion illustrates how the circulation of texts mediates relations of spiritual authority in evangelical networks. Baptized by the American missionaries who founded the Christian Center, the young pastor had encountered the teachings of Sunday Adelaja and Aleksandr Dzjuba during his stay in Moscow. In addition to selling books and tapes by these pastors at the Christian Center's book stall, the young pastor passed on their teachings in the form of named sermons. For instance, a sermon delivered by Pastor Aleksandr Dzjuba from Triumphant Zion during his visit to Joshkar-Ola in September 2005 was entitled "How to graft yourself onto the grace of the church." Announcing the topic, he asked everyone to take out pen and paper and take notes, and he invited the pastors among the audience (in addition to the pastor of the Christian Center, they had come from other churches in the Volga region) to "take this sermon for yourself" if they wanted to. At the Christian Center, such an act of appropriation had occurred a little more than two months earlier, when the young pastor preached on a similar topic ("Grafting yourself onto his grace") in his Wednesday sermon, addressed mainly to people who considered themselves leaders within the church. Through taking Dzjuba's sermons for himself, the young pastor served as an animator of Dzjuba's message, and drew authority from his association with the metropolitan pastor.

Both sermon performances offered advice on how to behave toward spiritual authority, especially when encountering differences between congregations and between clergy. Within this common theme, there were interesting differences in emphasis, indexing the unequal relationship between the two speakers and their churches. Both versions of the title were taken from Romans 11:17–18a: "But if some of the branches were broken off, and you, a wild olive shoot, were grafted in their place to share the richness of the olive tree, do not boast over the branches." Both sermons applied Paul's reflections on the proper attitude of the newly converted gentiles (the "wild olive shoot") toward the Jews as the original people of God ("the olive tree") to the situation of Charismatic churches within the landscape of more established denominations, as well as to that of newcomers to a particular congregation in relation to its long-standing members and leaders.

The related titles indicate the circulation of common themes, and the young pastor in Joshkar-Ola made it no secret that he was keeping up with the ideas of "his pastor," Dzjuba, through sermon tapes and visits to the "leadership schools" Dzjuba taught at Triumphant Zion. On several occasions, he referred to his work as passing on the "bread" which he received in Moscow and Kiev to the congregation in Joshkar-Ola, or as passing on the torch in a relay race. The commonality between these sermon performances extended to other Bible verses: both developed themes from Mark 2:22a ("And no one puts new wine into old wineskins") to discuss the need to lay aside old experiences in order to appreciate the message of a new pastor or a recently joined church. There was a common plotline, in which slightly humorous stories about proper behavior in unfamiliar worship settings illustrated the point about respect for the rules of a particular congregation as a precondition for sharing in its "grace" (see table 2). Finally, both pastors adopted similar performance techniques, enacting the message about the proper attitude of discipleship in the church with a small role play. Quoting James 4:6 ("God opposes the proud, but gives grace to the humble"), Dzjuba had the bandleader who had accompanied him from Moscow come up and act out a skit in which the musician was introduced as a proud person and Dzjuba pushed him back, showing how God opposes such people. Two months earlier, the young pastor had enacted the same skit with one of his ushers. Both pastors thus chose a subordinate from their own congregation to demonstrate a point about deference to divine will.

Differences between the two performances lay in those aspects that indexed the relationship of each speaker to the sources of the sermon's authority and to the congregation addressed (which in both cases was the Christian Center in Joshkar-Ola). The young pastor introduced his sermon

Aleksandr Dzjuba, "How to Graft Yourself onto the Grace of the Church," September 10, 2005

Each church has been provided by God with its own grace *[nadelena svoej blagodat'ju]*. And this grace is linked to the mission of the church. Each church has its own. When I repented, my mum was a Baptist. My first desire—well, to lead her out of that slavery, that is, to lead her out of the Baptist church. Mama, how can you go there? I went there to the Baptist church, they started to praise God, I came in right away like a Charismatic, hallelujah! [Laughter in the congregation] One of their deacons came up to me and stepped on my foot just like that, and I went on lalalalala [Raising his arms], thinking I'd show those Baptists. [Laughter] He came up to me and stepped on my foot, I didn't understand. He said put down your arms, here we don't do it that way. And I closed my eyes, but suddenly no one else is singing praise and all are looking at me. [Laughter] And I had come thinking to promote my church. But then I understood that I couldn't do anything there. And then, after a few years, God explained to me that I shouldn't change them, that it's a stupid task. There are people for whom—Mama, for instance, she comes into the church, sits down, and after fifteen minutes her eyes are closed. At most if someone is alert, well perhaps it takes half an hour until they are all asleep. The pastor comes out, and half an hour is enough to put everyone to sleep. I understand that there are people who, well, this makes them happy, they want to get some sleep somewhere. [Laughter] Why force them to clap their hands? Let them just go to the Baptists. [Laughter] Why force them? I don't fight over people, because I have understood that the grace of God is on that church too. And this grace carries with it a particular mission.

Young Pastor of the Joshkar-Ola Christian Center, "Grafting Yourself onto His Grace," June 26, 2005

Many people ask: There has been some experience in life, there has already been some experience. Even when someone first comes to God. I think that it is a rare person who hears about God for the first time. Probably there is already some knowledge, that here I know this is the way to pray, this is the way to praise God, or this is the way to read the Bible. That is, we already know somehow this is the way to act. And always any church, we have already said, carries its own particular grace. Any church. Remember, we said that in the Orthodox church, they have their grace, everything is calm, everything is quiet, there is such quiet there. And, for example, there are Baptist churches, also a Christian church, they also have their own grace, they dig in deeper in the word, know the Bible better. So they have more in this respect. You have to wear a headscarf there by all means. Among the Orthodox, a cross. They have their traditions. That is their own grace, their traditions, their teachings. Each church has its own characteristics, each church has its own particular measure of grace.

And each minister has his[1] own particular measure of grace. For instance, I meet with many other ministers, and I understand. For instance this week I met with a young Orthodox guy, we talked, and he serves in the Orthodox church. And when we talked, I felt that God is present in him. [Laughs] God is in him. He wants to prove to me that I don't believe correctly, but I can see that God is in him, simply there are some things that he has not understood. . . .

There. And, for example, different churches, for instance I see Baptist ministers, I see that God is there too. God is there too. There. Now if you take the Pentecostal church, God is there too. The Lutheran church, there is a Lutheran congregation here in town, God is there too. God is there too. There are many churches where God is present, and God, where he is, gives to the church, gives to the ministers, a certain measure of grace. All have grace, but the Bible says the measure, the measure is different for all. The measure of this grace is different. Grace is diverse [mnogorazlichnaja]. . . .

You must simply say: Praise God, if you have brought me here, then my task is what? To graft myself onto this grace, that is to become a part of this grace. Graft yourself onto this grace. If God brought you into a Baptist church, then you have to prepare, I don't know, a big Bible which is full of notes, well among us too, but there everything revolves around that. For praise you have to supply yourself with a hymn book, among the Orthodox perhaps you have to bring a cushion so as not to fall asleep there. [Laughter] That is, all of them have their own grace, that is their own measure of grace, you understood that, yes?

Note: 1. He used the Russian word *svoja*, which is a reflexive possessive pronoun indicating the gender of the possessed rather than the possessor. I translate it as "his" because the clergy in all the Christian churches in Joshkar-Ola were male, although female ministers were allowed in Triumphant Zion and the Embassy of God, the churches in Moscow and Kiev with which the Christian Center was affiliated.

Table 2. Two Sermons Developing the Theme of Manifestations of Divine Grace in Different Denominations

as being addressed primarily to people "who have come from a different church"; Dzjuba introduced his as deserving the special attention of people "from this church," placing himself as an outsider offering sympathetic criticism of the many changes in leadership the Christian Center had undergone. Dzjuba's call for people who like to sleep in church to "just go to the Baptists" may also be understood as a comment on his audience. Dzjuba and the husband-and-wife team of musicians he brought with him had spent much of the weekend criticizing local church members for being too passive in their responses to praise music, thus missing out on part of the grace offered by their church. While Dzjuba took the position of someone who was evaluating the congregation as a whole, the young pastor spoke to the problems of those members who failed to understand why God had brought them to this particular church.

Dzjuba also evaluated the young pastor, calling him a bearer of new grace for whom the congregation had to provide new wineskins, i.e., leave behind the things they thought they already knew. While thus throwing his support behind the young pastor, Dzjuba called him a *porjadochnyj chelovek* (lit. "orderly person"), a rather unenthusiastic term of praise denoting trust-worthiness and honesty but no outstanding qualities.

Finally, the pastors demonstrated their different relationships to their common "apostle," Sunday Adelaja in Kiev, in an anecdote they told to illustrate how not to behave toward authority. Both used the example of an unsuccessful Ukrainian pastor who came to Kiev to consult with Sunday Adelaja but, instead of listening to the more experienced and more successful minister, started to offer him advice. Dzjuba framed this story as his personal experience with a friend whom he introduced to Adelaja, while the young pastor told it as a story he heard from the protagonist (the unsuccessful pastor) at a seminar in Moscow. This indicates that there are several reasons for the similarities between the performances. The young pastor was probably familiar with a prior version of Dzjuba's sermon, which he heard in Moscow or on tape. But he had also had other opportunities to hear some of the same stories on which Dzjuba drew, through being part of the same network of seminars, tapes, literature, and joint worship. The differences between the two renderings anchored each performance in a chain of transmission in which one speaker was closer than the other to the original sources of wisdom.

Within the Knowledge Society as well as in evangelical churches, chains of transmission were also chains of authority, constituted through teaching and emulation. In both settings, it was in part the prospect of evaluation by superiors that motivated lecturers and preachers to put together ideo-logically correct collages from the loose associations of titles, illustrative examples, and methodical advice made available to them through a com-bination of mass media and face-to-face interactions. The association with these superiors was itself a source of pride, as shown by Dzjuba's and the young pastor's attempts to highlight their relationship with Sunday Adelaja. In the memories of two former lecturers of the Knowledge Society, there was a similar mix of dread and pride when they spoke about the academics who directed the society. One woman, a retired schoolteacher and lecturer of forty years, still conveyed the excitement of facing the "scholars" who evaluated her lecture before she could deliver it in public: "Fifteen people sitting there. You read your lecture. The first time they did not pass me, this and that and that you have to do, after all they are scholars. And the second time they said that it's okay to deliver this lecture." Her colleague, also a schoolteacher by training and later a full-time staff member at the Knowledge Society's planetarium in Joshkar-Ola, clarified the link between the scientific authority of printed sources and her responsibility to adapt them for diverse audiences when she discussed her use of *razrabotki,* or printed, "worked-out" versions of lectures:

> These *razrabotki,* methodical aids for the lecturer they were called, yes? For example, when I worked in a school myself, this is how these *razrabotki* helped me. So I already know, this was written by people with a doctorate, scholars, specialists. I already know approximately what I need to talk about. It's only the base, and then you take everything yourself, either from life, or from fiction, from scientific literature. So I had such [a topic of] unusual celestial phenomena, eclipses, all of this you explain and bring examples from the local, you ask people. That's why I love to talk to people [*obshchat'sja s ljud'mi ljublju*], because you can learn a lot from them.

Lecturers and preachers shouldered a double burden: they needed to please their superiors, who had definite standards of truth in mind, and to work with mass-mediatized materials in such a way that they created an actively engaged *public,* not the notoriously similar *masses* of passive, isolated spectators. But in the way they approached this problem, there was an important difference between late Soviet propagandists and post-Soviet preachers. Among the former, authority was derived from scientific standards that were ultimately buttressed by political institutions. Among the latter, the authority of the living word was much more personalized, since it resided in the divine inspiration that enabled a preacher to correctly interpret scripture and discern God's intention in the world. This belief in divinely inspired teachings led to a tendency to ascribe to didactic materials a spiritual status that went far beyond what Soviet lecturers would have felt comfortable with. But ultimately the preachers confronted the same all-too-human limits of ideological transmission that Soviet planners had to contend with.

Inspired Teachings

The tendency to both personalize media transmissions and sanctify teaching materials was exemplified by a course of the Institute in Basic Life Principles, sponsored by two Baptist congregations in Joshkar-Ola. The U.S.-based institute offers courses on Christian ethics to churches around the world. The curriculum consists of videotapes of seminars led by founder Bill Gothard (b. 1934) in the 1980s, combined with review questions and discussions led in person by an instructor from the regional office.

During the course I observed, the function of the Moscow-based instructor was largely to test audience comprehension; the course ended with an exam that qualified those who passed it to become instructors for the institute. He also seemed to play a gatekeeping role, making sure no one saw the videos out of sequence or outside the institutional setting where the local church was paying course fees to the institute. When I asked for permission to sit in on the second half of a two-part course sequence, the instructor, an expatriate American, said that normally he did not allow people to see the second part without having seen the first, because they might not properly understand it. He also explained that making tape recordings was forbidden, and the participants had to promise not to circulate copies of the supplementary materials they received.

Gothard's standardized and copyrighted curricula are an example of religious entrepreneurship not unusual in the era of mass media (Hunt 2004; Rudnyckyj 2009). But the participants interpreted these prohibitions as based in more than commercial considerations. The leader of a Bible study group in one of the Baptist congregations had participated in the course, and then refused to let a study group member copy the lesson on anger management. She first defended the prohibition by citing the institute's need to protect its copyright, but the irate member challenged her: "So where was the copyright of the apostle Paul?" The leader countered that, if these materials circulated freely, Orthodox Christians might use them for their own missionary ends. Besides, one should not study them out of sequence, because God always gave knowledge in the order in which it was needed most. Here, considerations of copyright and interconfessional rivalry were mixed with the idea that the instructional materials themselves had a sacred quality.

During the course itself, each lesson started with a prayer by one of the participants, suggesting that it was impossible to correctly process the information presented outside of a worshipful mood. On the videos, Gothard also prayed at the beginning and end of each taped lesson. The bandleader of the Christian Center had a similarly reverential attitude toward teaching aids. When I asked for copies of her lesson plans on the principles of praise-and-worship music, she warned that these materials had been written "in the Spirit" (i.e., by people who had invoked the presence of the Holy Spirit through prayer and praise singing) and that I should read them as I would the Bible, preparing myself through prayer and asking God to show me the meaning of the text.

Such reverential reading practices depend on people having been socialized into them through study groups, sermons, and other types of instruction (Crapanzano 2000; Luhrmann 2004), again tying the dissemination of media to personal internalization. Simon Coleman (2000: 171–172) calls attention to the exhortations to respond through prayer and pledges included in many evangelical instructional materials, and argues that the aim is to encourage a bodily appropriation of the teacher's words by the student. Turning his argument around, one could say that, through suggesting particular responses, the creators of instructional materials appropriate the future-oriented thrust of the learning process by attempting to retain control of the student's actions even after the lesson is completed. In a comparable way, the emphasis on the "activation" of the learner in Soviet pedagogical literature implied that this activity would be put to the service of centrally defined goals. Both Soviet era programs of study and religious curricula thus aim to harness the transformative energy of learning for larger projects of personal and collective change. But by privileging personal relationships with inspired teachers, evangelical networks exemplify some of the dangers of the personification of inspiration that Soviet networks after Stalin sought to diminish by bureaucratizing, rather than personalizing, the learning process.

Evangelical preachers would argue, of course, that secular attempts to harness the energy of the teaching process were bound to fail because they were based merely in human knowledge and sought human ends, lacking the divine wisdom that alone could bridge the gap between transformative promises and morally desirable outcomes. The further circulation of materials from the course on Christian ethics in Joshkar-Ola showed, however, that postsecular attempts to outdo secular predecessors faced similar challenges in the unpredictability of human learning.

Like the methodicians of the Knowledge Society, Bill Gothard made copious use of lists in his teaching. Lessons included lists of the twelve kinds of heart of which "God speaks" in the Bible, the three ways of enlarging our heart, and the thirteen steps on the path toward immorality. Other observers have noted a general tendency toward quantified lists among evangelical Protestants as an aspect of their penchant for standardization (Crapanzano 2000: 77, 157; Erzen 2006; Sullivan 2009). With its impression of completeness and easy replicability, the list promises to convey insights in a universally comprehensible way, providing teachers with an effective methodical tool to direct their students to action. In practice, lists turn out to be easier to disseminate than to replicate in a new performance. When a group of young Baptist women attempted to recreate one of Gothard's lists in their study group, they struggled to translate the sense of definitive direction conveyed by its form into classroom activity. The youngest member of the group, a student around sixteen years old, tried to model the discussion on a lesson dealing with the "principle of creation" (*printsip tvorenija*). The materials she had copied from the course workbook consisted of two lists, one of the "unchangeable characteristics" of a person and one of "signs of self-rejection." She simply read aloud the first list without discussion or modifications, although earlier she had announced that she thought there were more "unchangeable characteristics" than the ten points included by Gothard.

Before reading the second list, the student tried to have the other members of the group generate it themselves by asking what they thought the "signs of self-rejection" were. Obviously discouraged when the first volunteered answer, "people scold themselves" (*rugajut sebja*), was not an item from the list, she started to read the eleven signs together with the explanations and supporting Bible verses, occasionally stopping to ask the group what they thought a term meant, but quickly reverting to the text when what followed was silence or an unforeseen answer. For instance, under point 5, "self-criticism," she asked: "What is that? I mean, why?" Without waiting long for an answer, she continued: "No, let me explain. It is when a person always thinks, 'I could have done better.'"

Sociolinguistic analyses of classroom exchanges often interpret such a lack of uptake of student utterances by teachers as an expression of the teacher's authority (Collins 1996; Mertz 2007: 54–58). In this case, the presenter had very little authority over the other members of the group, being the only secondary school student among college-age "sisters." Rather, her lack of uptake may show how she was constrained by the authority of the curricular materials, which she sought to reproduce at the price of curtailing divergent answers. In their emphasis on exact replicability, such detailed curricula only underscore the limits of method's capacity to produce predictable effects, pointing to the paradox of claiming divine guidance and methodical exactness at the same time.

Didactic networks seem to work best when they rely on methodical prompts that are not quite as detailed and prescriptive as Gothard's courses. Most Soviet and evangelical methodicians worked in contexts which encouraged individual initiative and creativity in teaching, but held the instructor accountable for the effects of the message transmitted and for its faithfulness to preexisting models. They measured effectiveness by the degree to which teachings produced changes in students that were then reflected in observable indicators, such as the increased productivity of a work collective or the growth of a church. Both models thus sought to capture and direct something that is notoriously difficult to apprehend (Miyazaki 2004): the movement toward a different future that is present in a learning interaction. Given the risks involved, only those who urgently need rapid change seem likely to adopt didactic methods of mobilization. Khrushchev's didactic populism helped generate hope and engagement during the uncertain transition from Stalinism (Fitzpatrick 2006), but his successors found it too unstable to uphold. And as post-Soviet denominations are settling into a new religious order after the initial years of revival and proselytizing, those who work hardest to harness didactic dynamics are also among those who have the least to lose.

4

Marginal Lessons ·

Khrushchev era didacticism owed a great deal of its persuasive power to the palpable social changes that manifested in reconstructed cities, new apartment blocks, promises of more consumer-friendly production targets, and opportunities for participation in volunteer campaigns. While some hopes of impending change proved short-lived, the altered cityscapes brought about through the accelerated construction methods pioneered in the late 1950s remained, and imposed ongoing constraints on post-Soviet developments (Collier 2001). Religious life in Joshkar-Ola also had to adapt. By the end of the Soviet era, legal as well as illegal religious practices were increasingly confined to the outskirts of the city: the Orthodox met in the church of Semënovka, Muslims gathered for prayer in private apartments, and Baptists and Adventists established unregistered houses of prayer in the "private sectors" of single-family wooden houses outside the zones of reconstruction. The center, by contrast, was occupied not only by administrative headquarters, but also by the institutions of secular didacticism—theaters, cinemas, institutions of higher education, the Palace of Young Pioneers, and the planetarium of the Knowledge Society.

After the collapse of Soviet socialism, this spatial division changed, but slowly. In the city center, two Russian Orthodox churches reopened in the 1990s, and the diocese started to rebuild a third one. Other religious groups occupied the spaces of increasingly underfunded didactic institutions, meeting in houses of culture or former cinemas, largely in more peripheral areas. Great was my surprise, then, when I returned to Joshkar-Ola in September 2008 after an absence of two and a half years, to find both the city and the religious landscape altered by an ambitious construction project led by the republic's presidential administration. Under the label of historical reconstruction, new brick buildings were replacing Soviet public buildings and filling areas that had deliberately been left as green spaces by socialist city planners. The Knowledge Society's planetarium, located on valuable property directly across from the republic's administrative offices, had been torn down. In its stead, a large open square was flanked on three sides by an office building/exhibition hall whose arched galleries were apparently intended to evoke Byzantium. The square's centerpiece was a clock tower where, every hour, an icon of the Mother of God of Three Hands rode out on a donkey and entered a mosaic depicting a church which resembled the new Assumption Church in the garden behind the president's offices. That church, whose single-dome, cross-shaped structure also gestured toward Byzantine styles, had been completed in 2006, despite public misgivings about this sign of preeminence for Orthodox Christianity in a multireligious republic.

In addition to this transformation of the formerly unassuming environs of the Khrushchev era government buildings, other changes could be found along Karl Marx Street, involving the construction of Russian Orthodox structures on formerly public ground. At the site where only a commemorative cross had stood in February 2006, the outer shell of a new version of Resurrection Church was almost finished, built in a different style and on a smaller scale than the destroyed cathedral. Farther south, on the site of a former public beach on the banks of the Little Kokshaga River, a belfry marked the construction site for a larger, completely new cathedral modeled on the Savior on the Blood in Saint Petersburg, a late nineteenth-century church constructed at the site where Tsar Alexander II was assassinated in 1881, and hence a powerful symbol of Russian national unity. The republican archives, formerly located on Karl Marx Street in a wooden structure built on the site of a convent that had been destroyed in the 1920s, had been moved to a residential neighborhood on the other side of the river. There were plans to reconstruct the former convent church, but suspicious residents speculated that at least part of the site would be used for upscale apartments.

Like the Khrushchev era construction projects, these evictions, reconstructions, and rezonings gave palpable form to more elusive social and political shifts. Funding for building the new churches came from the Ministry of Culture, and the architects in charge of designing them confirmed that the churches' outward appearance had been decided by the republic's president, Leonid Markelov. The plans for Resurrection Church, for instance, were based on photographs of a church in Saint Petersburg that Markelov had given to the architects, along with the order to adapt the design so that it could be built entirely from local brick. Once finished, a sketch of the facade had been taken to the archbishop for his blessing.

Though benefiting from the sudden wave of state expenditures, the diocese seemed to have little control over spending priorities—at the same time as a number of churches were built in the center within a few blocks of each other, the city had taken away a projected church construction site in one of the Soviet era residential areas where most of the population actually lived. Archbishop Ioann, who three years earlier had told me that the time

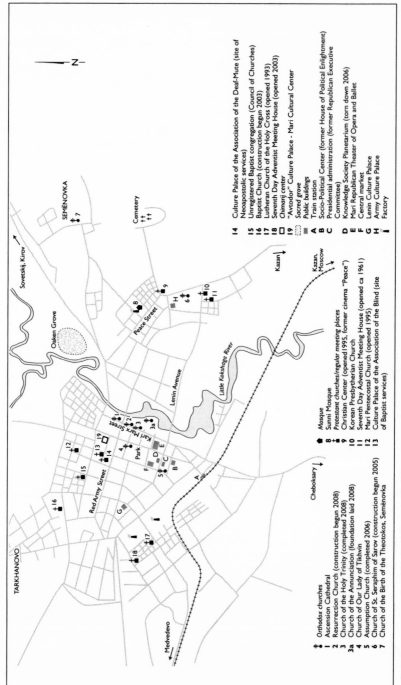

Religious centers and public buildings in Joshkar-Ola, early twenty-first century. Houses of worship are marked with numbers, public buildings with letters. The large street grids represent areas of city-managed apartment buildings; the smaller-gridded areas, where many of the Protestant churches are located, represent so-called private sectors with primarily wooden, single-family houses. [Map by Bill Nelson]

for the physical construction of church buildings was over and the task now was to work for the enlightenment of the believers, now spoke in glowing tones about the benefits of such construction work: whenever a new church was opened, he claimed, it filled up with believers, and thus promoted the spiritual rebirth of Russia.

While priests wondered who was going to serve in all those new churches, and icon painters complained that none of the architects had any idea of the interior fittings needed in an Orthodox church, there was only speculation about the government's motivation for funding the construction projects. Although republics continued to elect their presidents even after Vladimir Putin had started appointing the governors of Russia's regions, Markelov had won two consecutive elections as the candidate most widely considered to have Moscow's backing. His predilection for models from Saint Petersburg may have been a way to demonstrate Marij El's loyalty to the federal government, in contrast to the Turkish models that inspired the new Qol Sharif mosque in Kazan', the capital of neighboring Tatarstan. During a modest economic upswing in Russia, caused by the high price of oil on international markets before the stock market crash of 2008, there was also an economic motivation behind making formerly public areas available for commercial development. In addition to churches, there were plans for shopping centers on the riverbank and a "children's entertainment center" in the city park.

Whatever the precise constellation of economic and political interests may have been, the new reconstruction program threatened to marginalize the buildings of Soviet secular culture, which had once displaced religious structures from Joshkar-Ola. The archbishop's newfound enthusiasm for construction projects—subordinates often struggled to locate him as he rushed from one site to another—perhaps showed his awareness that it was best for his diocese to decrease its dependence on the infrastructure of Soviet didacticism, a dependence that remained substantial for the other religious groups.

Materializing Precariousness

Religious resurgence in the late twentieth century, after the end of the Cold War called the existence of both Western and Eastern models of the welfare state into question, has sometimes been interpreted as the defensive response of those marginalized by neoliberal reforms (Comaroff and Comaroff 2000). Fitting in with this interpretation, the years of capitalist "shock therapy" in the early 1990s did see a rise of religious commitments across Russia. As elsewhere in the world, a good part of this revival did not happen in traditional religious centers, but was made possible by religious entrepreneurs who were willing to occupy spaces made available by economic restructuring in the sphere of secular culture and leisure, such as empty storefronts and shuttered cinemas (Meyer 2006). In Joshkar-Ola and other postsocialist cities (Balzer 2005; Yang 2004), the link between religious revival and socioeconomic precariousness is evident in the spatial struggles among diverse religious groups (and between them and secular institutions) over the remaining structures of secular culture-building. But in Russia's Volga region at least, there have also been interesting differences between denominations in terms of their reliance on such Soviet leftovers, indicating that it is not the state of the economy alone that determines the rhythms and strategies of religious resurgence.

By the second post-Soviet decade, the buildings and networks that had allowed Soviet citizens to experience their link with human contemporaries continued to be used by groups that sought to connect people to the divine, but only when they had no other choice of meeting place. In Joshkar-Ola, newly built Orthodox churches aggregated around the centers of political and economic power, while everyone else made do with the spaces left behind by Soviet projects of cultural and industrial construction: Chimarij activities were coordinated from a small office in the culture palace of the Road Construction Authority, Muslims had built their mosque in the green belt surrounding a factory, and Protestant congregations struggled to rent auditorium space in houses of culture or to secure plots in the private sector, where wooden houses remained underserved by municipal infrastructures of gas, heat, and water. Economic precariousness, including high unemployment, affected the great majority of citizens in this republic regardless of religious affiliation, while those denominations that clung most tenaciously to the structures of Soviet didacticism did so out of a more specifically religious sense of precariousness: while Russian Orthodoxy's place in public culture was guaranteed by politicians eager to clothe themselves in its political legitimacy (Garrard and Garrard 2008; Mitrokhin 2004), other groups had to connect to the public sphere through the almost outdated, but widely recognized model of a didactic network.

Though not supported by a massive state bureaucracy, didactic approaches in post-Soviet religion resemble Khrushchev era mobilizations in the sense of being ways to work with limited resources during uncertain times: building organizations that are at once centralized and able to generate and exploit local enthusiasm. Looking at the Orthodox strategy of "Christianizing" Russian cityscapes (Kozelsky 2010) by occupying key sites without worrying much about winning hearts and minds through rhetorics of persuasion, it is clear that didactic networks are not the only approach to religious revival in the post–Cold War world. But as a familiar way of inhabiting the present on the way to its transformation, didacticism still appeals to those who see themselves as marginalized by ethno-confessional, political, and economic inequalities. Chimarij attempts to gain the status of a denomination through networks of teaching and learning show the enduring appeal of the model for building institutions from scratch.

Networking in the Countryside

When Chimarij activists attempt to harness the remains of Soviet didactic mobilizations to establish a foothold in the post-Soviet public sphere, there is a double irony: Soviet didacticism was not only part of an effort to build an explicitly secular culture, but it was also centered in cities and treated the rural sites of Chimarij rituals as recipients, rather than sources, of knowledge, aid, and instruction. Soviet agit-brigades sent out to the countryside to promote a speedy harvest often reported back the wishes and grievances of rural dwellers, who were assumed to be in need of both enlightenment and material help.[1] Even in the narratives of methodicians who worked with rural audiences across relatively small social distances, because they had themselves grown up in a village or even still lived in one, the movement from centers to peripheries played a role. A rural schoolteacher in her thirties remembered how her father, an elementary school principal and member of the Knowledge Society, set out on foot rain, shine, or snow for early morning lectures at outlying complexes of the collective farm in whose central settlement the family lived. Soviet didactic activities thus had a spatial direction in which towns were giving centers and the countryside was the receiving periphery.

As post-Soviet Joshkar-Ola was transformed by the modest wealth of the Putin years, the disparities between city and countryside increased: in many villages, a majority of houses still had no indoor plumbing, and their residents relied on woodstoves for heat. Meanwhile, legal reforms had lifted the prohibitions that formerly kept urban-based religious organizations from practicing rural outreach comparable to that of the Knowledge Society. The Lutheran satellite congregation in Ljupersola was an attempt of a Protestant church to establish its own network, creating pathways of knowledge and assistance between town and country. Laypeople from the village traveled to Joshkar-Ola to receive training as youth workers, Sunday school teachers, or humanitarian aid workers, while the deacon, the cantor, and a changing contingent of youth from the city boarded the church's minibus every Sunday evening to conduct the service in Ljupersola, sometimes bringing loads of donated clothing from Finland, and sometimes taking back sacks of potatoes. But only one other Protestant congregation—a Pentecostal group led by an ethnic Mari couple—was investing a comparable amount of effort in the countryside. The others concentrated their human and financial resources on evangelizing in the city.

The Orthodox Church also organized training sessions for rural teachers at the diocesan center, which, in Marij El as in many other republics and regions of the Russian Federation, was identical with the seat of regional government. But for Orthodox Christians, town-country relationships have been somewhat more complicated: while rural residents are considered to be in need of material and moral support from urban church institutions, the countryside is also the realm of holy sites and monasteries that attract urban dwellers as pilgrims seeking to receive healing and inspiration, rather than as missionaries seeking to direct and transform (Kormina 2006).

Rural places are even more central to Chimarij Paganism. Its high priest is the only major religious leader in the republic who lives in a village, not in the capital, and even urban adherents travel to villages in order to participate in rituals, which take place on garden plots or at sacred sites associated with particular villages. But for purposes of post-Soviet revival and recognition as a denomination, activists seem to find it necessary to balance an obligatory respect for rural ritual centers with structures of dissemination from city to country that resemble Soviet didacticism and the outreach work of other religious groups.

A case in point was a seminar in July 2005, which began in a culture palace in Joshkar-Ola and ended in a Mari village in the Morki district. Ambitiously entitled "The preservation of ethnic immaterial culture as a means toward state integrity and spiritual security," the seminar was organized by the Joshkar-Ola-based Mari Cultural Center, with funds from the federal Ministry of Culture. The participants included employees of culture clubs and museums in addition to practicing Mari priests (known by the Mari term *onaeng* or the Tatar *kart*). Invitations had gone out through the pyramid of cultural institutions, asking each district in the republic to send one or two cultural workers. In addition, cultural centers serving the Mari diaspora in the Perm region, Bashkortostan, Udmurtia, and Saint Petersburg had been invited to send representatives. Joshkar-Ola thus figured in the seminar as a center of knowledge and infrastructural support for matters concerning Mari ethnic culture, much as it did during the Soviet era.

The seminar coincided with important dates in the rural festival calendar, but without the spirit of competition which such timing would have brought during the era of Commissioner Nabatov and his successors. Instead of drawing people away from traditional festivals, the seminar was scheduled to allow attendees to participate in the celebration of *sürem,* a midsummer Mari ceremony, in the Morki district, where it has been held on St. Peter and Paul's Day (July 12) since the nineteenth century (Kalinina 2003: 19; J. Wichmann 1913: 105). Starting in Joshkar-Ola on July 11 with lectures by two Mari ethnographers in the culture palace of the republican Road Construction Authority (Avtodor), the event then turned into an excursion to the countryside. Participants were loaded onto two buses and taken on the three-hour drive to Morki town, the district center, where the day ended with a concert, dinner, and informal disco in the dormitory of the local technical college. On the next day, additional lectures by the same ethnographers informed the cultural workers of norms of dress and behavior at Mari ceremonies; the priests had already driven the remaining thirty miles to Shorun'zha village to prepare the ceremony under the instruction of the high priest of the republic and the local *onaeng.* The buses with the cultural workers reached Shorun'zha toward noon, after two stops in Morki: at the market to buy the headscarves that many female participants had not known to bring, and at the church to buy candles. In the village they joined a delegation of photojournalists from Finno-Ugric republics and a flock of journalists and visitors from across Marij El.

After the ceremony, the seminar participants visited the sights of Shorun'zha: the beehives, the library, and a workshop for traditional embroidery set up by the local collective farm. But at the urging of the two guests of honor from the federal Ministry of Culture in Moscow, the delegation did not stay for the evening concert that had been prepared for them. Instead, most of the participants returned to Morki, while a car took the Moscow guests back to Joshkar-Ola to catch the night train. I spent the night in Shorun'zha at the home of the methodician of the village clubhouse, whose efforts to prepare children for the concert had thus come to nothing.

We met the remaining members of the delegation again on the next day for the more informal part of the festival, which involved various forms of "play," such as horse racing, the blowing of ceremonial horns made from elm bark to drive out evil spirits before the impending harvest, and a long procession along a village street led by women from the local folk choir. The procession stopped frequently to partake of the food that the households along the street had put out on long tables in front of their gates.

On this day, the visible master of ceremonies was the chairman of the collective farm,[2] a former Communist Party secretary and a current member of the republic's parliament whose birthday was on Peter and Paul's Day.

He was widely credited with making this kind of ceremonial life possible in Shorun'zha, but had kept in the background during the ceremony proper, not appearing in the sacred grove. The chairman led the procession down the street and finally presided over a banquet in the collective farm's dining hall. There, he acted as the *tamada* (a pan-Soviet term of Georgian derivation for the master of the table) and called on guests to pronounce toasts, all of which included well-wishes for the future plans of the collective farm: building a hotel suitable to host comparable seminars in the future, and attracting ecotourists and students from ethnographic field schools in Finland. After posing for a group photograph on the steps of the dining hall, the delegation of cultural workers left, while the journalists stayed for another day, visiting a sacred spring and mountain in the vicinity. I also stayed behind to visit with the methodician's family and participate in the ongoing hay gathering in neighboring Shin'sha.

Becoming a Denomination

Like the workers assemblies of 1960, this seminar required more intricate preparations than immediately met the eye. And the Chimarij organizers could not rely on the well-established structures of party, trade union, or Knowledge Society that supported Soviet methodicians, but had to piece together comparable networks themselves, relying on the remnants of Soviet cultural institutions. The main organizers were the methodician of the Mari Cultural Center (sponsored by the republic's Ministry of Culture) and her husband, a retired army officer. In addition to organizing weekly evenings of Mari music and other forms of entertainment in Joshkar-Ola, the couple collaborated with the high priest to coordinate "events connected with the traditional Mari religion." The latter phrase was the title of a large hand-drawn planning chart hanging on their office wall, containing the annual scheduled dates of the big prayer ceremonies of republic- or district-wide significance.

Occupying rooms on the second floor of the Avtodor culture palace, made available by virtue of old acquaintance, the Mari Cultural Center had a rather tenuous hold in Joshkar-Ola. But its rival in the quest to provide Chimarij adherents with an institutional base in the capital, the cultural-political association Mari Ushem, had a more troubled relationship with the republic's government and was itself constantly in danger of losing its offices in the former House of Political Enlightenment. In the context of the unstable relations between Mari activists and a republican government dominated by ethnic Russians (Sokolovskii 2006), the title of the *sürem* seminar, with its allusion to Russia-wide anxieties about perceived threats to the

"security" and "integrity" of the state posed by ethnic and religious sepa-
ratisms, was probably designed to reassure federal sponsors of the loyalty
of its organizers. During the event itself, the organizers spent most of their
time entertaining the two guests from Moscow, even riding with them in a
separate car. But efforts to standardize and didacticize religion should not
be confused with political conformity: Mari Ushem, too, sponsored lectures
on Mari Paganism in Joshkar-Ola and distributed videotapes and literature
on the topic. The two organizations collaborated at some ceremonies, and
some cultural workers who received materials from the Mari Cultural Center
were also members of Mari Ushem.

One purpose of creating a teachable Mari religion was, then, to present Chimarij adherents as worthy of standing on a par with members of
other religious groups. The institutions that participated in the emerging
network—the culture palace of an enterprise in the capital, district cultural
administrations, and a district technical college and rural collective farm
headed by a former party secretary—had developed in the Soviet period
to spread knowledge and cultured behavior from the cities to the countryside. But, different from a Soviet era institution, the Mari Cultural Center
could rely on administrative command through the Ministry of Culture to
obtain the support of only some of these institutions. The director of the
culture palace and the chairman of the collective farm, for example, had to
be persuaded to support the project by virtue of personal connections or
common interests.

Like the institutional supporters, the two groups of students gathered
together as recipients and future transmitters of the imparted knowledge
were quite different: onaeng seeking to improve their knowledge of the ceremonies, and methodicians interested in Mari culture. From what I was
able to learn from the organizers, the hope was that the latter might organize similar ceremonies in their towns and villages, or at least give positive
treatment to Mari religious traditions during educational events. Through
gathering and instructing onaeng, the high priest was asserting the authority
of his own interpretation of Mari rituals and also acting to remedy the lack
of experienced priests after the Soviet period. Too many onaeng had been
killed under Stalin (Sanukov 2000: 129) to continue the previous system of
hereditary priesthood with informal training in the family.

This disruption confronted the high priest and his supporters with the
need to quickly train specialists, creating pressures of change comparable
to those that had prompted the Soviet reliance on standardized methods.
In the quest for standardization, the high priest had worked with the ethnographer Nikandr Popov to put together a book, *Jumyn jüla* (lit. "God's

customs," a neologism meant to be equivalent to "divine law," the Russian Orthodox term for a catechism; Popov and Tanygin 2003), that described Chimarij prayers and ceremonies. He also hoped to establish a training center for *onaeng* in the hotel complex in Shorun'zha once it opened. The reasons he gave for planning to do so in a village rather than in the capital showed both his awareness of the relative weakness of his group within the confessional politics of the republic—"it's better there than in the city, so that Ioann [the Orthodox archbishop] won't see, so that it doesn't bother him"—and the primacy of the countryside for the ritual and social life of Chimarij adherents: "it's better for the priests [*karty*] there."

The degree to which the high priest's authority was recognized in the republic seemed to vary from village to village. I attended one *agavajrem* ceremony in a small village where the presiding *onaeng* claimed never to have heard of the high priest. But there was a group of eight to ten priests from different districts who regularly co-officiated with the high priest during ceremonies at different locations. These priests sought to establish a network that mirrored the administrative structure of districts and republics, in the quest to achieve registration first in more and more districts, and finally at the republic level. In order to achieve this, the schedule of ceremonies they worked out annually ordered events in a hierarchy of local, district, and republic-wide significance. Replacing earlier distinctions between ceremonies held by a village, those organized by an association of neighboring villages, and rarer ones designated "all-Mari" or "world" prayer ceremonies (*mer kumaltysh*; Popov 1996), this model also involved a "hierarchy among *karty*," as the head priest of one northeastern district, a former police officer, explained: some could only officiate in their village, some in their district, some at any place in the republic. He seemed to consider this an important achievement, and told me to note it in my study.

By trying to create centralized teaching institutions in order to secure recognition and reconstitution as a religious group, Chimarij activists mirror the adherents of other indigenous religions in post-Soviet Russia. Sakha and Tuvinian shamans in Siberia (Balzer 2005; Walters 2002) as well as Pagans in the fellow Finno-Ugric republic of Mordovia (Shchipkov 1998) have tried to establish educational centers. They thereby not only accept Soviet era ideas of religion as a bounded system of knowledge (Broz 2009), but also place their hopes in Soviet models of a centrally directed public sphere, modifying the ritual geographies of neighborliness. For activists and their supporters among village leaders, precarious religious networks are among the few remaining alternatives to the secularist culture-building that once promised an end to rural isolation.

Organized Knowledge

Chimarij attempts to build a didactic network involved processes of standardization and canon-building that have been described as "rationalization"
(Weber 1972 [1921]), "internal conversion" (Geertz 1973), and "Protestantiza-
tion" (Gombrich and Obeyesekere 1988) by scholars in other parts of the
world. As changes instituted in a bid for recognition as a legitimate religion, they have precedents in the prerevolutionary Kugu Sorta (Big Candle)
reform movement, which abolished animal sacrifice and presented its tenets
in textual form as a way to claim parity with other religions of the Russian
Empire (Werth 2001; Y. Wichmann 1932). What distinguishes post-Soviet
didacticization from other types of religious reform is the way in which
activists approach the need for easier and speedier teachability as not only
a textual problem, but an organizational one. By making their rituals teachable, Chimarij not only claim equality with other religions and the right to
registration, but also strive to give religious life a society-building power
familiar from Soviet cultural work.

At the seminar, the didactic task fell largely to the two ethnographers,
Nikandr Popov and Ol'ga Kalinina, both researchers at the republic's Institute for History, Language and Literature. Popov lectured on "The social
concept of the Mari traditional religion as a factor in the strengthening
of the spiritual security of the country" and "The foundations of spiritual
morality of the Mari people." Kalinina's topics were more directly oriented
toward the practical application of the experiences gained at the seminar. In
her lecture "Calendrical folk festivals of the Mari in ethnographic materials," she provided a guide to the existing ethnographic literature on Mari
festivals, inviting participants to draw on such literature when organizing
events. And on the morning of the ceremony, she gave a short briefing on
how to dress and behave in the sacred grove.

The lectures of both scholars included efforts to package features of the
Mari religion into lists, a promising teaching tool for anyone interested in
easy dissemination. Kalinina had prepared a handout listing eighteen num-
bered rules for behavior before, during, and after the ceremony, referred to
by the organizers by the Russian term *metodichka*. Popov acknowledged the
lack of just such lists of rules as a problem within the Mari religion. Lecturing on the social concept of the Mari religion, he admitted that the Maris
had no such thing as the Ten Commandments, but, as God had revealed
himself to different peoples in different ways, the Maris also possessed moral
directives in the form of "god's sayings" (*jumyn oj-vlak*). Different sayings
had been preserved in different places, but, if put together "like a mosaic,"

they had "great meaning." In both lectures he elaborated the plan of gathering together Mari moral precepts from folktales (*jomak*) and proverbs (*kalykmut*), in which Maris articulated ideas about good and evil, and precepts on "how to relate to God, how to relate to other peoples, how to build up respect for the family, how to enrich our own culture."

Popov's efforts recall those of nineteenth-century folklorists who assembled European folk epics from individual verses and themes (Honko 1987; Knight 1998), or, more generally, the attempts to formulate coherent, decontextualized systems out of disparate and situated sources for which anthropologists have long criticized one another.[3] These lectures can certainly be situated in a particular tradition of European folklore studies. But they also show the power of a didactic model of religion. Listable precepts are not only convenient for structural analysis, they are also easy to disseminate, recite, and memorize, and hence teachable even in a short seminar or in the classes on Mari religion whose introduction into the school curriculum Popov advocated. Chimarij activists obviously considered lists of moral precepts and other forms of didactic entextualization as crucial to mobilizing the networks of teachers and cultural workers that they needed to revitalize Mari ritual life.

For ritual specialists, the appeal of methodical aids seemed to lie not so much in their usefulness for learning how to conduct a ceremony, but in the way they signaled conformity to a religious hierarchy. One *onaeng* in Shorun'zha displayed the book *Jumyn jüla* and a collection of Mari prayers compiled by Popov on a kitchen shelf, but when I asked whether he used them, he said no, he knew the prayers and actions without looking at a book. When someone came to him and said they did not know what to say in the sacred grove, he recommended reading some of the prayers; after that, people could pray by themselves. Like the lecture and sermon titles of other didactic networks, printed texts authorized the personal imagination by keeping it within approved bounds, promising a common direction to personal efforts to relearn Mari traditions.

Chimarij activists were not alone in feeling the pressure to codify their practices into easily teachable tenets. Popov's attempt to derive a "social concept" from proverbs and sayings echoes the "social concept" passed by the Moscow Patriarchate of the Russian Orthodox Church at its millennium council of 2000. This text, in turn, is a response to analogous statements in the Catholic Church, whose more centralized and explicit doctrines gave it an initial advantage in the post-Soviet quest to gain a voice in matters of contemporary social dynamics (Agadjanian 2003). Although the need to engage in social outreach has long been deeply disputed within Orthodoxy (Kenworthy 2008; Mitrokhin 2004), a variety of Orthodox dioceses have negotiated contracts with regional governments in the effort to fill the niche of charity work that the socialist state once reserved for itself (Caldwell 2008). In Marij El and elsewhere, permission to do volunteer work in schools, orphanages, prisons, and army garrisons was an object of competition between Western Christian churches, the Russian Orthodox Church, and other Russia-based religious groups. In this context, guiding statements and social conceptions were also instruments through which a religious organization could become socially effective by offering a sense of meaning and direction, which secular attempts at culture building no longer provided. Within this scramble to replace secular institutions, Chimarij efforts focused on the countryside, seeking to recreate the dynamics of Soviet networks while correcting the way they had marginalized villagers.

Lessons of Village Life

The seminar revealed some of the challenges of reinstating the promises of Soviet networks to the countryside. As a didactic event, it addressed three constituent groups assumed to be in need of methodically packaged knowledge about the Mari religion: the superiors in the federal government and the subordinate ritual specialists and cultural workers, many of whom came to Joshkar-Ola from more rural places. While this could have been the participant structure of a regional seminar in the Soviet era, the event departed from Soviet models in two ways. The first was the use of the Mari language almost throughout, except during some of the official welcoming addresses and in the printed program—something that, as several participants remarked, would never have happened during the Soviet period, when Russian would have been used to accommodate the non-Mari speakers. Second, the seminar transposed urban and small-town participants into a rural setting, whose residents and ritual sites had an authority of their own to support or obstruct the seminar's message.

Departing from the usual urban-rural vectors of Soviet didacticism, the seminar cast the urban visitors not as counselors and experts, but as prospective ritual participants who were themselves in need of instruction. Since Chimarij rituals were not practiced evenly in all parts of the republic, many participants had never attended a Mari ceremony before, or not since childhood. Many of them knew so little about ritual etiquette that they had not brought the proper attire: headscarves and skirts for women and caps for men. At the same time, they did not come with an expectation to be pure observers, but also as participants. For instance, some methodicians expressed embarrassment when they were told just before the ceremony that participants were not supposed to drink alcohol for a day in advance, whereas vodka had flown quite liberally at the dinner the previous evening. Two women from the district surrounding Joshkar-Ola, baptized Orthodox Christians, expressed anxiety over whether it was right for them to participate in a Chimarij ceremony. Doubting the ethnographer's explanation that Tünjambal Serlagysh, the Savior above the World, and Mer Jumo, the God of the World, corresponded to Jesus Christ and the Christian God, they decided that it might be better not to offer candles, coins, or other gifts, but just to stand back and watch. Conflicting religious commitments only reinforced the idea that a ceremony is an occasion for participation, never purely a didactic spectacle to be observed.

The rural setting of the seminar was thus neither the object of instruction nor simply a teaching tool. Rather, participants encountered the rural sacred space as a potential source of power with its own rules of engagement. The rural hosts also treated the ceremony as a combined occasion for self-display and for accomplishing aims that departed from those of the outsiders. Parallel to the seminar, the organizers of the ceremony in Shorun'zha had accomplished their own organizational feats. Having previously visited a much smaller ceremony on St. Nicholas's Day in May, I could tell that the sacred grove had been carefully prepared for this more important occasion: a wooden gate now marked the entrance to the sacred ground, and water containers hung nearby for handwashing before entering the grove proper. New wooden benches for worshipers stood near some of the five trees at which sacrifices were made. These preparations had been undertaken through the joint efforts of the collective farm and the village administration, as I later heard from the collective farm's chairman.

Village leaders also carefully managed Shorun'zha's reputation as a stronghold of Mari traditions. An announcement posted at the village bus stop alerted residents to the upcoming festivities, and asked everyone to appear in Mari costume. My hostess's sister, who lived on the street which the procession followed on the second day of the festival, reported that the collective farm leadership had asked all the neighbors to prepare tables with Mari dishes. Unsure what would qualify as a Mari dish, she tried to remember how to prepare something the organizers explicitly asked for, a kind of custard made from creamy, heated milk.

None of these displays of rural neighborliness would have been possible without the organizational skills of Shorun'zha's leadership, and observers from elsewhere in the republic were quick to acknowledge that. In Joshkar-Ola and Shin'sha, people often pointed to Shorun'zha as a model village, where people *zhivut druzhno,* live in unity, as friends. Many considered the way in which the collective farm and rural administration could mobilize residents to participate in community events to be exceptional, and saw it as the reason for the village's ability to conserve both religious customs and a functioning agricultural collective. As elsewhere in rural Russia (Rogers 2009: 227, 256), it only seemed possible to create a communal ritual life in those places where institutions of the Soviet collectivized economy survived.

While actively participating in constructing Shorun'zha's image, the chairman displayed a studied aloofness from outside attention, as if to avoid giving the impression that he was gaining personal fame from his village's reputation. He did not attend the ceremony on St. Peter and Paul's Day because July 12 was also his birthday, and he did not want that to take up all the attention, he explained during his speech at the concluding banquet. He also minimized any role that either his own planning or orders from town might have played in shaping the festivities: "No one prepared, no one summoned us from town. We sing ourselves, we dance ourselves, we distill [moonshine] ourselves and drink ourselves." When I asked in a subsequent interview if he thought that religious events like the *sürem* ceremony helped agriculture, he said no, they did not help agriculture, they helped the people. From this short answer, he launched into a reflection on the changes in the forms of leisure and sociality available in post-Soviet society, and asked me if I liked to go to the cinema. Even in Joshkar-Ola, no one could afford it any longer, he claimed: "No one goes to the cinemas now, what for, [to] watch some horror movie for 300 rubles?[4] We support each other, when someone is sick, when there is grief, you have to help, and we help from the workplace. Now we live like that, it's the primitive-communal order [*pervobytno-obshchinnyj stroj*]."

With this reference to historical-materialist theories of social evolution, where primitive communism represented the oldest form of social organization, the chairman pointed to the uncertain place of marginal rural communities in the attempts to rebuild former didactic networks along religious lines. According to him, the organization of religious ceremonies was not a result of thriving town-country networks, but one of the few compensatory measures available when past networks had fallen apart. During the 1980s, when he was first a club director and then party secretary, networks of cultural institutions and social services provided country dwellers with opportunities to spend free time watching movies or engaging in other pursuits. The present, by contrast, was characterized by isolation and abandonment. In his pessimistic assessment, religion was something for the village to fall back on when left to the devices of neighborly help, but it was a poor replacement for the Soviet promise to raise rural standards of living to urban levels.

The chairman's resigned skepticism brings us back to the link between networking strategies and social precariousness. Knowing full well that the new network could not provide the same kinds of subsidized resources that Soviet didactic organizations had made available to rural peripheries, he nonetheless embraced it as a better alternative to disintegration and isolation. From this perspective, the regeneration of Chimarij practices is not an end in itself, but a way to keep the village within the widened horizons of sociality that Soviet secularism had once opened up, even though not everyone believes in new chances or dynamic futures.

Disillusioned Nostalgia

Work on Turkish secularism has emphasized nostalgia for the hopes inspired by a strong developmental state as a motivation for abiding secularist attachments (Navaro-Yashin 2002; Özyürek 2006). Religious actors in post-Soviet Russia can be susceptible to the same nostalgia as they seek to recreate familiar structures of Soviet mobilizations. But people who came of age during the last decades of the Soviet Union have already lived through a number of disappointments as transformative energies died down and mobilizations failed to deliver on their promises of change. Rural people, in the experience of Shorun'zha's collective farm chairman, had always been low on the list of priorities of Soviet administrations, no matter what goals were proclaimed for a modernized countryside. And even in the city, successive waves of reconstruction had never brought about the promised communist future, in which all shortages of housing and goods would be solved.

For religious groups seeking to take over where secularist mobilizations left off, there are two options. One is to emulate the dynamics of secular didacticism, injecting them with the promise of divine agency. This is the model that has made global Pentecostalism attractive to the marginalized (Dombrowski 2001; D. Martin 1990), whose sense of precariousness and desire for change can come from poverty, but also from a sense of moral alienation. Larry Stockstill, the wealthy pastor of a megachurch, received God's call to reenergize his church through cell groups the night after Bill Clinton was elected president, apparently in anticipation of moral and political uncertainties (Stockstill 2001 [1998]: 13). Arising out of yet another kind of marginality, Chimarij trainings are a more sober expression of the hope that a didactic framework can create the momentum for directed change in a neglected countryside.

The other option for postsecular religion is to propose a different view of what transformation means. If the Russian Orthodox Church takes care to distinguish itself from didactic institutions, this is only partly because it recognizes their fading importance. Another reason is that Orthodox responses to modernization have foregrounded those theological resources for thinking about change that stand in tension with the search for standardized curricula. Though all sides share the idea that larger social change is brought about through deliberate personal transformation, they differ on the means by which such transformation can occur, and the ends which it should achieve.

III. Fissures

Не звоните, не презвоньте
Во всю мощь колокола.
Не заманят меня в церковь
Вера в бога отжила.

Don't ring, don't toll
The bells with all your might.
They won't lure me into church
Faith in god has outlived itself.

—*Chastushka* from "Evening of Miracles without Miracles," April 1972

5
Visual Aid

Before he died, the dormitory supervisor's husband saw a sign in a dream. Or rather, a poster. During his terminal illness, he had long resisted his wife's attempts to get him to declare his faith in Christ. But, as she later recounted in her testimony in the Lutheran church where she was in charge of the dormitory for visitors, he slowly began to learn prayers, laughing when he forgot the words. Then, one day, he told her: "I saw a dream: a colorful poster [*krasochnyj plakat*], on which was written 'In the name of the Father, and of the Son, and of the Holy Spirit.'" From this she had concluded that he died a believer, and was waiting for her in heaven.

In Russian, people "see" dreams instead of "having" them, so the visual nature of the divine sign is perhaps predetermined by grammar. But that it took the form of a poster with colorful writing and that the dying man's wife interpreted it as making manifest the culmination of a complex spiritual process resonate in curious ways with other uses of visual materials in Soviet and post-Soviet pedagogy. The focus on calligraphic rather than pictorial depiction also departs from another visual imaginary that is reasserting its presence in the region: the icons of Russian Orthodoxy.

In the various secular and religious approaches to learning that competed for attention in Soviet and post-Soviet Russia, the proper use and expected effects of visual materials were a prime area of methodological reflection. The creation and display of images and graphics were a matter of much effort and pride everywhere, at the same time as the proper use and potential dangers of visual interactions were debated between different groups. Reflections on the transformative value of visual interactions thus provide a good window onto the particular pedagogical traditions at play in the Volga region, highlighting affinities as well as tensions between their transformative ambitions.

In the Soviet advice literature for lecturers, known to many of today's religious activists from previous professional training, a specific set of expectations was attached to the use of so-called *nagljadnye posobija*, visual teaching aids. Such aids were supposed to make a lecture intellectually accessible, persuasive, and emotionally engaging, thus facilitating the transfer between acquired knowledge and changed actions that propaganda was supposed to achieve. Through the specific semantics of the adjective *nagljadnyj*, which can be translated as "visual" but also as "intuitively persuasive," the call for *nagljadnost'* included more than just a use of pictures. Figurative speech, effective examples, and statistics all counted as "visual" tools through which a lecturer could engage an audience and bring propaganda "closer to life." *Nagljadnost'* thus encompasses material pictures that are put in front of an audience as well as images that arise in a listener's head in response to the speech of a lecturer. This distinction turns out to be important to some of the religious traditions in Russia's postsecular landscape. If we read the theory of *nagljadnost'* as an exploration of the connection between visual perception and persuasion, we can see post-Soviet religious debates as attempts to problematize that same link.

Nagljadnost': Learning by Seeing

"Ten thousand words cannot replace one image," states a Khrushchev era brochure on film in atheist propaganda, quoting a Chinese proverb to argue that the clarity and accessibility of visual media could help viewers give up "the idealist agnosticism characteristic of religion, that is the notion of the fundamental unknowability of the world" (Zil'berberg 1956: 4). In assuming a direct link between seeing and knowing, Soviet atheists may sound like uncritical heirs of what Martin Jay (1993) has called the "ocularcentrism" of the enlightenment. But the semantic range of the noun *nagljadnost'* and its derivatives points to ideas about the link between vision and human motivation that are more complex than they at first appear.

Most crucially, *nagljadnost'* belongs to the vocabulary of methodical approaches, where it is a recipe for making knowledge effective rather than simply a metaphor for knowing. That propaganda must be *nagljadnaja* was a recurrent statement in the advice literature for lecturers of the 1960s and '70s, often supported by such standard authorities as recent party resolutions and the works of Lenin. An article on the use of visual aids in party study circles, published at the beginning of the 1972 academic year in the Russian-language newspaper of the Medvedevo district in the Mari ASSR, starts with a quote from Lenin: "The art of every propagandist lies precisely in this, to influence a given audience in the best possible way, making a known truth as convincing for it as possible, as easy to assimilate as possible, as *nagljadnaja* and impressive as possible." The author, the facilitator of a school of basic economic knowledge at a state farm in the Mari ASSR, goes on to say that visual media (*sredstva nagljadnosti*) constitute "one of the effective means for the activation of cognitive activity among the participants," especially in a heterogeneous group of students.[1]

Given what we have learned about didactic uses of textual media in Soviet propaganda networks, it will come as no surprise that not only audiences, but also instructors and cultural workers were among the targets of such "activation" by visual exposure. Checking on the "state of visual agitation" in a given work collective or institution provided a standard criterion for evaluating the performance of local propagandists.[2] The advice literature for cultural enlightenment work contained detailed instructions on how to produce and display all kinds of visual aids from posters and wall newspapers to exhibitions and slides, thus relying on local generative competence in a manner similar to the lists of lecture titles (Luehrmann 2011). Since this literature often spelled out the intended effects of methodical devices, it provides insights into the ideas about human motivation underlying Soviet uses of visual media. The following description of an evening on the topic of "Science and religion" comes from a manual on atheist propaganda in cultural institutions written by Mikhail Nekhoroshkov, the biologist from the teachers college who also organized the Evenings of Miracles without Miracles. In preparation for the event about science and religion, conducted in 1966 in the Medvedevo district's house of culture, visual media helped attract the audience and direct its attention to the seminar's key themes:

In order to attract a wide audience, the House of Culture, in addition to colorfully designed signs [*krasochno oformlennykh afish*], uses the local radio, invitation cards, notifies the leaders of public organizations, firms and rural institutions by telephone. . . . Before the evening began, the listeners acquainted themselves with *exhibitions of atheist literature,* and of *paintings* by Russian and Soviet artists unmasking religion. The *skillfully designed visual material* [*umelo oformlennaja nagljadnost'*] *attracted the attention* of those present, *caused not a few reflections and even disputes.* (Nekhoroshkov 1967a: 8; my italics)

The combined intellectual and emotional effects of the visual impressions—attracting attention, causing "reflections and even disputes"—continued during the evening itself, where sights, music, and words all complemented each other. After the choir sang "March of the Enthusiasts" on a stage illuminated by a single beam of light, the cinematic projector was turned on, "and on the screen appear[ed] images from the newsreel on the launching of a space rocket." This was followed by a talk on the topic of "Science and religion" by a teacher from a local school, an overview of scientific atheist literature in the holdings of the district library, a demonstration of chemical experiments unmasking religious miracles, a recital of atheist poetry, and a performance of the Russian genre of humorous folk song known as *chastushki,* with atheist texts sung by two female students "dressed in brightly colored Russian costumes." The evening ended with a short dramatic sketch "about a fortune-teller and a trusting girl" (Nekhoroshkov 1967a: 8–9).

While the purpose of the sketch was to promote emotional engagement with the victim of religious deceit—all present reportedly "felt compelled to sympathize" with the girl (*nevol'no perezhivali*; Nekhoroshkov 1967a: 9)— Nekhoroshkov does not specify the intended effects of the newsreel images of the space rocket. Given the abundant references to Soviet space exploration in propaganda materials of the 1960s (Bazykin and Komarov 1961; Nekhoroshkov 1964: 31), he seems to take for granted that a technologically reproduced image of this triumph of Soviet science would predispose people to accept the assertions of the lecture that followed, namely that science and religion were opposed to each other and that science was superior in its ability to improve human life. Assuming that this was the rationale behind the clip from the newsreel, the evening on "Science and religion" used visual materials for three different purposes: to attract attention (the announcement posters and the exhibits of books and pictures), to elicit intellectual and emotional responses (the exhibits and the visually striking aspects of the performances), and to reinforce the persuasive effects of verbal arguments. All these effects presuppose a capacity of images to bundle information and emotional appeal with a degree of compactness that words cannot approach, making the whole available for intuitive apprehension.

A closer look at the semantic field of *nagljadnost'* shows that its unifying element is reference to just such an intutitive form of learning, which is based on demonstration and observation rather than verbal explanation. While the abstract noun *nagljadnost'* may be a Soviet era neologism, the adjective *nagljadnyj* and morphologically related terms were part of the prerevolutionary Russian language, combining meanings of seeing, supervising, and learning. The root *-gljad-* refers to the faculty of sight, as in the noun *vzgljad* (gaze) or the verb *gljadet'* (to look). The common spatial prefix *na-* adds a connotation of "on," "over," or "from above." The 1905 edition of the dictionary of Vladimir Dal', the authoritative reference work for the Russian language up to the revolution, contains the verb *nagljadet'/nagljadat'* in the sense of "to look after, to supervise, to observe." The derivative noun *nagljadok* or *nagljadysh* means "a foster child, someone one has taken on responsibility to look after." Closer to the Soviet use of *nagljadnost'* is a related group of words which refer to a particular style of learning through observation: the nouns *nagljaden'e* and *nagljadka* refer to "the capacity of an autodidact [*sposobnost' samouchki*], a skill obtained by experience, through watching others [*na drugikh gljadja*]." The adjective *nagljadnyj* is defined as "learned by *nagljadka*; experienced, practical, applied; clear, comprehensible, reasonable." Examples come from pedagogical practices: "the *nagljadnyj* method of teaching," and "the geometrical method of proof is more *nagljadnyj* than the algebraic." A second adjective, *nagljadchivyj*, describes a person "who has *nagljadchivost'*, i.e., the capacity to learn by *nagljadka*."

In Soviet literature, the adjective *nagljadnyj* is used in much the same way as defined by Dal', combining meanings of "visual" or "accomplished through visual demonstration" with those of "persuasive" and "immediately comprehensible" (comprehensible "at a glance," to give an English analogy for the implied link between vision and speedy mental processing). By contrast, *nagljadka* as a designation of an informal way of learning through observation does not appear in Khrushchev and Brezhnev era literature. The new term *nagljadnost'* also refers to processes of intuitive learning, but presupposes a teacher who deliberately stimulates these processes by choosing appropriate visual aids. As part of a methodological discourse, the term encompasses both the materials used to visually enhance the learning process, and the quality that makes such materials effective. In the first sense, *nagljadnost'* might be translated as visual media (though it also includes figures of speech, statistics, and other ways to make information more accessible and relevant), in the second as "visuality," "intuitive intelligibility," or "persuasiveness."

The rich semantics of *nagljadnost'* point to the complex pedagogical tradition from which this concern with perception and intuition in the learning process springs. The semantic range of the Russian word closely corresponds to the German *Anschaulichkeit*, a term from nineteenth-century romantic philosophy that denotes the capacity of objects of contemplation to stimulate a cognitive process that combines sensory perception and intellectual generalization. Whereas for Immanuel Kant, *Anschauung* (intuition) as sense perception was distinct from the generalizing cognitive activity that is based on intellectual concepts, Johann Wolfgang von Goethe developed the argument that visual contemplation could generate generalizations of a different kind. In his work on the morphology of plants and the perception of color, Goethe argued that contemplation could provide insights that were neither abstract ideas nor mere additions of empirically observed traits, but rather holistic visions of the essential features of a species or phenomenon. The *Urpflanze* ("original plant") of his *Metamorphosis of Plants* (1790), for instance, was a construct that would combine the essential features of all existing plants, derived from observation of the infinite variety of plant life, without corresponding to any empirically observable specimen (Breidbach 2006; Burwick 1986).

Although natural scientists largely rejected Goethe's approach, the influence of his thought on European reading publics was great enough to inspire twentieth-century Gestalt psychology and early German and Russian abstract art of the Bauhaus and Brücke movements (Ash 1995: 85–87; Vitz and Glimcher 1984: 100–103). His questions about the relationship between sensory perception and human ways of learning and meaning-making were also taken up by philosophers like Hegel and Schelling (both read avidly by Russian radicals from the mid-nineteenth century onward; Malia 1965) and attracted the attention of reformist pedagogues in Western Europe and in Russia (L. Froese 1963; Zander 2008). It is thus perhaps no coincidence that the semantics of a term from German idealist philosophy survived in Soviet era Russian as a part of pedagogical vocabulary.

Nineteenth-century Russian movements for pedagogical reform developed in dialogue with Central European currents such as the kindergarten movement, Johann Pestalozzi's "object learning," and the eurhythmic exercises of Rudolf Steiner's anthroposophists, all of which involved ideas about integrating sensory experience into educational processes (Kirschenbaum 2001: 10–19; Maydell 1997). Even Lev Tolstoj, whose pedagogical efforts showed more Slavophile leanings, was aware of Western European reformist institutions, which he visited on a study tour in 1860–1861 (L. Froese 1963: 100–101). Although the relationship between pedagogical reformers trained before the revolution and the Bolshevik government of the 1920s and 1930s was fraught with mutual suspicion, some pedagogues placed such multisensory forms as the cultural excursion and the didactic spectacle in the service of socialist construction (Clark 1995; Fitzpatrick 1970; Johnson 2006: 97–123; Plaggenborg 1996: 217).

Postwar literature on *nagljadnost'* continued to explore the interaction of various senses in stimulating interest and understanding, both through theoretical studies on the combination of visual materials and speech in teaching (Zankov 1958) and through more practical advice literature on the use of visual materials in propaganda (Zil'berberg 1956; Gorfunkel' 1976). For example, instruction in the art of designing posters and decorating the interior of a clubhouse included rules about the different emotional tones created by colors from the warm and cold ends of the spectrum, recalling earlier pedagogical adaptations of Goethe's color wheels (Shchipanov 1961: 34).

It is doubtful that Soviet cultural workers would have known much of the intellectual genealogy of *nagljadnost'*. But the literature they produced nonetheless dealt with complex philosophical questions about the link between perception and knowledge. It did so by transposing the discussion into a methodological key, providing instructors with tools for engaging and convincing an audience through visualization. In addition to still and moving images, the recommended "visual aids" included illustrative examples, numbers, and performances that appeal to senses other than sight. In the words of P. L. Gorfunkel', whose manual "Psychological foundations of *nagljadnost'* in propaganda lectures" was available to lecturers in the Mari republican library, *nagljadnost'* is not only "what people look at," but "everything that enables the emergence of a visual image [*vozniknoveniju zritel'nogo obraza*]":

> If a person, looking at a chart, perceives only the visual image of the numbers placed on it, but not the phenomenon reflected through these numbers, then for him the chart is not a visual aid [*ne javljaetsja nagljadnym posobiem*]. On the other hand, if we play to the audience a recording of a speech by V. I. Lenin, then such a demonstration, addressed not to sight, but to hearing, has all the qualities of *nagljadnost'*. The listener is affected not only by the power of Lenin's speech, with its characteristic simplicity, accessibility [*dokhodchivost'*], iron logic, passionate conviction. In him arises also the visual image of the leader, stored in memory from portraits, photographs, films, which enhances the propaganda effect manifold. (Gorfunkel' 1976: 15)

In this logic, tables and statistical charts as well as sound recordings can serve as "visual aids" when they enable the audience to visualize something more than what they immediately perceive—the course of development represented by numbers, the personality of a political leader. Another manual praises Lenin himself for having mastered these principles: the statistical charts in his book *The Development of Capitalism in Russia* are said to "allow the readers to see the processes, the tendencies of development standing behind the numbers" (Kirsanov 1976: 41). The same author speaks about descriptive and figurative speech as "interior *nagljadnost'*," and formulates the goal of the lecturer as speaking about remote events "as if everything said was also seen, experienced [*perezhito*]" (55).

The division between "interior" and "exterior" *nagljadnost'* recalls the multifaceted meanings of the word *image* in contemporary media studies. As William Mazzarella (2003) has pointed out, the advertising industry uses the term *commodity image* to refer both to visual depictions of a product and to the associations that come to people's minds in connection with a brand name. Although pedagogical thought is absent from his genealogy of debates about the visual in nineteenth-century European philosophy, Mazzarella traces a dynamic, though sometimes antagonistic, relationship between state-sponsored didactic initiatives and commercial advertising in independent India, another society undergoing rapid modernization in which images were used to help audiences perceive the importance of abstract concepts and long-term processes. The difference between the pre-revolutionary *nagljadka* and the Soviet *nagljadnost'* seems to lie precisely in the problem of visualizing phenomena that are not readily accessible to the human eye, much like Goethe's *Urpflanze*. Whereas learning by *nagljadka* assumes a situation where a pupil can see and imitate what a master does, socialist propaganda often described phenomena with no observable shape, because they were either abstract processes or promises of future attainments. The intuitive resonance of the power of science over nature or the benefits of the latest five-year plan cannot be taken as given, but has to be produced in the same way as a commercial advertisement might produce an association between a commodity and qualities such as sex appeal, intelligence, or cosmopolitanism.

In their quest to visualize the invisible and give local relevance to projects initiated elsewhere, Soviet propagandists drew on the methodological repertoire of multisensory pedagogy. Nothing about this repertoire is necessarily "secular," and some influential pedagogical schools, such as Rudolf Steiner's anthroposophy, were in fact components of larger esoteric movements (Zander 2008). In their attention to the developmental effects of material qualities such as color and shape, these pedagogues opposed approaches that privilege learning as a purely cognitive process of understanding disembodied concepts. They thus present an alternative strand of nineteenth-century European thought that is often overlooked in genealogies that associate the development of liberal Western thought with an ever-increasing commitment to divorce symbolic representations from embodied practices (Asad 1993, 2006; Keane 2009; Mahmood 2005). Rather than any discomfort with materiality as such, it is their willingness to equate material images with imaginary representations that places reform pedagogues in an intellectual tradition with roots in Western European theology and philosophy, and brings their approaches into conflict with established uses of religious images in the Volga region.

The premises of multisensory pedagogy led Soviet atheists to take embodied interactions between religious practitioners and sacred images very seriously, while privileging sight over other channels of interaction. What separated the understandings of atheists from those of religious practitioners was not only the atheists' lack of attention to the materiality of an image as something that can be touched, kissed, and hidden as well as seen, but also the role that each side assigned to the imagination. Didactic uses of visual aids involved a tendency to equate "exterior" perception and "interior" visualization, which Russian Orthodox critiques had long associated with Western Christian traditions. As these critiques are revived in post-Soviet religious debates, what results is not a simple confrontation between "secular" and "religious" camps. Rather, the visual culture of Soviet didacticism provides a common reference point for adherents of different denominations, as they draw on divergent theological traditions to debate the safety and desirability of particular means of transformation.

Religious Images and Their Critics

In a republic inhabited by adherents of religions that have long been in opposing camps during ongoing controversies about the role of images in worship, one would hardly expect a single religious response to the visual culture introduced by Soviet modernity. Among the monotheistic traditions, both icon venerators, such as Russian Orthodox Christians, and iconoclasts, such as Muslims and evangelical Protestants, are represented. For all three groups, Chimarij neighbors who venerate sacred trees and other natural features are part of lived reality, rather than simply objects of polemics against Pagan "idolatry." But regardless of the diversity of theological stances on images, religious worship shares with modernist propaganda what Matthew Engelke calls the "problem of presence" (2007), a concern with giving some form of perceptible presence to phenomena and beings that are not immediately accessible to human senses. From this perspective, the difference between making divinity present in a tree or envisioning socialist construction in a chart may lie merely in the degree of abstraction. Valerie Kivelson and Joan Neuberger restrict the analogy to specific artistic traditions when they argue that an approach they sum up as "seeing into being" is characteristic both of "the transcendent viewing experience associated with medieval and early modern [Russian Orthodox] religious imagery" and of "the transformative quality ascribed to Soviet socialist realism" (2008: 6).

Suggestive as such analogies are, it is important to note that from the point of view of some of Russia's religious traditions, the capacity of an image to represent an already-existing spiritual reality does not necessarily depend on its visual qualities. And even where visual contemplation is important, the desired effect may be to restrain the viewer's imagination, rather than to stimulate her to visualize the future outcomes of a social transformation.

In spite of their overall commitment to sharp distinctions between "scientific atheism" and "religion," atheist scholars did much to popularize analogies between religious and socialist imagery, often describing religious images as dangerous competition to their own offerings of "transcendent viewing experience." Post-Soviet theological debates, however, tend to distinguish sharply between the visual culture brought by socialist modernization and religious uses of sacred images, with charges of idolatry being aimed at both sides, depending on the confessional identity of the speaker. Since these debates revolve around the relationship between images (exterior *nagljadnost'*) and the imagination (interior *nagljadnost'*), they show how different religious traditions engage the legacies of Soviet visual culture in their own decisions about transformative methodologies.

Since most Mari and Russian inhabitants of the region were at least formally considered Orthodox before the revolution, atheist propagandists worked in an environment where images of the saints and Jesus Christ were a crucial vehicle for religious sensibilities and permeated everyday life. Before the revolution, and far beyond it in many places, virtually every house in Orthodox villages had a "red" or "beautiful corner" (*krasnyj ugol*) where icons were kept on a shelf or in a case (*bozhnitsa*), before which the inhabitants of the house performed their prayers (Tsekhanskaia 2004). As late as 1967, the commissioner for religious affairs in the Mari ASSR claimed that most houses in the republic had icons.[3] Icons were also found in churches and were carried outside during processions (which Soviet law restricted to church grounds) and funerals. They were thus a visible and potentially public symbol of religious practice and belief, and it is not surprising that much anti-religious work targeted them. Denouncing the veneration of bleeding, weeping, or oil-exuding icons was a standard feature of atheist propaganda. In the Mari ASSR and elsewhere, chemical experiments demonstrating how substances resembling blood, tears, and oil could be deliberately made to appear by deceptive priests were part of the Evenings of Miracles without Miracles (Nekhoroshkov 1964).

As we have seen, the effectiveness of the denunciatory approach of the Evenings of Miracles was disputed even among atheist propagandists, and the more thoughtful among them certainly realized that the persistence of icon veneration could not be explained by deception alone. Taking recourse to theories of *nagljadnost'* which emphasized the psychological influence of images on viewers, alternative explanations interpreted icons as propaganda tools of the church, analogous to Soviet posters and banners. In a characteristic analysis, Nekhoroshkov repeatedly mentioned processes of sight as channels of interaction between humans and icons, in order to argue that the icon was a way for "church people" to influence people's thoughts and behavior in an even more efficient way than a propagandist could, because it happened in the intimate sphere of the home:

> The veneration of icons was inculcated in children from the earliest age. As a rule, icons were *colorful,* with a *shiny* wreath around the image, which unwittingly *attracted the interest and attention* of the children. In all the most important events in a person's life the icon inevitably participated. . . . All family members went down on their knees and prayed several times daily, *looking at the icon,* asking god to grant them better life and health. . . . Everyone who came into the house *turned his eyes* first of all towards the god-shelf [*bozhnitsa*], to the icons, and finding them, crossed himself, bowed and only after this greeted the inhabitants of the house. (Nekhoroshkov 1967b: 15; my italics)

Fully crediting the material effects of the icon's color and shininess, Nekhoroshkov interprets the image as a visual teaching aid, a tool to enhance the impact of ideological messages by making an audience emotionally receptive.

Post-Soviet religious critiques of icon veneration often display similar psychological understandings of icons, seeing them as persuasive tools to induce the viewer to worship the object depicted. For instance, the Finnish pastor of the Lutheran church pointed out that Orthodox churches have images of "many, many saints," whereas the interior of the Lutheran church was simply and unambiguously dominated by the cross and the image of Jesus. He thus implied that icons made it difficult to concentrate on the real object of worship, or even to identify it. In a more far-ranging critique, the Chimarij high priest told me that "Jesus Christ is an image painted by someone." His phrasing clearly evoked icons: *obraz, kem-to napisannyj*—a "written," religious image rather than a "painted" secular picture, which would be referred to as *kartina*. But he went on to talk about the ways the apostles had distorted Jesus' original teachings in the Bible, thus suggesting that it was not the veneration of icons as such that was problematic about Orthodox Christianity, but rather the church's reliance on human memory, transmitted in textual as well as pictorial form.

In these interreligious critiques, what is at issue is often the concern that material images can reinforce a demand for false concretizations of the divine. A final example comes from a Friday sermon by the mufti of Marij El. Pointing to the danger of "Wahhabi" infiltration with its literalist interpretation of the Quran, the mufti accused a dissenting faction within the mosque of asking: "It is written: 'Allah ascended on his throne.' How did he ascend? Where is the throne?" By looking for literal reference points for such passages, these Muslims forgot that "God has no beginning and no end, he was not born, he has no son and no father. They are already imagining an image [*predstavljajut obraz*], like Christians. The next thing they'll do is draw this image in the prayer niche."

Protestant, Chimarij, and Muslim critics thus join Nekhoroshkov in identifying icons as visual stimuli that lure the imagination into unsafe directions. While both secularist and interdenominational polemics against icon veneration predate the Bolshevik Revolution (H. Coleman 2007), what is striking about these post-Soviet debates is that all sides overlook the important nonvisual components of popular interactions with icons. In Marij El as elsewhere in rural Russia, devotees touch icons, pass under them, or place objects on them to absorb their power, all ways of obtaining blessing and healing that do not require looking at the icon (Tsekhanskaia 2004). Taking up W. J. T. Mitchell's distinction between "pictures" as physical media that hang on the wall and the "images" that are visually perceptible on them, one can say that an icon's character as a flat, rectangular, tangible picture matters at least as much as the image represented (Mitchell 1994).

Even icons kept in the house, contrary to Nekhoroshkov's description, remain largely unseen for much of the year in the rural areas of the Volga region. In Mari villages, most houses I visited had icon corners, whether or not the inhabitants were baptized Christians. In most cases, the shelf supporting one or more icons, along with other powerful objects such as Palm Sunday twigs, Easter eggs, and vials of holy water, was fitted into the corner opposite the entrance door and shielded by a lavishly embroidered curtain that created a niche in which the icons were barely discernible. The curtain was lifted during feast days and family events, but for most of the year the flowers on the curtain were far more visible than the images behind it, making the corner a visually dominating feature of the room, but preventing the kind of intense visual interaction with the icons that was crucial to atheist interpretations of their effect.

Curtained icon corners are by no means unique to the Mari, but are also common in Russian households of the Volga region and parts of central Russia. In other regions, icons are decorated with embroidered kerchiefs, which may also be used to cover them. Various ways of shielding the icons from view are often explained by the desire of the inhabitants of a house not to be seen by "the gods" in all their daily undertakings, i.e., to limit and direct the contact with divine forces which the icons make present (Tsekhanskaia 2004: 130–131). A slightly different rationale was suggested by an Old Believer in the Jurino district in Marij El, who told folklorist

Marina Kopylova in 2004 that she closed off her icons with a curtain because "they can still see us anyway," whereas passersby looking in from the street would not see the icons and be tempted to steal them (Kopylova, personal communication, January 4, 2007). Both explanations treat sight as an important aspect of the relationship between the residents of a house and their icons—but what matters is the image's own capacity to see, a dimension of visuality that is at least theoretically absent from Soviet understandings of images,[4] and also largely missing from the explanations of contemporary defenders of icon veneration. For some rural residents, sacred corners could even work without any image in them at all, as was the case in one house in Shorun'zha, the village known for its Chimarij ceremonialism. Here, the familiar embroidered curtain partitioned off a corner that contained no icon, but merely a candle fixed to a narrow board fitted across the angle. When I asked why there were no icons, the owner's sister, herself visiting, answered: "Oh, they simply haven't bought one." Her sister-in-law added: "We'll have to order one. Or no, they sell them in the church, you can buy them there."

I later learned that she and her husband had built the house seventeen years ago, so they obviously felt no great need for icons, and their professed intention to buy one may have been mainly for my benefit as a stranger with unknown religious sympathies. But the point is that the corner worked well for them without an image in it. Family videos showed that the curtain was lifted and the candle lit for birthdays and other important events in the lives of family members, as would be done in front of the icon in other households. Even though residents of villages where Orthodoxy has more of a foothold would probably not consider icons so dispensable, the fact that the use of an icon-less corner can be very similar to one with an icon seems to resonate with Margaret Paxson's observation that, in rural Russian households, "it is not strictly the case that the corner of the home is powerful because the icon resides therein; but the icon is powerful at least in part because of its placement in the corner" (2005: 219). The invisible forces that make the corner a powerful place in the house add a dimension to the icon that goes beyond the visual image depicted, but also beyond its material qualities as a picture.

What atheist critics failed to notice about rural icon corners is that they simultaneously create a perceptible divine presence and help restrict that presence to a particular location and to ritually sanctioned occasions for interaction. Far from presenting a constant avenue for "church people" to extend their influence into family life, these icons are part of rhythms of invisibility and appearance that are governed by communal standards for when and how to seek contact with the divine. Among religious critics, the mufti perhaps comes closest to this insight when he links attempts to depict God verbally or graphically to an urge to contain divine transcendence. Post-Soviet Orthodox defenders of icon veneration, by contrast, affirm the impulse to impose limits on human interaction with the divine, although they also ignore most folk uses of icons. Like their critics, these defenders focus on visual interactions with icons, but interpret these as necessary restraints in the rampant visual imaginaries of secular culture.

Reining in the Imagination

To venerate icons in post-Soviet Russia is to be necessarily aware of a multitude of possible criticisms, both secular and religious. In polemical literature on the subject, theologically educated defenders of icon veneration have pursued a dual strategy of argumentation. On the one hand, they draw analogies between icons and familiar visual forms, not unlike their critics. "A mother who kisses the photograph of her son," one "anti-sectarian notebook" encourages the defender of Orthodoxy to reply to Protestant questions, "does not cause you disgust. Why then is an Orthodox Christian kissing the image of the Savior an idol-worshiper?" (Rubskii 2003: 94). On the other hand, defenders of icon veneration have turned the charge of illicit psychological influence against secular visual culture, claiming that icons serve to protect people from being overwhelmed by visual stimuli. During a dispute in the Christian Center between representatives of Joshkar-Ola's Protestant churches and Orthodox clergy, Father Oleg Stenjaev from Moscow answered critical questions about icon veneration by relating a conversation he once had with a Baptist woman:

> She says: "I don't need icons, Christ is in my heart." I asked her: "And what does he look like?" You know, this woman gets a little confused, and says: "He is not very tall, red-headed." And somehow got even more disturbed. I say: "What is bothering you?" She says: "He looks like one man. When I was young I knew this one man. He was some kind of accountant, very religious." . . . When we speak about Christ, whether we want to have icons or not, in the mind of each of us some kind of image arises. One young Orthodox boy, he was thirteen, went to see the film by Zeffirelli, *Jesus of Nazareth*. And then for a whole month he could not free himself from that hallucination. He says: I get on my knees to pray and I have, he says, that actor before my eyes, and there's nothing I can do about it. The icon exists to filter out this sensual image, sensual apprehension. It shows another world, in a way. And sensuality goes to the sidelines a little bit.[5]

This priest was drawing a distinction between ordinary sense perception and the kinds of sensations one should have while praying, a distinction important to Orthodox liturgical practices. Within this distinction, he
described icons as a barrier to the visual influences that might assault even
the most iconoclastic worshiper. In this highly selective view of traditions of
icon veneration, critiques of secular visual culture merge with themes from
nineteenth-century Orthodox analyses of Western Christianity, which often
focused on the tendency of Catholic and Protestant spiritual practices to give
free rein to the human imagination. In a provocative turn of phrase, Father
Stenjaev went on to ask if the visualizing rhetoric of Protestant preaching is
really so different from a veneration of images: "And what if not icon painters
are pastor Timofej and pastor Sergij [Old Slavonic versions of the names of
his Protestant opponents] when they tell about Christ in their sermon? He is
crucified, the hands, legs pierced by nails, a crown of thorns on his head?"

The Orthodox priest was pointing out that images in today's world are
unavoidable, and that Protestant critics of Orthodox "idolatry" themselves
do not hesitate to appeal to visual imaginaries. As if to confirm this diagnosis, Protestants in Joshkar-Ola enthusiastically used films to propagate
their faith. In 2005, a Baptist church showed Mel Gibson's *The Passion of
the Christ* on Orthodox Maundy Thursday, and a montage of mute scenes
from the same film formed the visual backdrop to a lengthy song about
the sufferings of Christ during the Easter evangelizing concert organized
by a Pentecostal church. Immediately following these views of Christ being
flagellated, carrying his cross through the streets of Jerusalem, and dying
painfully on the cross, the pastor's exhortation verbally developed the imagery and encouraged listeners to go even further in their visual imagination:

> You know, it was no coincidence that Jesus died in just the way that
> you saw today in the scene from the movie. He was flogged, he was
> simply torn to pieces, the skin taken off, there was not a living piece of
> flesh on him, the blood was flowing and pouring in streams, maybe he
> would even have died from loss of blood most of all. So much blood all
> around! Why such a death? Why blood? No forgiveness without blood-
> shed. You remember what we said in the beginning? Passover—that
> is the lamb which had to be presented as a sacrifice for sin, sacrifice
> for salvation.

This style of preaching is intriguingly close to what Charles Hirschkind
(2006: 156–161) terms *word-as-camera* preaching in the equally iconoclastic
tradition of contemporary Egyptian Islam, and illustrates well what Stenjaev was referring to when he called Protestant preachers "icon painters."

The visualizing descriptions in the sermon presuppose a familiarity of speaker and audience with portrayals of violent scenes in film. Recalling the rhetorical style described as "interior *nagljadnost'*" in Soviet manuals, verbal imagery is used to stimulate the visual imagination and elicit emotional responses.

There is an ironic undertone in Stenjaev's analogy between preaching and icon painting, because these examples of Protestant *nagljadnost'* seem to be just what he had in mind when he claimed that icons are necessary to filter out sensual images that get in the way of prayer. As a priest known for his public arguments with various Protestant and Protestant-derived groups, Stenjaev is without doubt familiar with Orthodox polemics against the Western Christian tradition of visualizing biblical scenes, in particular those involving the suffering and death of Christ. Orthodox reactions to Mel Gibson's film have often appealed to these reservations about visualization as spiritual practice. Valerij Dukhanin, an instructor at a Siberian seminary writing with the blessing of his archbishop,[6] points out in a polemical tract that the idea of actors impersonating Christ's suffering on the screen is an outgrowth of the long history of uncontrolled "daydreaming" (*mechtanie*) in Western visual arts and spiritual practices, a common accusation from nineteenth-century Orthodox polemics against Catholicism (Dukhanin 2005: 99). In the Western tradition of such visionaries as St. Teresa of Avila or the painters of the Renaissance and Baroque eras, "the spiritual was . . . replaced by the soulful, prayerfulness was replaced by romanticism and sentimentality, contemplation by daydreaming" (92).

Using a common Orthodox distinction between the spiritual and the soulful that we will return to in the next chapter, Dukhanin urges viewers to question the sources for visual imaginaries of the divine. By challenging the legitimacy of portraying biblical events in film, his analysis stands in marked contrast to Western criticism of Mel Gibson's controversial film, which largely focused on the politics of its contents, for instance its alleged antisemitism (Burston and Denova 2005). Dukhanin argues that Western Christians have to resort to their own imaginations because they lack canonically established styles of icon painting and have departed from early Christian traditions of spiritual discipline. As examples, he cites the tendency of post-Renaissance Western art to portray saints with the faces of living human beings,[7] and juxtaposes Western spiritual disciplines with the warnings of Byzantine church fathers and their nineteenth-century Russian interpreters against allowing images to arise in the mind during prayer. In particular, he quotes from the polemics of the nineteenth-century bishop Ignatij (Brjanchaninov, 1807–1861) against Teresa of Avila and Ignatius of

Loyola, whose *Spiritual Exercises* contains instructions to visualize Christ, events from the Gospels, and heaven and hell (Dukhanin 2005: 98).

When I told educated Orthodox laypeople about certain Protestant practices of prayer and Bible study that aimed at "seeing God face-to-face," they often repeated to me that the Byzantine church fathers had warned against imagining scenes during prayer. Like Dukhanin, they were drawing on the nineteenth-century rediscovery of Byzantine monastic practices associated with the translation of a Greek compilation of spiritual texts known as the *Philokalia* (Love of Goodness; Slavonic: *Dobrotoljubie*). Consisting mainly of texts dealing with monastic ascetic practices, the counsels of the *Philokalia* were adapted to lay lives in the writings of St. Ignatij and Feofan the Recluse (1815–1891; see A. I. Osipov 2001). These Orthodox theologians and their contemporaries, concerned with recovering specifically Eastern Christian traditions after centuries of orientation toward Catholic theology, constitute major sources of inspiration for post-Soviet Orthodox publications (Stöckl 2006).

In the reprints of the *Philokalia* for sale in many Orthodox churches, readers find such lines as "Blessed is the intellect [Greek: *nous*; Russian: *razum*] that is completely free from forms during prayer. . . . Blessed is the intellect that has acquired complete freedom from sensation during prayer."[8] According to the works of nineteenth-century authors also available as reprints, ways to put this injunction into practice range from concentrating on the texts of the prayer books (Feofan 1991) to reciting a short invocation of the name of Jesus in a formula such as "Lord Jesus Christ, son of God, have mercy on me, a sinner" (Ignatii 2000). As Kallistos Ware (1985: 400) points out, this insistence on imageless prayer privileges a particular strand of spirituality, eclipsing other traditions of prayer in medieval Eastern Christianity that recommended imaginative meditation upon events from the life and passion of Jesus. Besides, all forms of prayer are usually carried out facing one or several icons, and thus have a visual dimension, albeit one that is carefully controlled by the canonically approved image.

One way to understand the critique of visualizing practices in this icon-venerating tradition is with reference to the distinction between material and imaginary visual signs, as made by media theorist Lambert Wiesing (2005). Distinguishing between two different aspects of what Mitchell calls an "image," Wiesing differentiates those visual signs that we perceive in the outside world from those that we form in our imagination. The imaginary signs are suspect in the tradition of Orthodox criticism discussed here, because they might be the consequence not of divine inspiration, but of pride or demonic possession. Protestant instructors traveling through post-Soviet Marij El, by contrast, actively encouraged exercises of imaginary visualization, in that respect showing a greater affinity with the Soviet methods of *nagljadnost'*. For example, during the Baptist video seminar on life principles, a lesson on "The Means of Success" extolled the benefits of memorizing biblical passages and mentally visualizing their content while reciting them aloud. According to Bill Gothard, it is through this meditative practice that the central "message of success and victory" of any passage of scripture becomes clear to the believer. One of the cumulative consequences of unrepented sin is an inability to visualize scenes from scripture, a state in which the devil could easily overcome a person.

The video lecture demonstrates the saving power of visualization with the help of animation. While expounding on the importance of imagining scenes from scripture, instructor Bill Gothard is shown making a chalk drawing of the "tree planted by streams of water" from the opening lines of Psalm 1. Once the drawing of trees in front of a radiant sunset is complete, the sunset gradually transforms into the face of Christ. This use of video animation to achieve an effect that would not have been possible in a live classroom resonates with Wiesing's observation that video and computer imagery more closely approximates the features of mental imaginaries than do traditional painting and photography (Wiesing 2005). Video and animated film share the capacity of the human imagination and dreams to visualize beings and objects that shift shapes and otherwise escape the laws of object constancy and gravity to which static pictures are more closely bound. As Birgit Meyer notes in her work on video production among Ghanaian Pentecostals, these technical possibilities make video a particularly suitable medium for reproducing the kinds of visions of divine and demonic powers that some forms of Protestant worship encourage (Meyer 2006).

From this foray into theological disputes, the role accorded to the visual imagination emerges as a crucial point of difference or convergence between various religious uses of images and the Soviet pedagogical tradition of *nagljadnost'*. Perhaps because they have common roots in Central European traditions of visual contemplation, Protestant and Soviet practices appear to be much closer to each other than current Orthodox understandings. This affinity may point to a dialogue between nineteenth-century reform pedagogy and older religious practices from both within and outside of Europe. The Orthodox position is influenced by the nineteenth-century Russian revival of Byzantine spiritual practices, which aimed to correct perceived Western influences in theology and liturgical art. But neither side of the debate can completely detach human learning from the capacity for visual perception.

Visual Learning: *Nagljadka* and *Nagljadnost*'

Orthodox polemics against daydreaming notwithstanding, neither the Soviet nor the Protestant approach advocates an entirely free play of the imagination. In both views, learners are directed by authoritative teachers and texts, and in Baptist and Pentecostal understandings the ability to visualize depends on the purity of one's heart and the fervency of one's prayer. Likewise, Orthodox authors who seek to distinguish icons from imaginary signs cannot rule out the ways in which any publicly available image will also become part of popular imaginaries. The historian Vera Shevzov (2004: 174–175, 177, 232–233) notes several cases from nineteenth-century Russia in which icons of Mary appeared, and sometimes spoke, to people in dreams or visions. In other cases, Mary or another saint appeared as a human being, but directed the dreamer to an icon that was hidden or had been forgotten (224–225). In these dreams, icons seem to have an imaginary agency not so different from Wiesing's videos. They may also crystallize psychological processes in a way similar to the calligraphic poster that reportedly appeared to the dormitory manager's dying husband. Not surprisingly, revelatory dreams and the icons to whose discovery they sometimes led were subject to careful scrutiny by church authorities. Different from the poster, however, icons were effective because of their ability to mediate the presence of actual persons (the saints and divine figures depicted on them). Here lies the difference in the kinds of didactic relationships that icons and posters were supposed to encourage.

In the Mari countryside and elsewhere in Russia, icons differ from posters in being not always and exclusively visual media, and not always and exclusively didactic tools. Rather, the treatment of icons is reminiscent of what the art historian Hans Belting calls an idea of image-as-presence. In this understanding, which Byzantine icon venerators shared with more widespread traditions in the Mediterranean world and beyond, the image is not primarily a visual reminder of a loved or venerated person (as it is in the understanding of image-as-representation more familiar to contemporary readers), but a medium through which absent beings—be they ancestors, the emperor, or gods—could extend their persons across ontological, geographical, and temporal divides. The visual resemblance of image and prototype is not necessarily decisive for images to work in this way, nor are channels of sight the most important way of interacting with them. An image might be hidden in a sanctuary, behind a curtain, or in a box, visible only to certain people or at certain times; touching the image or an object that has been in contact with it may be an integral part of partaking in its power, in addition to or even instead of looking at it (Belting 2000 [1990]: 54–59; Belting 2001; see also Gell 1998). While this understanding seems to emphasize the image as a material medium (or "picture"), the example of the empty corner in Shorun'zha shows that sometimes a delineated space alone can work to create a presence, with no need for any perceptible image at all.

When post-Soviet defenders of icon veneration such as Oleg Stenjaev present icons as visual barriers to restrain the imagination while praying, they privilege aspects of the theology of the icon that fail to account for tactile interactions with the present-making image. At the same time, they are not completely assimilating icon veneration to secular didactic practices. The Orthodox theology of icon veneration can provide ancient precedents for a number of different understandings, including that of icons as didactic media. Learning, in this understanding, has important visual components, but it happens through a relationship of personal emulation, rather than the imaginary abstractions encouraged by *nagljadnost'*. This idea of learning by example can be seen in a letter written by Byzantine emperor Leo III to Caliph Omar II between 717 and 720, in answer to the Muslim ruler's challenge of such Christian practices as the adoration of the cross and of images:

> We honor the cross because of the sufferings of the Word of God incarnate. . . . As for pictures, we do not give them a like respect, not having received in Holy Scriptures any commandment whatsoever in this regard. Nevertheless, finding in the Old Testament that divine command which authorized Moses to have executed in the Tabernacle the figures of the cherubim, and, animated by a sincere attachment for the disciples of the Lord who burned with love for the Savior Himself, we have always felt a desire to conserve their images, which have come down to us from their times as living representations. Their presence charms us, and we glorify God who has saved us by the intermediary of his Only-Begotten Son, who appeared in the world in a similar figure, and we glorify the saints. (quoted in Meyendorff 2001a [1964]: 107; his ellipses)

This letter, written on the eve of the iconoclastic crisis which would preoccupy Byzantine politics and theology for much of the remainder of the eighth century, can lend ancient authority to post-Soviet analogies between icons and photographs of loved ones. The idea that icons authoritatively represent what a saint actually looked like has gained renewed importance in the post-Soviet revival of "Byzantine" and "Old Russian" styles of icon painting (Kuteinikova 2005), reversing the eighteenth- and nineteenth-century trend toward adopting conventions of Western painting. As visually accurate, though stylized, reminders of saints who live on in heaven, icons enable viewers to sustain a relationship with their saint, who becomes a guide in a learning process more akin to the prerevolutionary meaning of learning through *nagljadka* than to the abstract representation of invisible phenomena implied in late Soviet *nagljadnost'*.

Leo seems to consider visual resemblance to be crucial for the present-making capacities of images, but Stenjaev's claim that icons allow a special kind of vision, different from ordinary sensory perception, is entirely absent from this letter. Scholars have argued that it was in reaction to the iconoclastic controversies which Leo himself unleashed a few years later, and to the later hesychast debate over the nature of the light that Jesus' disciples perceived during the transfiguration on Mount Tabor, that the idea that icons allow a spiritual vision of divine reality became widespread (Belting 2000 [1990]: 166–177; Meyendorff 2001b [1982]). Such mystical interpretations of icons are common in twenty-first-century publications that advocate for the Byzantine revival in iconography (Yazykova 2010). The painters of the icon workshop of the Mari diocese participated in this quest to recreate a visual language specific to icons (Kudriavtseva 2002). As post-Soviet Christians encounter a range of visual media, the theological and aesthetic division between icons and ordinary objects of perception gains renewed importance.

It would thus be wrong to claim that Orthodox defenders of icon veneration are entirely untouched by Soviet theories of *nagljadnost'*. Rather, the debate traced in this chapter exemplifies an antagonistic kind of affinity, brought about when evolving concerns from two separate areas of expertise suddenly speak to each other: icon veneration as an alternative approach to personal transformation has gained urgency and salience among people immersed in pedagogical discourses that emphasize the importance of visual interactions. All sides agree that what is in front of a person's eyes is uniquely important for their inner state and motivation for action. Instead of the *elective* crossing-over of chemical elements from old amalgamations into new, this *antagonistic* affinity implies a mutual reinforcement of elements from two different discourses that enter into critical dialogue with one another. Stenjaev's warning about the potential for visual contemplation to lead to idolatry, even when the medium in question has a morally beneficial message ("I get on my knees to pray and I have . . . that actor before my eyes"), is an instance of this antagonistic reinforcement of pedagogical and theological traditions.

Engaging the Secular Imagination

Soviet historian Richard Stites reminds us that Lenin, though critical of unqualified utopianism, wrote in *What Is to Be Done* (1902) that political activists need the kind of dreaming that "may run ahead of the natural march of events" (quoted in Stites 1989: 42). Communist daydreaming, in this view, encouraged the bold vision of a changed future that religious prejudice foreclosed. Keeping this in mind, we might see the religious controversies about the possibilities and perils of visual stimuli as concerned with the proper stance toward twentieth-century transformations: should religious practices parallel secular mobilizations, or should they form persons and communities that would be resistant to promises of radical change? Should images attract people's attention and commitment to the causes of evangelical outreach, or should they lead them slowly on a path to inner transformation? Should a religious community sanction the use of images, and if so, should these images differ in form from those proliferating in secular contexts?

Part of what gives these debates their vigor is the renewed ideological competition after the end of Soviet era restrictions on religious and philosophical expression. But the different positions also have roots in particular pedagogical traditions—selective lines of thought about the means and ends of human transformations. Soviet methodical literatures on *nagljadnost'* took up complex ideas about the developmental significance of human sense perceptions, and Soviet activists tended to understand religious images in light of those theories. Post-Soviet religious debates about images, by contrast, highlight a question that the Soviet literature rarely broaches directly: *should* an instructor use images in order to persuade and engage audiences? What could the unintended effects of such methods be? If these doubts play themselves out in debates about the imaginary, not just in the stances toward material practice that much of the literature in the anthropology of secularism explores, the reason may lie in secularism's special concern with untold human futures. Recognizing no extrahuman partners in the effort to either change or maintain the world, secularism perhaps cannot afford to distrust the human imagination too much. When facing the issue of how and to what degree to encourage citizens to daydream about change, atheists came closest to debating broader questions about the ethics of persuasion.

6

The Soul and the Spirit

Pedagogical traditions differ not only in the methods they espouse, but also in their desired outcomes, in the kinds of persons and communities they hope to create. One way to understand the different goals of secular and religious transformations is to look at the qualities each seeks to develop and promote, both in individuals as they go about their lives and in collectives. In late Soviet and post-Soviet Russia, a term that was used across several secular and religious traditions to describe the ideal outcome of transformation was "spirituality" (*dukhovnost'*). Despite common roots in European theological and philosophical vocabulary, the term meant something different to each group that used it. The relationship between transformative goals and the qualities and behaviors that count as signs of spirituality becomes apparent when comparing the three traditions that elaborate the most on the concept: late Soviet atheism, Orthodox Christianity, and Charismatic Pentecostalism.

As a term that crosses religious and secular realms of meaning, "spirituality" is an important quality of the persons and social relations that each group imagines itself to be producing, be it through didactic spectacle or religious liturgy. The differences in what each side means by the term reveal various strategies of managing the risks of transformation. Manifesting in very different sights, sounds, and movements, Orthodox and Pentecostal spiritualities nonetheless both point toward a more-than-human end point of human learning, whereas late socialist spirituality affirms the value of an ordered human community.

The Spirit of Advanced Socialism

The emerging scholarship on the Khrushchev Thaw and the subsequent years of "advanced" or "developed" socialism emphasizes the increased salience of various terms connected to spirituality as a departure from older, more militaristic and mechanistic, ways of imagining Soviet social relations. Under Khrushchev, campaigns for family and workplace morality and against drinking and "hooliganism" were often framed as being concerned with "spiritual values" (*dukhovnye tsennosti*; see Field 2007; LaPierre 2006).

165

The empirical social scientists who began to investigate Soviet society during those years also saw the "spiritual development" (*dukhovnoe razvitie*) of citizens as a major area in need of study and intervention. For instance, a large collaborative study conducted by the Institute of Philosophy of the Soviet Academy of Sciences and the Knowledge Society in the early 1960s included empirical materials from twenty-five Soviet factories to illuminate the "spiritual world" of workers in the transition from socialism to communism (Stepanian 1966). At a 1963 conference devoted to the book project, the managing editor, Tsolak Stepanjan, explained some of the rationale for this shift to the spiritual. Under conditions of the imminent transition to communism, he claimed, consciousness no longer merely reflected being, but could advance ahead of it—progressive workers in a socialist society could already have a "communist" consciousness. Obviously under the influence of the promise of the new Communist Party program to build communism by 1980, Stepanjan proclaimed the most pressing social task to be "the all-around development of personality and the final overcoming of survivals of the past."[1]

Even as such hopes of imminent transition faded under Brezhnev, the focus on spiritual values remained. Sociologists such as Viktor Solov'ev saw the growth of the "spiritual needs" (*dukhovnye potrebnosti*) of Soviet citizens as an opportunity to convince them of the benefits of atheism, but warned that state failures to fulfill these needs were a major factor that was holding underserved populations back in religious attachments. "It is not enough to liberate a person from the captivity of religious ideas, it is necessary to provide for his all-around spiritual development," Solov'ev commented on survey results on religious belief in the Mari ASSR (1977: 110). In the logic of these studies, such spiritual development was measured mainly in terms of participation in a humanistic culture of reading books, attending the cinema, and striving to enlarge one's circle of friends and acquaintances. Being spiritual was thus almost the same as being a good Soviet citizen, or at least had the same outward manifestations.

Soviet methodicians saw themselves as standing in competition with religious institutions in providing for spiritual needs, and the renewed emphasis on secular festivals during the Brezhnev years was their attempt to hold their own in this competition (Smolkin 2009). But spirituality, in Soviet parlance, was squarely placed in the framework of human sociality, expressing itself in the need for entertainment, companionship, intellectual growth, and useful labor. Brezhnev era secular festivals focused on showcasing and rewarding labor productivity, and, as Caroline Humphrey observed, tended to take the form of official meetings, "almost as though people can think of no other 'Soviet' way of doing things" (Humphrey 1998: 399). The final measure of the effectiveness of cultural work in a given collective was always whether or not people fulfilled their work obligations: in the optic of party superiors, spiritual values and a state-centered work ethic amounted to the same thing.[2]

Body, Soul, and Spirit

For Brezhnev era methodicians, a spiritually developed person was an economically productive member of society who also appreciated literature and art. Such appeals to spirituality may have been part of the wider attempt to tame change by paying routinized homage to it. As Dominic Boyer has shown, "spirit" in its Hegelian sense has provided citizens in a variety of political settings with an antithesis to structure, a way of talking about the forces of history that may move a society toward unknown outcomes (Boyer 2005). In Russian as in other European languages, the term for Hegel's spirit, *dukh,* has a long, predominantly religious genealogy and a great deal of semantic overlap with the equally multivalent term *dusha* (soul). In literary and everyday speech, both are conceptualized as essential elements of being human that can grow or contract, acquire strength or wither at different times in life (Pesmen 2000). Having a soul and/or a spirit is thus an important part of what keeps a person open to change.

Though affirming the idea of working toward progress, Brezhnev era bureaucracies were wary of the unintended directions change might take. It could, for example, pull people into ideologically undesirable directions, exploring avenues of transformation that lay outside of Marxist secular frameworks. Since "spiritual" often meant "church-related" in the Russian language (*dukhovnaja seminarija*: a theological seminary; *dukhovnaja muzyka*: religious music), it must have been especially hard for Soviet methodicians to wrest the ideal of spiritual development away from connotations of religiously motivated practice. In casting improved human relationships of labor and pleasure as the ultimate aim of change, they also had to erase an important theological distinction within Orthodox Christian thought: the distinction between the soul as the seat of the human psyche and human needs, and the spirit as the potential for moving beyond those needs.

In Orthodox polemics about images, we have already encountered a discourse that opposes "soulfulness" (*dushevnost'*) or "sensuality" (*chuvstvennost'*) to spirituality (*dukhovnost'*). In Dukhanin's writings about film, the opposition was applied to the contrast between Eastern Orthodox and Western Christian uses of sacred images; in Father Oleg Stenjaev's apologetics, sensuality was embodied by secular visual culture. Both refer to a theory of the human psyche that traces itself back to the writings of St. Paul and the Greek church fathers. Here, intellect and emotions are not seen as end points of human possibilities, but as stepping-stones toward another kind of faculty. This faculty, labeled "spirituality" (*dukhovnost'*), is associated both with the Holy Spirit as the third person of the Trinity and with an innate human potential to transcend the present fallen state and become reconnected to God through a life of Christian discipleship. In the writings of some of the desert ascetics whose counsels are collected in the *Philokalia*, an opposition between *psyche* (soul) and *pneuma* (spirit) from the epistles of St. Paul was elaborated into a theory of three life stages, labeled physicality, soulfulness, and spirituality (*telesnost'*, *dushevnost'*, and *dukhovnost'*), which are characterized by the increasing renunciation of bodily and emotional impulses.[3] Feofan the Recluse, one of the nineteenth-century bishops who popularized these teachings among Russian laypeople, wrote: "The human soul makes us little higher than the animals, but the spirit reveals us as little less than the Angels" (Feofan 1991: 33).

Crucially, these ideals of spiritual life as a way of drawing closer to divinity were originally elaborated in monastic settings, where monks and nuns strove to attain them through withdrawal from all worldly relations. The original Greek edition of the *Philokalia* was compiled on Mount Athos, an important monastic center in northern Greece, in the eighteenth century, and the first translation was published in Russia in 1793 in Church Slavonic. Both versions were addressed to monastic audiences as part of a general revival of monastery-based spirituality (Florovsky 1991 [1937]: 175–177). It was only in 1877 that a modern Russian translation of the *Philokalia* made these teachings accessible to large numbers of lay readers, who faced very different issues of how spirituality might be practiced.

While in the monastic context the movement from one stage of spiritual development to the next was achieved primarily through ascetic contemplation, laypeople found ways to realize it through social service in brotherhoods and sisterhoods, as well as in public church rituals (Kenworthy 2008: 23). In that context, spirituality came to denote a piety that relied on divinely instituted sacraments rather than on the human sociality that was promoted in secular cultural work. During the Soviet period, prohibitions on charitable or other social initiatives by religious organizations left sacramental piety as the only avenue for those laypeople who wanted to pursue a spiritual life within the framework of the Orthodox Church. But during the later decades of the Soviet Union, the church was increasingly not the only place for spiritual development: at the same time as official policy sought to promote a secular discourse on spiritual values, many Soviet citizens began to experiment with the esoteric sides of yoga, psychic healing, and magical practices inspired by a range of sources (Lindquist 2006). Some healers and seers achieved popularity among Communist Party hierarchies in the Soviet Union and abroad, and their abilities even became objects of study at state-sponsored research institutes (Valtchinova 2004).

Spirit-Infused Routine

The common effect of these phenomena was to preserve a meaning of spirituality that could not be measured in terms of work ethics alone, allowing people to explore avenues of transformation that Soviet methodicians would have preferred to close off. Some alternative ways of pursuing spirituality could be dismissed as little more than individual hobbies, but some sustained communities designed to put spiritual dynamics into practice (H. Coleman 2005; Wanner 2007). Among Christian denominations outside of the Russian Orthodox Church, Pentecostalism places the most emphasis on the notion of the spirit. Pentecostal congregations took root in the western parts of the Russian Empire before the revolution, and small groups have been present in the Mari ASSR at least since the 1970s. With their ecstatic interpretation of spirituality, they departed as much from Brezhnev era routine as they did from Russian Orthodox notions of what was advisable during worship. Invigorated through Western missionary input since the early 1990s, Pentecostal and Charismatic communities continue to present a challenge to post-Soviet notions of public order.

Despite vast differences in their soteriology, social ethos, and ecclesiology, Pentecostalism and Eastern Orthodoxy share an idea that sets them apart from secular festival planners: the necessity of the presence of the Holy Spirit, evoked through proper liturgy, as a precondition for a human gathering to reach its transformative potential (Berzonsky 2004; Shaull and Cesar 2000: 145–159). The two denominations differ radically, however, in their ideas about the qualities of such a spirit-infused community and the practices that create it. As divergent ways of seeking spiritual development in a world shaped by secularist concerns, the forms of Orthodoxy and Pentecostalism that emerged from the Soviet era can be compared to the divergent religious movements in late twentieth-century Sri Lanka as described by Richard Gombrich and Gananath Obeyesekere (1988). In their analysis of changes in urban Sri Lankan religiosity over the course of the twentieth century, these authors trace a process where monastic ideals of restraint and serenity spread among lay Buddhists and underwent a transformation reminiscent of post-Soviet rediscoveries of the nineteenth-century popularizers of Byzantine spirituality. Facing the problem of how to live out monastic values without detaching themselves from the secular bonds of kinship and professional life, middle-class Buddhists frequent short-term retreats and courses in meditation, events that often take on a more emotionally charged quality than their monastic models. For working-class migrants to the cities and others who are unable or unwilling to invest in such means of spiritual development, the ecstatic worship of various spirits that can possess people provides an alternative way of achieving out-of-the-ordinary experiences, comparable to that opened up by Pentecostal worship (cf. Meyer 1999).

Different from Brezhnev era attempts to equate spiritual development with good citizenship, religiously inspired spiritualities of the late twentieth century dramatized a tension between spiritual and social commitments.[4] While the meditative response of Buddhism and Orthodoxy tries to recreate the "otherworldly individual" (Dumont 1983) of monasticism under this-worldly conditions, the ecstatic response of spirit religion and Pentecostalism aspires to a Durkheimian kind of "collective effervescence" (Durkheim 1998 [1914]) as a path beyond everyday experience. Each approach recognizes different markers to distinguish spiritual from secular communities, and allows for different linkages between personal and social change.

The Christian Spirit and Its Place in Liturgy

Orthodoxy and Pentecostalism are not the only Christian denominations to consider the presence of the Holy Spirit as a defining feature that sets apart an ecclesial from a secular gathering. German Lutheran liturgies start with an invocation of the Holy Spirit, and Quakers value silence to ensure that the few utterances made during worship have a properly "spiritual" source (Bauman 1983). Throughout the Christian world, ecclesiastic institutions claim to be guided by the activity of the Holy Spirit, which is identified with the "comforter" whose descent Jesus promised to the disciples in the Gospel of John (John 14:26).

A more specific commonality between Orthodoxy and Pentecostalism lies in the fact that both denominations have teachings on what liturgy must be like in order to be spirit-filled. While other denominations tend to take for granted that the Holy Spirit will be present wherever people gather in the name of Christ, both Eastern Orthodoxy and Pentecostalism identify particular liturgical conditions for such a presence (Meyer 1999: 142–143; Schmemann 1966 [1961]). Both groups also share a view of the human being as itself endowed with a spirit, which is capable, under the right conditions, of entering into contact with the Holy Spirit. Theologically, these "right conditions" create the distinction between a liturgical event and a social gathering. So for both groups, ensuring that a religious gathering has its intended effect involves a commitment to orthopraxis that is commonly noted for Orthodox churches, but has often been overlooked in discussions of Pentecostals that focus on the alleged individualism of their beliefs and spontaneity of their worship.[5] In very different ways, both liturgical theologies deal with the problems of managing collective dynamics that Soviet secular methodicians were also intensely aware of.

Among Orthodox Christians in Marij El, judgments about spirituality and soulfulness were often made in a contrastive manner, comparing Orthodox worship to Western Christian and secular practices. Several priests and lay believers commented that Baptist and other Protestant services were "merely concerts," because they revolved around the singing of songs without sacramental acts such as confession and communion. The judgment that Protestantism is more conducive to pleasant sociability than to spiritual growth was also made by a more sympathetic observer, a rather loosely practicing Orthodox woman who often visited the Lutheran church in Joshkar-Ola. She commented favorably on the atmosphere of that "comfortable, homey church" (*ujutnaja, domashnjaja tserkov'*). But the Protestant teaching of salvation by faith alone struck her as "a childish faith," a desire for the instant joy of salvation that denied the responsibility to constantly work on oneself.

During the Protestant-Orthodox dispute in the Christian Center, Father Oleg Stenjaev presented a similar view of Protestant doctrine as not necessarily wrong, but representing a standstill at a low stage of development. Stenjaev identified the core Protestant virtue of "faith" as merely the first step of a Christian life, to be followed by the development of the other two Christian virtues of hope and charity (Russian: *ljubov'*, which literally means "love"). The utmost goal was not just to gain forgiveness of sin, but to achieve the "reconstruction of the image of God" in oneself. Such reconstruction required personal prayer and participation in the sacraments of the church (cf. Zigon 2011).

An identification of Protestantism with sensual indulgence may be surprising to Western readers who associate Eastern Orthodoxy with lavishly decorated churches and beautiful music and Protestantism with grim austerity. But the ethnomusicologist Jeffers Engelhardt reports comparable judgments from Estonian Orthodox choir singers, many of whom converted from Lutheran backgrounds. These church musicians contrast the sentimental pleasure of Lutheran congregational singing to the more restrained, prayer-oriented styles of those Orthodox choirs that strive for a return to what they term Byzantine musical traditions. In Orthodox singing there is a subordination of musical to verbal formulas and a discouragement of ostentatious displays of skill that make worship into "something certain," as one of the Estonian converts put it (Engelhardt 2009: 97).

The contrasts drawn by these Orthodox practitioners echo film critic Dukhanin's accusation that "the spiritual was . . . replaced by the soulful" in Western Christendom (2005: 92). During the Soviet period, the same charge of soulfulness could be leveled against secular gatherings and the interpersonal relations they created. Lectures on pastoral theology by Archimandrite Veniamin (Milov, 1887–1955), given at the Moscow Spiritual Academy at Holy Trinity–St. Sergius Monastery in 1947–1948, provide a glimpse of Soviet era elaborations on the subject. Veniamin applies the diagnosis of soulfulness to erroneous ideas about priestly authority, but also to Soviet-style politics. Having left the foundation of divine grace bestowed through the apostolic tradition of sacraments and prayer, Catholic priests base their authority on merely human structures, while Protestants, revolting against this priestly authority, often replace it with an exalted faith "in the calling of [church leaders] through the Holy Spirit and their immediate divine 'empowerment.'" In the most extreme cases, "blind followers deify [their presbyters and elders] for sentimental excitement of the soul [*sentimental'noe dushevnoe vozbuzhdenie*] and religious intoxication [*morfinizatsiju*], although in reality these only weaken any real spiritual love for God" (Veniamin 2002: 153). Among Orthodox priests the danger of replacing a grace-inspired spiritual influence on others with soulful human pressures also existed, for instance when priests placed all their hope in fiery sermons (155) or in measures for the "religious-moral enlightenment" of the laity (158). Ways of fighting the "temptation of soulfulness" (155) included humbling oneself before God and "remembering the true power of only the grace-filled [*blagougodnykh*] ways of influencing the believers," i.e., through the sacraments (156).

At first glance, Veniamin's emphasis on liturgy and personal asceticism rather than public sermons and educational or charitable initiatives seems very much in line with the restraints which the Communist Party placed on the Orthodox Church as a price for the end of the worst physical persecutions (Kolymagin 2004; Shkarovskii 1995). Delivered just a few years after the Spiritual Academy's reopening as one of three institutions of Russian Orthodox higher learning in the Soviet Union, the lectures can appear as an example of political conformism. Such a reading would overlook, however, that Veniamin emphasizes the radical difference between the kind of community created by Orthodox liturgy and the community associated with the public events of Soviet life. For instance, he reminds his students of the antipathy of such famed preachers of the Byzantine church as St. John Chrysostom against applause in the churches, "suitable only for secular spectacles" (2002: 154), and of the fight of the apostle Paul in Corinth against the "soulful-fleshly party-mindedness of the local Christians" (148). Applying the Leninist term "party-mindedness" (*partijnost'*) to the divisions among first-century Christians in Corinth, he gives this Soviet virtue a negative twist and suggests that it implies the same kind of "soulful" attachment to human leaders which he imputes to Protestants, "equal in effect to the service of idols and demons" (ibid.).

By identifying the cultural vehicles of Soviet modernization with emotional exaltation rather than rational control, Veniamin's work foreshadows post-Soviet Orthodox discourses on the importance of keeping the spirituality of the church free from soulful influences. Reliance on canonically sanctioned sacraments assures priests that they are not merely influencing people with their own ideas. Proper liturgy, guided by the Holy Spirit, is thus also a safeguard of proper authority in the congregation. Pentecostal engagement with the spirit is also concerned with such liturgical safeguards, but assumes very different criteria for legitimate authority.

Strength to Grow

Although Pentecostals in Joshkar-Ola did not use the contrasting term *soulful,* they also thought of spiritual life as lying beyond the limitations of ordinary human possibilities. Pentecostal worship, in both its more traditional forms (going back to the early twentieth century) and its more recent Charismatic adaptations, is geared toward enabling members of the congregation to receive and exercise the gifts of the Holy Spirit. Without these gifts they will still go to heaven after death if they have accepted Christ as their savior, but they lack the capacity to fulfill the plan which God has for them in this life, which is to serve others and facilitate the coming of God's kingdom. The tasks which the Holy Spirit helps Pentecostals accomplish are often just as mundane as those for which late Soviet spiritual education sought to mobilize people, but they encompass a wider range, from the intimately familial to behaviors which call human norms into question. One member of the Christian Center in Joshkar-Ola explained the strength[6] of the Holy Spirit in terms of the dissatisfaction she started to feel a few years after having joined a Baptist church, which did not practice speaking in tongues, prophecy, or other spiritual gifts. Using a comparison of the recently born-again to infants that is common among evangelicals,

she identified her need to move beyond Baptist teachings with the growing
need for a kind of strength that she did not naturally have:

> In the Bible it says that we should grow and go on from infants into
> the full age of Christ. We must always grow, grow, grow. If at first you
> guard and guard children, if there are scissors lying around, a needle,
> you say don't take it, don't touch, and then they grow a bit and they
> should already not touch it on their own. They have already learned
> something and should do it on their own. And the Lord also wants
> us to walk by ourselves, that is, to search for Him now. At first He
> was leading us, I went there, and He went there, I went here, and He
> went here, like a mother who walks and walks behind her little one,
> and then comes a point [when she says] how much walking around
> can one do, where is he going now? And the Lord is like that also:
> it's necessary for us to walk on our own and look for Him now. And
> then, one could say, the necessity for strength has arrived.

From the Orthodox point of view, the most vivid expression of Pentecostal spiritual strength—praying in tongues—is the epitome of emotional
exaltation. But for this woman, the spiritual nature of this strength lay
in the fact that it expressed abilities that she did not naturally possess,
causing her to act in unexpected ways. Her most poignant example came
from the time when she had just converted to Pentecostalism, while her
ten-year-old son was dying from leukemia. After receiving the baptism
of the spirit with the help of two American women visitors, she was able
to find comforting words for her son when he was in pain. In answer to
his question if he was suffering for sin, she told him that he was suffering
because God was preparing him to be a great preacher, like an eighteenth-
century Protestant minister they had read about. Unexpectedly, the words
she said gave her son visible joy, an effect she attributed to the new strength
she had received:

> These words, they carried this divine spirit, this strength in these
> words. If there had been no strength, I would have said ordinary
> words, and there wouldn't have been this divine strength, I would
> just have put knowledge into them and would not have given him
> joy, would not have given him a glimpse of the love God has for him.
> In this situation, I on my own would not have thought of this and
> would not have dared to say such a thing. I would never have dared
> say such a thing to my own child. Well, how would I say something
> like that and he would feel better? Really, this just came and came,
> I don't even know how it came and came out of me just like that. I

wasn't even thinking any of that. I wasn't thinking, but whatever came out of the heart, I said. And afterwards, he wasn't thinking any more why he was in such pain.

The caveat "I would never have dared say such a thing to my own child" suggests that without spiritual inspiration, this mother would have found her explanation either too prideful (you will be a great preacher) or too cruel (God is deliberately making you suffer). Like another parent of a dead son, described in Susan Harding's well-known essay on her interview with a Baptist pastor (1987), this woman's understanding of spiritual growth made her endow a devastating loss with a significance that went against her feelings as a parent. Where the Baptist pastor used the story of how he accidentally killed his son to remind Harding of the fragility of her own life, this Charismatic parishioner took our interview as an opportunity to "witness" to times when the task of tending to ordinary human responsibilities requires more-than-human strength. Different from the late Soviet equation of spiritual values with interpersonal and productive ethics, Pentecostal spirituality seems to thrive on the limits of what self and society can provide, sometimes requiring adherents to relativize cherished emotional attachments.

In this woman's account, the process of gaining spiritual strength was a very personal experience, so that what she presented as outside inspiration might be interpreted as springing from some little-acknowledged part of her own self. Thus, Tanya Luhrmann explains born-again Christians' sense of personal communication with God as their discovery, through redirected attention and new concentration practices, of the fragmentary, multivocal nature of ordinary self-experience (2004: 524). But solitary introspection is not the only way to experience and diagnose spiritual strength, and neither is personal transformation its intended end point. As we have seen, the church that this woman eventually joined, the Joshkar-Ola Christian Center, had very specific teachings on the need for collective learning and discipline as conditions for congregational growth. With such teachings, the Pentecostal search for spirituality goes beyond individual psychology and, like its Orthodox counterparts, intersects with liturgical theology.

The Sounds of the Spirit

That right liturgical action was as important among Charismatics as among the Orthodox was brought home to me when I noticed the great lengths to which the young pastor and his Moscow mentors went in order to teach the congregation proper ways of praising God through music and dance. Having heard frequent exhortations during services to dance harder and follow the lead of the band more enthusiastically, I began to ask church musicians about the significance of this practice of "praise" (*proslavlenie*). The bandleader of the Christian Center, a woman in her late twenties, prefaced her answer by identifying the ways of praising God as a central issue in interdenominational disputes:

> Differences between denominations happen most of all because of praise [*iz-za proslavlenija*]. Remember in the Gospel according to John the fourth chapter, where Jesus talks to the Samaritan woman. She asks him a variety of questions—oh, I see that you are a prophet, this and that. But in the end, it all comes down to the question of how to worship [*kak poklonjat'sja*]. And he says, you [pl.] don't know what you worship [*chemu klanjaetes'*], but we know. From here comes even the name of some confessions, that is, denominations. Ortho-dox [*Pravo-slavnye*]. Those who praise in the right way [*Pravil'no slavjat*].

Indeed, the Russian term for Orthodoxy, *Pravoslavie,* takes up the aspect of the Greek term which refers to "right praise" rather than "right doctrine," and the Eastern churches have traditionally maintained that there is a unity between doctrine and doxology, between teachings on the faith and teachings on how to worship, meaning that doctrinal truths become part of lived experience through liturgy (Felmy 1984; Schmemann 1966 [1961]). For a Protestant denomination, by contrast, the Charismatic insistence on the centrality of questions of "how to worship" is unusual. A Russia-born Lutheran pastor, whom I interviewed in his capacity of director of a radio and television mission in Moscow, used the same story of the encounter between Jesus and the Samaritan woman to make a point about the irrelevance of ritual to spiritual development. In answer to my question about the specific challenges of rural missionary work, he explained:

> Of course the level of real knowledge of God among people is very low. You can compare it to the Gospel of John in the fourth chapter, when Jesus was talking to the Samaritan woman at the well. He talks to her about very spiritual things, very high ones, and she tells him what she knows. Yes, yes, yes, I remember, we are told that we have to worship [*poklonjat'sja*] on Mount Gerizim. He talks to her about very spiritual things, and she talks to him about what she knows. When we talk to such people from villages, they usually say to us: yes, we have icons at home too; yes, me too, I have holy water standing at home. You have to start from such very elementary things, gradually going on to somewhat deeper things.

The Gospel story to which both referred is in John 4:7–30, where Jesus rests near a well outside a Samaritan city and asks a woman for water. At the end of a long conversation, she comes to the question of right worship and the different teachings of Samaritans and Jews in this respect:

> [The woman said,] "Our fathers worshiped on this mountain; and you say that in Jerusalem is the place where men ought to worship." Jesus said to her, "Woman, believe me, the hour is coming when neither on this mountain nor in Jerusalem will you worship the Father. You worship what you do not know; we worship what we know, for salvation is from the Jews. But the hour is coming, and now is, when the true worshipers will worship the Father in spirit and truth, for such the Father seeks to worship him. God is spirit, and those who worship him must worship in spirit and truth." (John 4:20–24)

The Charismatic bandleader and the Lutheran pastor offered very different interpretations of this passage. While the Lutheran interpreted the woman's question about the proper place and way of worship as an expression of her ignorance of true spiritual issues, the bandleader stressed that knowing how to praise God is what "everything comes down to." In the study materials she designed for musicians, she quotes the above passage to say that leading the congregation in worshiping God "in spirit and truth" is the purpose of the praise-and-worship band.[7]

For Pentecostals and Orthodox Christians, worshiping "in spirit and truth" involves bodily motions carried out to the rhythms of liturgical music. In the Russian Synodal Bible translation, Greek and Hebrew terms rendered as "worship" and "worshiper" in English correspond to terms like *poklonjat'sja, poklonnik*, etc., literally meaning "to bow down," "one who bows down." The Pentecostal and Orthodox liturgies translate these terms into quite different gestures and rhythms, but preserve their bodily connotations.

In her explanations the bandleader used terms related to "worship" (*poklonenie*) almost interchangeably with those denoting "praise" (*proslavlenie*). The link between the two has long been present in Jewish and Christian liturgical texts, for instance in the practice of blessing food offerings through giving thanks and praising God's deeds over them (Felmy 1984: 196; Lang 1997: 29), and in the language of the Psalms, which treat public praise as the proper response to experiences of divine power (Assmann 2002: 166–170; Bornkamm 1968). Orthodox services stand in this tradition when they treat "praise" as one way of accomplishing "worship." The vespers, for instance, start with a call to worship followed by a psalm of praise. The priest or a reader calls:

Come, let us worship God, our King.

Come, let us worship and fall down before Christ, our King and God.

Come, let us worship and fall down before the very Christ, our King
and our God.

Come, let us worship and fall down before Him.[8]

In response, the choir or a reader chants verses from Psalm 104,[9] "Bless the
Lord, my soul," which praises God for the works of creation. While praise
is expressed verbally through prayers and hymnody, worship also involves
bodily acts of bowing down, for instance when the gates of the iconostasis
open to reveal the altar, or during the Gospel reading. In response to the
prayer petitions read by a deacon or reader, people cross themselves and
then either bow from the waist (*pojasnyj poklon*) or kneel and touch their
head to the ground (*zemnoj poklon*), depending on their personal piety and
the liturgical season—prostrations to the ground are a penitential practice
more common during periods of fasting and are omitted during Easter week.

Pentecostal theologians are also fond of pointing out the many words
for "praise" and "worship" in biblical Hebrew and Greek (Munroe 2000).
But in the fashion of list making as a tool for teaching and dissemination,
they arrange different terms into a sequence of stages, each with its own
associated musical and bodily forms of expression. In the understanding
that had circulated to the Christian Center through its North American
and Ukrainian/Nigerian connections, "praise" (*khvala* or *proslavlenie*), calling the presence of God into the church with loud, fast music and dancing,
preceded "worship" (*poklonenie*), a state of contemplative surrender to God
by each worshiper. The latter found performative expression in people standing with both arms raised and face turned upward, eyes closed and body
slightly swaying, sometimes singing softly or praying in tongues. Ideally, the
sequence culminated in the "entry into the holiest of holies" (*vkhod v svjatoe
svjatykh*), a state of close contact of every member with God that was the
goal of each service, but was not always reached. This last stage seemed to
have no physical signs, but looked and sounded much like "worship." But
people sometimes discussed after a service whether or not the congregation
"got through" (*probralis'*).

Both Orthodox and Pentecostal theologians look to the Old Testament
for instructions for correct, spirit-filled worship, but they draw diametri-
cally opposed conclusions, most of all when it comes to the use of beautiful things and sounds in worship. During the Orthodox-Protestant debate
in the Christian Center, representatives of the Orthodox Church defended
the use of icons with reference to the images of cherubim which decorated
the ark of the covenant and the walls of Solomon's temple, counterbalanc-

ing the commandment against the making of images (Exodus 25:18–22; 2 Chronicles 3:7, 10). Descriptions of Solomon's temple were also popular at the Christian Center, but its leaders interpreted them as saying that the presence of God during worship was hindered rather than enhanced by the beauty of earthly things. At the beginning of the first service during the Christian Center's anniversary conference in September 2005, the male lead singer of the praise-and-worship band explained the necessity for enthusiastic praise with an example from the second book of Chronicles:

> You know, the Holy Spirit reminded me of a passage in the Bible. It's . . . Second Chronicles, the fifth chapter. We won't read the whole chapter, but in this chapter it is written that when Solomon built the temple, it was marvelous. There was so much gold there, there were so many stones, there was so much of everything that just looking at it one could, well, I don't know, trip over and fall, that's how beautiful and marvelous everything was. But you know, in order for people to really experience something, for them to start seeing something unusual, something was still lacking. It was very beautiful, there was gold, there were stones, everything. But you know, in this temple, God wasn't there yet. Everything was beautiful, everything was there, except for this. And you know, friends, I feel as if we're in that temple. . . . There was a lot of gold, but *something* was missing [Laughter in congregation], although everything was just great. But then came the glory of God. Let us now seek this glory, let us now seek God. Let us in this praise, in this glorification [*v etoj khvale, v etom proslavlenii*], let us stand up now, let us pray, so that God, so that He may be found by us.

Part of the reason that Charismatics and Orthodox drew different conclusions from descriptions of the same temple was that they were reading biblical texts through the lenses of different musical practices. In both denominations, music is materially important for the practice of worship, but it is used to create very different dynamics. In Orthodox churches, only a cappella singing is permitted. Byzantine and old Russian choral works have variable meters that allow the rhythm of the text to determine the rhythm of the melody (Martynov 1997). In interviews with two lay conductors of church choirs and an Orthodox priest who was a former choir singer, I was told again and again that the purpose of church singing was to support the priest and the congregation in praying. In the words of one conductor, prayerful concentration depended on singing that did not "attract attention to itself," but was uniform in style and tonality and enabled listeners to follow the liturgical texts. Western-influenced choral works of the eighteenth and nineteenth centuries, said the priest, "attract attention by their musicality" and were therefore fit only for concerts, not for worship. "Prayer and aesthetic sentiment—spirituality and soulfulness—are after all somewhat different things." As an example of how liturgical music could remain distinct from the "soulfulness" of secular settings, he pointed to a current trend among church choirs to return to harmonizations based on the Byzantine system of "eight tones" (Greek: *oktoēchos*; Slavonic: *os'miglasie*; a system of melodic phrases that succeed each other through the weeks of the church year; see Engelhardt 2009; Headley 2010).

Charismatic bandleaders in Joshkar-Ola and Moscow, by contrast, expressed the common Protestant position that any style of music is appropriate for worship, if performed for the glory of God. But in practice, music was almost always provided by a band with synthesizer, drums, and electric guitar, and its strong rhythmicality and variable tempo were crucial to leading the congregation on the progression from praise to worship. Internationally, contemporary Protestant praise music is known for its cyclical structure with short refrains and stanzas that can be repeated as long as necessary to allow congregations to reach the desired physical and emotional response (Hawn 2003: 233n21). In a discussion of the role of music in West African spirit possession, ethnomusicologist Veit Erlmann (1982) rejects the assertion that any particular musical rhythm or tempo physiologically causes trance, but notes the importance of an overall rhythmic structure quite similar to that of services at the Christian Center: alternation between slower and faster tempi, with an overall acceleration in the course of the ceremony.

During the opening service of the anniversary conference, the bandleader's exhortation to search for God was followed by a lengthy appeal to be joyful against a backdrop of calm music, after which the band broke into a fast-paced song. As usual during services, the music became calmer after two or three fast songs involving clapping of hands and jumping. During the worship stage, slow, meditative songs (repeating lines such as "I want to touch you / I want to see your face" or "We are thirsting for you, Lord") overlapped with scripture readings and prayers led by the pastor. This was usually the first time in the service when people started praying in tongues, forming the backdrop to the pastor's praying, which often alternated between standard Russian and glossolalia. Sometimes, the praise-and-worship phase could go on for well over an hour before the start of the sermon. Sometimes, it continued after the sermon; at other times, the pastor asked members of the congregation to come forward with specific pledges or testimonies. Generally, the pace of the service slowed down toward the end, with an altar call for newcomers who wanted to commit themselves to Christ, a collection of money, prayers for the evangelization of the city, and announcements.

Different from the steady state of unperturbed concentration that is the ideal of Orthodox worship, Charismatic musicians aim for contrasts between moods of extreme excitation and relaxing calm. They achieve this through varying tempi, rhythms, volume, and harmonies in a technique reminiscent of a disk jockey who encourages dancers to switch between moments of faster and calmer movement. Indeed, many observers of Pentecostal or faith-theology-inspired churches have little to say about praise music except that it is rock music with Christian texts. Tanya Luhrmann remarks on the inward-turning effect of singing "songs *to* God, not *about* God" (2004: 523), and with that makes an important observation about the intimate nature of the relationship implied by the texts. But, at least according to the teachings which the Christian Center was receiving through Triumphant Zion and the Embassy of God,[10] such an inward focusing of "emotional attention," as Luhrmann puts it, was not the point of these lengthy and often physically exhausting exercises. Neither was it to attract rock music fans to Jesus. Rather than being aesthetic or emotional, music according to the Charismatic ideal was "spiritual," in the sense that it helped both individuals and the collective transcend the bounds of natural emotions. But, different from Orthodox understandings, spirituality was not a state of calm concentration, but an overwhelming presence that could only be invoked through personal sacrifice.

Music and Sacrifice

In our interview, the bandleader emphasized discipline both in the band and in the congregation as a condition for effective praise. As leader of the praise band, it was her job to pass on the "vision" of the pastor to the musicians as well as to make sure that the band prepared the congregation to receive the words of the sermon: "Depending on how much praise there is, what the praise is like, its quality, that's how open the heart of the person will be to accept the word." In order to achieve this spiritual receptivity, it was important that people not just be present during praise, but actively participate through bodily motion, particularly in ways they found painful or embarrassing:

> The one who offers the sacrifice of praise [*zhertvu khvaly*], it says in the Psalms, that person honors Me. That means God doesn't need simply—ah, why do we lay ourselves open like that? Sometimes you

have to shout, because you simply don't know what else to do. So that it'll be a sacrifice. So that there'll be a sacrifice, and a sacrifice is something you don't want to do. Something that is uncomfortable for yourself. Many people think that I am like that in real life. No! [Laughs] No, I am a very quiet person. I know what is a sacrifice for me, and I know on what sacrifice God will come: on that which I want to do least of all.

In some ways, the sacrifice of praise is a very individual affair, which each person has to carry out according to his or her particular fears and discomforts. The most important thing is to ask God "in the spirit" what the proper sacrifice is and then carry it out without delay:

You can't tell God, during praise [vo vremja khvaly] you can't say, God, let me shout to you tomorrow, when no one will hear. Or let me get on my knees before you tomorrow, when no one sees it. Let me do it later. When God prompts [pobuzhdaet] you to do something, you have to do it right then, or else it's no longer a sacrifice.

One purpose of the public framework of congregational praise was thus to enhance personal sacrifice, forcing people to go beyond their inhibitions. But public praise was necessary not just for the individual's sake, but for the sake of the whole church, and this made it a requirement for all members, not just an optional exercise of personal piety. Successful praise brought on the presence of God, as it had in the story of Solomon's temple. When this presence was strong, it could heal people, bring them to repent, and help everyone correctly understand the sermon.

For this reason, the bandleader was unforgiving toward people who said that they disliked the music of a particular church, but liked "the word," i.e., the sermons. "I am not even sure if they correctly understand the word. Do they hear what is said, do they understand it correctly?" She found it equally unacceptable for people to just stand still with raised arms during the entire period of praise, saying, "I am at the stage of worship [u menja poklonenie idet], and everyone else is still at praise [khvala]." Stillness and raised arms were appropriate for the slow, advanced stage of worship, but one had to observe the order of "entering the courtyard, praise, [and then] worship in the holiest of holies." It was like the order of body-soul-spirit, she explained, taking up the same Pauline distinction that is so important in Orthodox teachings.[11]

At the Christian Center, worshiping "in spirit and truth" thus entailed going beyond one's own inhibitions and disregarding emotions such as shame, embarrassment, or fear. According to the congregation's mentors at Triumphant Zion, it was the task of the people in authority within the church to encourage others to go beyond their emotional comfort zones. The leader of Triumphant Zion's band found that the Christian Center suffered from a lack of "character" in its praise and linked this to a basic problem of authority common to many Protestant congregations in Russia:

> They have a very good heart. There. Which is thirsting for God. They have a very good heart, which loves God. There. What they lack—their character is not trained [*nevospitan kharakter*]. Not the character of the people, but the general character, the collective character of the praise group. It is obvious that the praise group had no vision, and so failed to form a defined character [*chetkij kharakter*]. . . . I think that this is the basic problem: when there is a change in leadership. . . . From that follows a constant change or lack of vision; this does not form the character of the ministry. From that follows an insufficient number of ministers, an insufficient number of musicians, insufficiency and again insufficiency and again insufficiency. This is only because the spiritual goal [*dukhovnaja tsel'*] was lost at some point.

A "spiritual goal," when it existed, enabled people to go beyond the natural goodness of their heart and form a disciplined group that could achieve the aims of effective evangelizing and church growth. The idea that relentless and consistent music and dancing were both a sign and a precondition for a successful church manifested in preachers verbally berating the congregation to be more outgoing. Musicians, who overlooked the auditorium from their place on stage, sometimes spoke privately to members of the congregation who were not jumping, dancing, and clapping actively enough. As the bandleader told me, she and her musicians would offer such reticent members a pact, saying: "Don't close your eyes. Look at me and I will look at you, and we will dance together."

These demanding teachings about praise met with mixed reactions within the congregation—some members ignored them, while some found them helpful for shutting out the thoughts of worldly obligations that might distract them from prayer. For example, the bereaved mother who interpreted spirit as strength also told me that she needed reminders to shout loudly during services, because otherwise unwelcome thoughts would "attack" her: at home, her two surviving daughters were hungry, her husband was angry (he remained a Baptist and was not completely happy with her choice of religious affiliation), she would accomplish nothing anyway, and the laundry wasn't done. The liturgical creation of divine presence thus enabled the kind of tearing loose from ordinary, habitual attachments that Pentecostal spirituality requires. Achieved through musical and bodily practices of self-sacrifice, "spiritual" worship meant connecting the ideal of intimate spontaneity in relations with God to the value of collective discipline in a corporate body that could obtain "victory" (a key term in this and other Charismatic congregations) over the forces of evil that beset the world.

In some ways, Orthodox visual and musical forms—designed to help congregants concentrate on proper objects of worship as defined by the church—come closer to promoting the kind of inward-turning experience of personal change that Luhrmann ascribes to Pentecostal worship. An employee of the Orthodox diocese, who had attended some of the early meetings of the Christian Center in a culture palace in 1993, contrasted the pressure to conform to collective spatial arrangements there to the more individualized patterns in the Orthodox churches. Sitting in the back of the auditorium, she felt as if the music were placing a ring around the congregation, and she was uncomfortable when young ushers standing in the aisles asked her to move closer to the front. In an Orthodox church no one tried to stand behind a worshiper, and if someone wanted to leave, no one persuaded them to stay, she pointed out.

Although Orthodox piety also calls for acts of intercession and service to others, expansive evangelizing is problematic because salvation is not assured by a simple act of conversion, but must be won through a slow process of working on oneself (Kenworthy 2008). In the theology of "spiritual warfare" (O'Neill 2010: 88–90) espoused by the Christian Center, by contrast, the ultimate purpose of liturgical gatherings was to reclaim the city from the spiritual forces of evil. Church members performed liturgical acts oriented toward transforming Joshkar-Ola, such as prayers over a city map (Luehrmann 2010) or nighttime prayer patrols during which small groups of church members spread out through areas where the church planned evangelizing concerts, softly praying in tongues to reduce the impact of demonic forces. During an evening service in which the pastor scolded the congregation for not dancing enough, he went on to talk about the necessity of "pumping your spirit" (*kachat' dukh*, as one would say about muscles in body-building; cf. S. Coleman 2000) so that God could entrust the church with the great things it was destined to do. "God sees us as people who solve the problems of the state" was the message that summarized the ultimate purpose of divine election and spiritual fitness.

In this idea of spirituality as a perpetual, aggressive struggle, the point of the similarity between praise music and secular rock may be to conquer a prominent site of secular culture through incorporation. Orthodox spiritual

Orthodox	Charismatic
Routine	Spontaneity
Restraint	Exaltation
Humility	Demonstrative strength
Guidance from tradition	Guidance from prophetic inspiration
Words from prayer book/liturgy	Speaking in tongues or in spontaneously inspired words
Beauty, formality	Disregard of form, overcoming of desire for form
Materiality transformed through blessing and aesthetic convention	Materiality minimized
Unity of purpose	Unity of purpose

Table 3. Markers of Spirituality in Russian Orthodox and Charismatic Worship

practices, by contrast, maintain a deliberate distance from secular cultural forms, along with skepticism about the instant transition from a secular to a spiritual lifestyle that evangelical conversion promises.

The Qualities of Spirit in Three-Way Critique

The spiritual is perhaps best thought of as a style (Gell 1998: 167) that involves very different qualities in late Soviet, Orthodox, and Pentecostal contexts. One commonality between the two Christian denominations is that some modification makes an object, action, or person different from what are considered to be its "natural" characteristics (see table 3). But while Pentecostal worship is made spiritual by ecstatic effervescence, an Orthodox gathering becomes spirit-filled when there is a commonality of aesthetics and purpose that unites individual worshipers in an unobtrusive fashion. In line with the idea that the material world is included in the divine plan of redemption (Goltz 1979), Orthodox worship quite unapologetically fashions stylistic coherence from ordinary materials, such as wood, paint, and human voices. Pentecostals, famously aspiring to a "complete break with the past" (Meyer 1998), distrust even the desire for beautiful things and sounds in worship. But neither side can escape the need for theological ideas to take on recognizable form, and this "inescapable materiality" (Keane 2007: 41) makes religious styles available for secular activists to imitate or measure themselves against, creating both dilemmas and creative possibilities.

When Soviet atheists turned toward ritual as a means for promoting their own understanding of spiritual development, they took it to be a form of didactic spectacle. Similar to their didactic understanding of icons, Soviet atheists described religious rituals as tools used by religious organizations to persuade people to follow their doctrines. To distinguish religious and secular rituals, they generally emphasized the rationality of secular didacticism, as opposed to the false emotional pressure exerted by religious activists. But atheist planners also came to argue that some degree of emotional appeal was necessary to make ritual effective. This is where the debate over which features of religious gatherings to imitate and which ones to shun joined ongoing Soviet concerns with the role of collective emotions.

The Soviet attempt to secularize spirituality by placing it firmly within the bounds of ordinary human intellectual achievement went along with a strong suspicion of agitated affective states. Abhorring Pentecostal ritual, late Soviet methodicians seemed to have an easier time understanding Orthodox aesthetic preferences. However, they also recognized similarities between their own didactic networks and evangelical forms of organization, similarities that both troubled and fascinated them.

When describing Orthodox ritual, the attitude of atheist propagandists was often straightforward envy and competition, focusing most of all on the perceived beauty of Orthodox liturgy. For instance, discussing the results of a survey of Russian Orthodox peasants in selected regions of the Mari republic carried out in 1967–1968, Nikolaj Sofronov, an instructor of philosophy at the technical college in Joshkar-Ola and a member of the atheist section of the Knowledge Society, found that over 50 percent of respondents who admitted to attending church named the beauty of the singing and of church interiors as a reason. This led Sofronov to a reflection on the process by which church art helped turn a casual visitor into a committed believer:

> Having been to church, having heard the polyphonic singing, having felt the influence of church art, the person returns to the temple again and again, in order to experience himself [oshchutit'sja] again and again in unusual surroundings. Gradually he begins to take an interest not only in the music and the paintings, but also to listen [prislushivat'sja] to the words of the preacher and, without noticing, becomes a believer. Receiving satisfaction from choral singing, paintings and church architecture, the person counts their effects to the credit of religion and finally begins to argue with conviction for the beneficial influence on himself not of art, but of religion. (1973: 29)

Like analogous Soviet understandings of the impact of icons in the home, this passage probably exaggerates the impression that the sights and sounds of impoverished and ill-attended rural churches could have made on visitors. But what is interesting is the mechanism by which beauty is said to affect its audience. Perhaps influenced by Pavlovian ideas about conditioned reflexes (Todes 2001: 244–248), Sofronov understands beauty as satisfaction derived from stimuli that are themselves ideologically neutral, but that become linked to particular messages through association with words, in this case, the sermon. Through habitual association with beautiful sights and sounds, verbal messages receive positive emotional reinforcement. Being content neutral, the use of beauty in the church can be appropriated for Soviet propaganda, even though the mood of the art must be changed from "pessimism" to "optimism":

> In order to end the influence on people of church art, pessimistic in its foundations, it is necessary to significantly improve the work of aesthetic enrichment of rural toilers: take all measures to develop folk amateur art [narodnoe samodejatel'noe iskusstvo], help the works of the best masters of music, painting, sculpture, and graphics take broader root in everyday life. (Sofronov 1973: 29–30)

Both Orthodox and Pentecostal musicians would reject this mechanistic understanding of liturgical beauty, though for different reasons. Orthodox faithful indeed often pointed to the beauty of services as something that should immediately convince all visitors of the correctness of Orthodoxy. But practitioners understood this effect to be brought about not by coincidental association, but by a unity of purpose between the music, the text, and the prayerful concentration of all involved. One choir conductor spoke of a feeling of "grace," which was created not through melodic beauty alone, but by its correspondence to the intentional state of choir and clergy:

> [And people say:] grace filled the church. This is because that person [the reader] himself was praying, or the choir was praying, and this immediately spread [peredalos'] to everyone. It spreads to the priest in the altar, and his prayer also spreads, because the priest is already praying himself, and when the choir sings, it must help him in his prayer.

Beautiful music "gives wings to the soul," and singers in church become like angels, explained the priest whom I interviewed on liturgical singing. His statement points to the tradition of Greek theology that accords transformative power to human encounters with beauty far beyond the simple enhancement of ideological messages that Soviet methodicians sought (Pelikan 1993: 286).

For musicians from the Christian Center, by contrast, beauty detracted from opportunities for spiritual growth. During a meeting of her cell group, the bandleader discussed a former church member who had moved to Moscow and was having difficulty accepting Triumphant Zion because she found it "too loud." Her husband was Orthodox, and she had also attended Orthodox churches: "there she filled her ears [*naslyshalas'*], they have harmony, ideal sound, while in Triumphant Zion there is noise, shouting." As a consequence of her attachment to beautiful sound, this woman was unable to "graft herself onto the grace" of a spiritually strong church.

Rejecting any idea of spiritual possibilities beyond the play of human attachments and habits, Soviet methodicians failed to grasp these different ways of thinking about beauty. As we have seen in discussions about the Evenings of Miracles without Miracles, their worry was more about the legitimacy of cultural enlightenment work relying on the same methods of emotional pressure that religious groups were allegedly using. But they also acknowledged that positive emotional appeal could help rituals connect with intimate aspects of people's lives. When methodicians in the 1960s and '70s compared religious ritual to Soviet propaganda, it was often to note the emotional deficit of the latter. In the published version of a lecture on "Reasons for the vitality of religious survivals in the USSR," a member of the Knowledge Society stated: "The weakness of the emotional impact [*emotsional'nogo vozdejstvija*] of scientific atheist propaganda significantly lowers the effectiveness [*rezul'tativnost'*] of all this work, leads people to dissatisfaction and a cold, indifferent attitude toward the events carried out" (Ignatov 1963: 211). The task now was to reach both "feelings and mind [*chuvstva i razum*]" (ibid.), and the answer was a return to the strategy of secularizing folk traditions, which had begun in the 1920s, combined with admonitions that Soviet ritual should be "more beautiful, more interesting, more content-laden than old traditions" (Anonymous 1963: 60). The religious distinction between "soul" and "spirit," between inciting emotional responses and transcending them through a common focus on a nonhuman presence, has no place in this model, but neither is it pure behaviorism. People's emotional responses are assumed to be governed by rationality, and legitimate propaganda must address them as beings with both "feelings and mind." The accusation against religion is that it fails to respect this duality by overwhelming people's rational faculties and presenting what is actually an aesthetic effect as dogmatic truth.

Reservations against religious aesthetics highlight the ambivalent relationship of Soviet methodicians to the potential emotional impact of their own mass spectacles. Anxiety about the use of emotion in public gatherings was expressed in occasional comments about the "theatricality" of Orthodox ritual (A. A. Osipov 1963: 71), but more often in visceral reactions against the worship styles of Pentecostals and other Protestant "sects." Ironically, these were the very groups whose structures Soviet observers had long recognized as akin to their own (H. Coleman 2005).

When discussing organizational strategies, atheist propagandists had to acknowledge the uncanny affinities between evangelical groups and the Soviet apparatus. "Each sectarian is a propagandist according to the rule book [*po ustavu*]," said a participant in a 1959 seminar in Moscow, noting the parallels to Soviet cultural work that are used by Baptists to attract new members:

> They organize artistic evenings, organize evenings of leisure, excursions, outings to the countryside, but everywhere deliver sermons on themes of everyday life and morals [*propovedi na bytovye i nravstvennye temy*]. They have their mutual aid fund, give material aid. They assign [*prikrepljajut*] each sectarian [to potential converts] according to the principle of personal acquaintance for the purpose of catching souls [*dlja lovli dush*]. They distribute handwritten flyers, sometimes even put them into mailboxes in Moscow.[12]

If one changes the word "sermons" to "lectures," the only expression that is not in line with describing the activities of a party cell would be "for the purpose of catching souls." Which raises the question that probably made this parallel disconcerting for Soviet methodicians: what were their own artistic evenings, excursions, and lectures for? What distinguished the way they "caught" people from the illegitimate pressure used by religious groups?

One solution for methodicians after Khrushchev's denunciation of Stalin was to displace such parallels onto the "personality cult" of the recent past. In the words of the same speaker, sects were built "according to the principle of a political party" with particular practices of intimidation: "During the obligatory candidacy stage for each member there is a full-fledged investigation [*slezhka*], they constantly threaten them, down to physical threats. They prescribe who should live with whom, which profession to choose."[13] Since this was said at the height of the Communist Party's efforts to de-Stalinize, it may not be too far-fetched to assume that a speaker in 1959 might have intended a parallel to now-condemned practices of his own ruling party when he criticized the "investigation" of members and interference with their family and professional lives.

If Soviet propagandists thus recognized a certain kind of uncanny double in how sects behaved, the sharpness of their reaction also shows some real differences between late Soviet and evangelical Protestant understandings of the value of rational control. While evangelicals recognized liturgical conditions under which such control might be relinquished to spiritual forces, Soviet ideas of human development included no extrahuman force such as the Christian Holy Spirit to maintain a unity of purpose even after rational restraints are abandoned. This may explain why, for all of the experimentation with multisensory pedagogy, the lecture always remained the dominant form of cultural enlightenment work, and the verbal report of the newspaper remained the model for other mass media (Sherel' 2004: 84).

In the 1960s and '70s, the visceral force of the commitment to rational control was most apparent in reactions against Pentecostal worship. Soviet law prohibited the registration of religious organizations whose rituals were "harmful to the health of citizens" or whose teachings discouraged the fulfillment of the duties of a Soviet citizen (Barinskaia and Savel'ev 1973: 24). Pentecostals fell under the first provision unless they pledged to refrain from speaking in tongues during worship. The second provision referred to organizations that encouraged their members to refuse military service, including some Pentecostal, Baptist, and Seventh-day Adventist groups.[14] The rationale for why glossolalia was considered a health risk is apparent from notes included in the file on a Pentecostal group that came to the attention of authorities in Krasnogorsk, a railroad settlement in the Mari ASSR, in 1975. On a sheet of paper evidently containing notes from a conversation with members of the group, the commissioner for religious affairs, Savel'ev, had jotted down:

On Pentecostals or Christian believers of evangelical faith:

Speaking in an incomprehensible language (glossolalia)

So-called "angelical tongue" in which a person converses with god— wild shouts [dikie vykriki], etc.

Prayer gatherings are carried out under circumstances of extreme nervous excitation, religious exaltation and fanaticism. People prepare for such gatherings over long periods of time, exerting themselves through prayers and fasts. As a result of being in the sect, "P[entecostals]" turn into mentally and psychically unfit people. There are known cases of severe psychiatric illness, [and] cases of murder on the grounds of religious fanaticism.[15]

These notes, probably copied from instructional materials received from Moscow, reiterated rumors about unregistered sects, which had faced increasing ostracism since the 1961 split among Soviet Baptists over the issue of whether to accept state registration (Iarygin 2004: 119–120). The notes also expressed a special abhorrence of ecstatic worship practices, which would not have been an issue in an encounter with Baptists. Accusations of

ritual murder among Pentecostals were a staple of the anti-sectarian campaigns of the 1960s and were dramatized in the film *Clouds over Borsk*
(*Tuchi nad Borskom*, 1960, directed by Vasilij Ordynskij), which tells the
story of a Komsomol girl who is drawn into a Pentecostal congregation and
eventually crucified.

Further down in the notes, Savel'ev stated that the group in the Mari
ASSR could register if they "renounce[d] the perverse [*izuverskogo*] character
of their cult." The concept of perverse cults comes from Russian imperial law,
where it applied to groups such as the Skoptsy, who practiced self-castration
as a way to escape the sinful bonds of sexual reproduction (Engelstein 1999).
In its suspicion of uncontrolled crowds, the secularist Soviet state was thus
continuing to make distinctions among religious groups that favored the
routinized, highly clerically controlled worship style of Russian Orthodoxy.

Risks and Limits

In Savel'ev's description, nothing about Pentecostal worship seems to recall
Soviet cultural events—"wild shouts," "incomprehensible language," and
"exaltation" are not among the standard descriptions of any Soviet gathering.
In fact, such behavior seemed so un-Soviet that enthusiasts of rock music in
the 1970s also encountered accusations that their practices were detrimental
to mental health and incompatible with Soviet society, as becomes clear from
some private correspondence between teenagers quoted by Alexei Yurchak.
In the same year in which Savel'ev had his argument with the Pentecostals in Krasnogorsk, a Siberian university student named Aleksandr and a
friend in Leningrad corresponded about the resistance to rock music they
met among their teachers and Komsomol leaders. Rejecting such criticism,
Aleksandr wrote about the "psycho-aesthetic pleasure" afforded by rock,
which takes the listener "beyond his morals or beliefs—in short, beyond
his intellect," in contrast to the mere "aesthetic pleasure" provided by classical music (Yurchak 2006: 231). In its improvements upon the classics, rock
music was "an unprecedented phenomenon of our life that in its impact on
the human mind is, perhaps, comparable with the space flights and nuclear
physics" (234).

As Yurchak points out, these students were creatively using the interpre-
tive possibilities opened to them by official Soviet discourse. In its positive
orientation to the future, Marxist historical narrative endowed the communist future with untold possibilities, so why not include new aesthetics
and new mental and emotional capacities? Similar points have been made
about Soviet science fiction as both growing out of Soviet enthusiasm for

science and threatening to destabilize its claims to rationality (Kats 2004 [1986]). In this sense, transformative outcomes that went beyond present human boundaries remained possible even in the routinized world of late Soviet secularism. If such epitomes of Soviet progress as space flights could incite dreams of mind-altering effects, and if religious methods of orchestrating group dynamics could appear indistinguishable from Soviet ones, then dealing in change remained risky business throughout the Soviet era.

For all the insistence on human limits, the critical relationship of Soviet methodical work to what it saw as religious competition recalls a core meaning of "affinity" in the Volga region: the interdependence of neighbors who belong to distinct communities but who have contributed so much to each other's existence that none would be imaginable without the others. In the biographies of methodicians, the boundaries between secular and religious sensibilities appear even more fluid, subject to the rhythms of human life rather than once-and-for-all commitments.

Preparing bread and other food offerings before a prayer ceremony, Novyj Tor"jal district, November 2005. The preparatory work of local methodicians is evident in the painted sign with the names of the gods worshiped at this tree and in the fresh wooden bar placed to hang cloth offerings. [Photograph by Sonja Luehrmann]

On the way to Shorun'zha. A folklore group from Morki meets a delegation of *onaeng* (in white hats) and cultural workers at the district's boundary during the seminar on Chimarij ritual described in chapter 4. [Photograph by Sonja Luehrmann]

Resurrection Church, Joshkar-Ola, viewed from the west during the interlude between its reopening in 1944 and its destruction in 1960. The razed bell tower is visible to the right of the entrance. The tips of the fence in the foreground belong to the Lenin Park across the street. [Photo from Starikov and Levenshtein 2001, courtesy of the authors]

The new Resurrection Church under construction, September 2008. [Photograph by Sonja Luehrmann]

Icon corner in a Mari household in Bajsa village, Kirov region, June 2005. Barely visible behind the embroidered curtain are small icons, Easter eggs, and twigs blessed on Palm Sunday. [Photograph by Sonja Luehrmann]

"Worship"—a time of quiet prayer during the service in the Charismatic Christian Center, September 2005. [Photograph by Sonja Luehrmann]

IV. Rhythms

Самое дорогое у человека—это жизнь. Она дается ему один раз, и прожить ее надо так, чтобы не было мучительно больно за бесцельно прожитые годы.

There is nothing more precious to a human being than life. It is given to him just once, and must be lived in such a way that one does not look back in agony at aimlessly squandered years.

—A popular epigraph for atheist works, from Nikolaj Ostrovskij, *How the Steel Was Hardened,* 1932–1934

7

Lifelong Learning

After the closing and destruction of Resurrection Cathedral in 1961, the village church of Semënovka was the only Russian Orthodox house of worship in the immediate vicinity of Joshkar-Ola. When I asked an aged priest who had served in Semënovka since the mid-1970s why that church remained open, he replied laconically: "If they had closed it, there would have been no place to sing off the deceased." The phrase "singing off" (*otpevat'*) refers to Orthodox funeral services, and the priest's assertion was that even Soviet officials would not have wanted, or dared, to deprive the population of the republic's capital of a place to hold such rites. For a study of the interaction between religious and secular spheres, this matter-of-fact assertion raises a number of questions. While it is tempting to treat the Soviet era as a purely secular background to post-Soviet efforts of religious revival, funeral rites are just one area where religious practice not only persisted under socialism, but did so with a measure of public recognition. Soviet secularity could never quite exclude religion, and post-Soviet religiosity relies on the secular training and skills of former methodicians. We should thus think of the religious and the secular not so much as characteristics of long historical eras that succeed each other, but as sites of engagement that alternate and overlap in the lives of both societies and individuals.

As the public balance of power between secularist and religious institutions began to shift during perestroika, residents of the Mari republic adjusted their aspirations accordingly, but they did so with the help of more long-standing ideas about the place of this-worldly and other-worldly commitments in life's trajectory. In the biographies of local methodicians, we find evidence of the kind of "dispersion" and "inversion" of religious elements that Hans-Joachim Höhn (2007: 36–38) considers to be markers of post-secular modernity. But it is often hard to tell if such phenomena are purely consequences of Soviet secularization or simply modifications of older patterns of living out a variety of human possibilities. In competition as well as complementarity, secularist and religious commitments laid uneven claims to people at different stages in their lives, sometimes speaking in almost indistinguishable languages, sometimes pulling in different directions.

Competition: Ideological Seasons

When they interpreted icons as visual teaching aids, and liturgical beauty as a means to mesmerize an audience, atheist activists upheld the idea of functional equivalence between Soviet ideology and religion. One reason that they perceived such analogies between their own efforts and those of the "church people" may have been that, particularly in rural communities, secular events and religious observances competed for the limited amount of time available for nonproductive activities.

Emile Durkheim (1998 [1914]: 307) famously argued that religious experience among Australian Aborigines was a function of otherwise dispersed groups coming together for collective endeavors at certain times of the year, and that such patterns of gathering and dispersal divided the year into "sacred" and "profane" seasons. Although this model may work well for hunter-gatherers whose ordinary economic activities happen in dispersal, the sacred and the collective had a more tension-ridden relationship in large-scale Soviet agriculture. Religious affairs commissioner Nabatov and his colleagues displayed special concern about ritual activities during spring sowing and fall harvest because these were the times when economic managers most needed people to be focused on collective production. Increased didactic interventions by methodicians at these critical times exhorted people to focus on collective farm work, discouraging religious festivals as well as work for individual households in the private plots (Grossman 1977; Humphrey 1998: 302–306). Summer and early fall were major times of "Soviet presence" in the countryside (Fitzpatrick 1994: 174) because at the height of the agricultural season it was especially important to combat the dispersal and diversion associated with neighborly patterns of production and ritual practice. But agitational brigades also made their rounds during this time simply because the roads were in relatively good shape, and high school and university students were free to travel. While designed to enhance productivity, conducting and attending propaganda events took time away from agricultural labor, or from necessary rest periods during lunch breaks and after dark. Even under socialism, the relationship between spiritual development and good work ethics was not free from tension.

As times of heightened contestation between the demands of collective agriculture, individual family plots, and cultural enlightenment work, seasons of intensive agricultural work thus embodied the contradictions that could arise between different ways of measuring economic productivity and communal cohesion. Village religious observances, by contrast, seemed more successful in straddling divisions between the concerns of individual households and the village as a whole. Contrary to Soviet denunciations, Mari village festivals were timed to accompany important events in the agricultural cycle without directly competing with them; ceremonies were held before or after spring sowing, midsummer hay making, and fall harvesting. What is more, Chimarij and Russian Orthodox rituals recognized households as the main participant units, as both the providers and recipients of blessed foodstuffs and objects. But when it came to sustaining larger ecclesial institutions, the plans of Russian Orthodox and other Christian clergy stood in a similar tension with the demands of agricultural subsistence as those of Soviet ideological workers. For clergy in Joshkar-Ola and smaller towns, summer was a time of special opportunities and special problems, much as it was for Soviet propagandists. Summer weather facilitated pilgrimage and evangelization, but the garden work with which many residents of post-Soviet Marij El were occupied from the time the snow melted until the first frost also constituted a drain on everyone's time and strength (cf. Ries 2009). "Don't all go off to your gardens right away. If someone wants to work, you can help dig the church garden," said the Russian Orthodox priest of a district center in his Easter homily in 2005, making a futile attempt to protect the holiness of the "bright week" that follows Easter. Throughout the summer, I heard his colleagues in the Lutheran church and the Charismatic Christian Center address the issue of gardens with comparable resigned disapproval, even as they tried to take advantage of the warm weather for evangelizing efforts.

The competition between secularist cultural work and religious observances can thus be seen as one side of a triangular relationship, in which both stand in tension with the demands of rural (or deindustrialized suburban) subsistence. Within this triangle, religion is neither a harmful diversion from agricultural work, as atheist propagandists portrayed it, nor does it stand in easy harmony with the rhythms of village and partially urbanized life. Much like the Pentecostal Baptists on Papua New Guinea described by Joel Robbins (2004: 255), Christians in Marij El have found that the need to tend their gardens is at odds with their efforts to come together frequently as a Christian community. In the seasonal rhythm imposed by the Russian climate, any activity that involves regular communal gatherings—whether to listen to a lecture or to attend religious services—is easiest to sustain in the winter. But because weather conditions restrict long-distance outreach during that season, it remained up to village teachers and film projectionists to trudge through the snow and spread messages of the Soviet future to rural audiences. If the palpable signs of post-Soviet religious revival have remained mostly confined to cities, the Russian climate still plays a role:

during the times when rural audiences would be most receptive to visitors with religious messages, they are also hardest to reach.

The competition with the rhythms of rural life seems to be most intense among ideological movements that expect their participants to be economically active at the same time as they develop spiritually, as do evangelical Protestantism and Soviet systems of lifelong learning. Rural religiosity in Russia, by contrast, is geared to a far more fragmented social reality. Confronting the tensions between being productive and pursuing a spiritual life, local religious traditions have tended to resolve them through complementarity, where different commitments are deemed appropriate for different life stages. In particular, the association between intensive religious practice and old age adds a new set of meanings to the phrase "postsecular religion."

Complementarity: Learning through Old Age and Death

The priest from Semënovka claimed that the need to give the dead a liturgical "singing off" remained so pervasive throughout the Soviet era that even officials intent on closing churches had to take it into account. Indeed, Soviet statistics on religious rituals consistently showed that the percentage of deceased people who received religious funerary rites was noticeably higher than that of children who went through baptism or other religious rites of passage, and far higher than that of couples who were married in a religious ceremony.[1] Elsewhere in socialist Eastern Europe, funerals also retained the strongest religious symbolism compared to other life-cycle rituals (Kligman 1988). In spite of these trends, evidence suggests that funerals received less attention in the struggle for secular rituals than other observances. For instance, they rarely figured in the literature on new secular holidays, although scenarios for secular funerals had existed since the 1920s (Lane 1981: 82–83).

As Christel Lane (1981: 83) suggests, part of the reason for this relative indifference lay in the philosophical difficulties of making entirely secular sense of a funerary rite. More precisely, dead people were beyond the reach of didactic intervention, making it harder to conceptualize how their treatment mattered to the society of living human beings. Socialist funerals addressed the surviving kin with messages about the meaning of life and the death-transcending power of labor, but that same theme was elaborated in many other contexts. For example, workplace festivities sometimes played on the theme of continuity between generations (Petrov 2003: 143), as did the public commemoration of dead heroes, such as Lenin or the fallen of the Second World War, whose role in Soviet life has been well documented (Merridale 2000; Tumarkin 1983, 1994; Weiner 2001).

Compared to other life-cycle events, increasing the number of secular funerals does not seem to have been a major concern for methodicians on the ground. As elsewhere in the Soviet Union of the 1960s and 1970s, in the Mari ASSR there was abundant discussion of "new rituals" in newspapers and advice manuals. But the only call for more attention to funerals that I found struggled to define the proper addressee of the ritual's didactic message. In his book *The Family and Religion,* Mikhail Nekhoroshkov quotes the letter of a miner published in the central newspaper, *Pravda:*

> [A]s long as a person is alive, above him there is the party committee, the mining committee, and the rest of the leadership—we demand, we educate, we care for him in whatever way we can. Because this person is ours, and we're not willing to give him up to anyone. But once he dies—then what, all of a sudden he stops being one of ours? Take him, priests [*popy*] and deacons, lay to rest the sinful soul—is that how it goes? To the dead, of course, it's all the same, but the living are looking at us! Children, grandchildren are growing! And for us also, as long as we are alive, it's not all the same what trace remains behind. We need to know that we have not walked the earth for nothing, that we have left something behind in people. (quoted in Nekhoroshkov 1967b: 51–52)

The letter argues that holding religious funerals for people who lived secular lives sends their surviving kin and friends a message about the fragility and powerlessness of the secular community just at a moment when its continuity and solidarity most need to be affirmed. "To the dead . . . it's all the same" what kind of funeral they receive, but the living need to reaffirm the enduring strength of a community of human beings who are irrevocably "ours."[2] Such an exclusively humanist understanding of community might have been expressed in funeral rites that acknowledged the finitude of individual life and the commitment of colleagues and family to carry on the achievements of the deceased. But the fact that Nekhoroshkov quotes from a Moscow newspaper, omitting the usually obligatory local examples, suggests that there were few experiments with secular funerals to report on in the republic.

This neglect was due in part to a view of community membership as involving susceptibility to teaching. Note that in the above quote, the living person develops ties to the secular community through the didactic efforts of party and trade union offices: "we demand, we educate, we care" (*trebuem, vospityvaem, zabotimsja*). From an atheist point of view, there was no way in which these efforts could continue after death.

Soviet atheist didactic interventions more typically targeted youth and middle age, and could thus coexist quite comfortably with traditions which associated intensified religious practice with old age (Rogers 2009). In the Volga region, as elsewhere in Russia, such a complementary view of secular and religious stages of development survived Soviet socialism fairly intact, though it depended on an idea of learning that was at odds with the promises of Soviet didacticism.

The happy convergence of Soviet atheist and local religious ideas of life stages can be seen in the statistics on life-cycle rituals. The lowest percentages of religious rituals were for marriages, i.e., rituals conducted for mature adults. Rituals connected to young children and to people at the end of their lives, by contrast, remained more strongly religiously marked. Atheist observers also associated old people, young children, and women with religious activity—the three groups assumed to be less fully integrated into socialist work collectives (Dragadze 1993; Paert 2004). A study by Viktor Solov'ev concluded that grandparents were the major force in deciding on the baptism of newborns even against the preferences of the parents (Solov'ev 1982). The commissioner for religious affairs, Savel'ev, claimed in several reports that most religious believers were women and pensioners. In 1974, he backed up such statements with statistics compiled from the reports of registered Russian Orthodox congregations, which showed that most registered (*dvadtsatki*) members of the eleven functioning Orthodox churches in the republic were female pensioners with no more than elementary educations.[3] The composition of the "church *aktiv*," as Savel'ev called it in analogy to mobilized party or trade union members, reflected associations of religion with social marginality and led him to call for the familiar didactic solution to the religious problem: specialized cultural programs for housewives and pensioners.

One might see the emphasis on the social marginality of religious practitioners as a self-serving move by atheists intent on minimizing the significance of the phenomena they were trying to eradicate. Indeed, historians have sometimes interpreted the tendency to ascribe greater religiosity to women as primarily an expression of the gender biases held by Soviet activists (Husband 2000: 102–105; Peris 1998: 79–83). Others have noted the opportunities for accommodation and disguise provided by official ideas about gender and religion. With respect to the "women's riots" (*bab'i bunty*) against the 1929–1930 collectivization campaigns and church closings,

Lynne Viola (1996) argues that women's association with irrational, inconsequential behavior made it possible for them to express the dissent and dissatisfaction of the whole village, while shielding the community from state retaliation. A man might privately agree with his wife, but protect himself and the whole family by publicly denying any knowledge of her activities. During the anti-veiling campaign in Soviet Central Asia, the feminization of overtly religious behavior gave men a similar option of public disavowal (Northrop 2004: 176).

A similar argument about the benefits of marginality can be made for the association of religious practice with pensioners. If grandparents took the initiative to have children baptized, this served the interests of the parents, who had much more to lose in terms of educational or career opportunities. It also served the interests of the atheist activists, who could argue that high rates of baptism did not constitute evidence of the failure of atheist education among key social groups. Soviet regulations recognized the risk of such strategic disavowals of responsibility and tried to curtail them by forbidding churches to perform baptisms of minors unless both parents signed the baptismal register.[4]

But beyond such strategic considerations, particular characteristics of rural Russian religiosity facilitated the compartmentalization of religion by age and gender. Douglas Rogers (2009: 45) makes this argument for Old Believers in the Urals, pointing to their tradition of "deferring ritual participation," where youth and middle age were times for attending to this-worldly affairs, while old age meant turning toward the spiritual formation of one's soul in the interest of salvation. Rogers points out that this habit of uncoupling ritual practices from the affairs of the fallen world, documented since before the revolution, allowed Old Believer communities to adapt quite successfully to the demands of Soviet rule, while they reproduced religious life through the activities of the old and the very young.

The forms of old-age asceticism espoused by Rogers's priestless Old Believers are extreme, involving withdrawal from commensality with younger family members and other acts of quasi-monastic abstention. Among Old Believers in the Mari republic, some female elders even prepared their coffins during their lifetime and reportedly lay in them for days at a time "in expectation of some kind of miracle."[5] But patterns of intensified religious practice during those life stages when an individual is less preoccupied with activities of production and reproduction have also been reported in mainstream Orthodox communities. For twentieth-century Greece, Renée Hirschon (1989: 220–232) and Charles Stewart (1991: 74, 109) have noted the association of religious activity with women and old age. For Russia,

Tat'iana Bernshtam (2005: 241) argues that the trend in the late nineteenth century was that only women and the aged kept fasts, while younger men increasingly did not.

Studies of Protestant and Catholic Europe have interpreted a similar compartmentalization of religious and secular involvement by gender and age as an effect of secularizing processes (Brown 2001; Christian 1972). The Greek and Russian examples are certainly open to the same interpretation. But compartmentalization has older precedents, such as the Muscovite tradition of people entering monasteries at an advanced age, after having lived lay lives (Smolitsch 1953: 262–263). Comparable to Hindu expectations about renunciation in old age (Hawley 1987), a general ethics of social complementarity became a resource for engaging the demands of secular society.

In the Mari republic, this notion of complementarity was not restricted to Orthodox Christians, but was part of the shared neighborly assumptions about how religious practice worked. A group of mainly elderly women cleaned the floor of the Russian Orthodox cathedral after services on Sundays, and one participant said that she would do this for her children's sake as long as she could, after which they would have to do it for her. A Tatar schoolteacher to whom I mentioned the problems of Muslim students at German universities, where the fasting month of Ramadan sometimes coincides with major exam periods, expressed bafflement as to why young people would observe the fast. She explained that she was nearing retirement and would perhaps take up fasting then, though it would be hard. For her, fasting and increased piety were necessary for people who were withdrawing from productive life and preparing their souls for death.

An elderly couple in a Mari village recalled how notions of gender complementarity had helped them conduct household-level sacrificial ceremonies during the Soviet period. With her husband's knowledge, the wife conducted the rites at home while he was at work, so as not to endanger his job at the post office. The couple explained their division of religious labor as a strategic accommodation, but this accommodation was made possible by a prior understanding of ritual as intercession: what counted was that the ceremony be performed by someone in the household, not that the whole household be present. As they prepared to participate in a communal sacrificial ceremony in the fall of 2005, it was still the old matriarch, rather than her husband, grown son, or daughter-in-law, who said the prayers before the icon corner before everyone left the house. She also stood in line to hand the *onaeng* the family's sacrificial offering, a duck, and receive his prayers, while her husband joined other men in tending the fires under the kettles in which meat from all the sacrificial animals was cooked together. Even after the lifting of Soviet restrictions, the task of ritually representing the household still fell to the oldest married woman.

Although none of these instances excludes the possibility that the feminization and deferral of religious practice might have increased during the Soviet period, they make it unlikely that these phenomena either were invented by Soviet observers or simply reflected strategic reactions of religious believers to Soviet policy. In terms of the logic of local understandings, restrictions on who could participate did not significantly impact the efficacy of religious observances, just as devotion to constructing the socialist society during youth and middle age did not preclude turning to intensive religious practice after retirement. The relationship between the religious and secular spheres was thus shaped in part by the religious traditions of rural Russia. But the alternation of religious and secular commitments also depended on movement between different approaches to learning that not everyone found easy.

Wasted Time; or, Complementarity's Shadow

The link between secular attachments and particular learning contexts became clear in a conversation with a retired journalist and former anchor of an atheist radio show. When I interviewed her in 2005, she was wearing a Russian Orthodox baptismal cross around her neck and was clearly embarrassed when I asked about the show she had worked on in the 1970s. But she still spoke with indignation about a specific episode, when in the course of visiting a "sect" whose exact denomination she had forgotten, she learned that this group used children who had learned to play the piano "in Soviet music school" to play religious music during services: "this baffled me." The idea that the skills that children acquired in the Soviet educational system could be used for religious ends went against her sense of the purpose of knowledge. Legal prohibitions against the involvement of minors in congregational life—the reason for splits in the 1960s within Baptist, Adventist, and Pentecostal groups, parts of which refused to comply with these laws (Lane 1978: 146–148; Sawatsky 1981)—show a similar concern with ensuring that schoolchildren would be exposed to exclusively secular influences. In what may have been the same case remembered by the journalist, Commissioner Savel'ev asked the city executive committee to take action against an Adventist congregation in Joshkar-Ola in 1977. The leadership, he stated, had "enlisted [*vovlekli*] for participation in the divine service—playing the piano as accompaniment to the choir of believers—Sasha Trusjuk, son of the presbyter, student of the seventh grade of middle school No. 24 in Joshkar-Ola."[6]

As the example of France shows (Bowen 2008; Ozouf and Ozouf 1992), such a visceral association between schooling and secularity does not have to lead to militant atheism, but can simply enforce a secularist version of compartmentalization: students in state schools are expected to leave whatever religious attachments they have outside the classroom. In the Soviet Union, the hope was that the secularizing influence of the school *would* extend into the family and into a graduate's productive life, but the mechanisms of control weakened outside the school fence. Though they did not always succeed in turning people into lifelong atheists, the constant claims that Soviet educational offerings made on the time, energy, and aspirations of children, adolescents, and working-age adults had an impact on their ability to look beyond secular knowledge. While they were proud of their professional accomplishments, many post-Soviet religious activists spoke of the ignorance and lack of skill with which they had approached religious practice late in life, and many expressed regret for time spent pursuing other kinds of learning.

Often, changes in their family status pushed people to seek religious expertise and venture beyond the society of human contemporaries. The teacher of Quranic reading at the mosque recalled how the thought of her own and her mother's future death spurred her desire to acquire knowledge about Islam. Her mother had been illiterate in Arabic, but knew the prayers she had heard "from the grandmothers." The daughter grew up with a sense that God existed, but in school all she heard was that "God does not exist." As she grew older, the question of religious knowledge became more pressing for her:

> I thought: I am going on forty; I thought: sooner or later I'll have to die. My hair is cut off, what sort of a Tatar-Muslim am I? I thought of myself as a Muslim, not understanding that being a Tatar doesn't mean that you're a Muslim yet. . . . So at forty I already started to think that, for example, my mother was old, and that I can't do anything, don't know anything, how to pray, which prayers to read, I didn't know anything. When I turned fifty, I started to go to the mosque. At that time the first abc's [*pervye azy*] started here, the mosque wasn't finished yet, we went to this temporary shed heated by a stove. I started to go there, received my first abc's there. And then when I wanted to know more, and couldn't get it here, I went to the *medrese* [in Kazan']; my mother had already died at the time, I didn't have to take care of her.

This former factory worker was born in 1942, so her forties coincided with the end of stagnation and the onset of perestroika. She took up religious practice as she was nearing retirement age (fifty-five for women), during a decade of growing religious activism in all denominations in the republic. The spirit of the times must have made it easier for her to take on the responsibility of an elderly woman: to say prayers for the generations that preceded her and those that followed. Her approach to religion came from the framework of lifelong learning, familiar from her time as a trade union organizer. She enrolled in distance education at the *medrese* in Kazan' while taking care of her infant granddaughter and allowing her daughter to go back to work. Although she successfully completed her diploma thesis under these difficult conditions, she later told me that she and other women active in the mosque regretted that they had "wasted" so many years without saying prayers and observing fasts; if they had started earlier, embodied forms of ritual knowledge would now come more easily.

A Mari schoolteacher of the same generation (b. 1945), who had started attending sacrificial ceremonies after retirement, also mentioned her mother's death as a key moment when she realized the inadequacy of her own knowledge. Thanks to an aunt's explanations, the bereaved daughter, who had spent her working life away from her native Shorun'zha, found out how much she had to learn about commemorating the dead. While her mother had been alive, she had allowed her daughter to visit the village cemetery whenever it suited her schedule, but now it turned out that graves should only be visited on special days, such as the spring festival of *semyk*.

> Before, I didn't know either how to behave in the cemetery. I arrived from the city, and my mother and I [said], let's go to the cemetery. It turns out there too you have to know the right procedure. Even here in our neighbor's family, the grandmother has already died now, her neighbor died and, she said, appeared to her daughter in a dream: "My daughter, visit me in the cemetery when everyone else goes, too, and come through the main gate." All of us stand there and watch when all the people are coming.

For this retired teacher, learning how to properly commemorate her mother (and, later, her husband) became part of a quest for spiritual knowledge that led her to consult with Mari ritual specialists and to take classes with a psychic healer. Both women actively sought knowledge about religion in old age, seeking to compensate for their lack of preparation with the kind of on-demand, methodical learning that was part of the promise of Soviet didacticism. But both also felt that participation in Soviet life had disrupted their relationships with their elders, and that their own mothers had practiced only a compromised version of older religious traditions.

These women belonged to a generation whose parents were born after or shortly before the Bolshevik Revolution, and both reported having had limited exposure to religious exemplars in their own families. In 1952, Commissioner Nabatov noted with his characteristic astuteness that, although Tatars claimed that only old people fasted during Ramadan, observation of the daily schedules of two working-class families had shown that all members adjusted their meal times to fall after dark, so that effectively the whole family adhered to Islamic restrictions.[7] For members of later generations, such religious ordering of family life was no longer available as a source of learning. She had been able to learn little about Islam from her mother, said the teacher of Quranic reading, since even her mother had just been a little child when the mosque in their village was destroyed. The Mari teacher had heard about prayer ceremonies in her childhood "from the tales of the elders," but had not been taught prayers herself.

A glimpse at another family suggests that it was only toward the very end of the Soviet era that engagement with secular learning replaced more tacit forms of religious transmission in the family. The principal of a rural primary school, born in 1963 in an Orthodox Christian Mari family, converted to Islam when she married a Tatar. Though considering herself an observant Muslim, she contrasted the religiously influenced dispositions modeled by her parents to her own generation's inability to provide their children with the same kind of example. Her father, a party member whom she called "a true communist" (*istinnyj kommunist*), died in an accident after throwing her mother's icons out of a new house. But although she thought that her father's atheist convictions were firm enough to eventually cost him his life, the school principal maintained that he prayed for the health of the family every morning while cutting the bread for breakfast. When I asked what words he used in the prayer, she said that as a "true communist" he would never have prayed aloud, but she was sure that "in his soul" (*v dushe*) he was praying. He always insisted that no one start eating until he had handed each child their portion, and allowed no one to exchange their food with anyone else's. Her husband, by contrast, only cut a slice of bread for himself and let everyone else serve themselves, abdicating the responsibility of the head of household to intercede for the family. For her, this illustrated the failure of her generation to exemplify religious sensibilities for their children in the way even atheist parents had done in the past.

The complementarity of religious and secular spheres thus helped keep socialist society permeable to nonhuman forces, but exemplars from whom one might have learned how to engage these forces became increasingly hard to find. People of postwar Soviet generations felt that they lacked the long-term exposure that would have helped them build up the disposition necessary for taking up religious practice later. When they complained about "wasted time," they acknowledged the difficulty of using methodical study to make up for missed opportunities to form the necessary habits. Once as I was waiting among petitioners to be received in the Orthodox archbishop's office, two visibly nervous elderly women whispered to each other that they did not know any of the "church rules" of behavior. A middle-aged man suggested that they use the present time of Lent to learn. "It's too late for us to learn," replied one woman with obvious regret.

Like many of the religious methodicians in this book, these nervous petitioners were of a generation that had spent their working lives under Soviet socialism, and whose parents had done likewise. Having reached retirement age around the time that restrictions on public religiosity were lifted, they struggled to remake themselves into the kind of religious adepts they imagined their grandparents and great-grandparents to have been. The difficulties many of them encountered show the limits of Soviet didacticism, with its promise of speedy and lifelong transformation. For some members of this and younger generations, the response was to embrace the learning practices of evangelical Protestants, whose expectations seemed easier to meet through short-term, concerted effort. Another solution for recuperating secular learning into religious practice can be to theologize the discoveries as well as the methods of Soviet science, as has happened in post-Soviet encounters with occultism.

An Atheist Yogi: Theologizing the Spirit of Science

My discussion in this book has focused largely on activists who sought to conform to specific religious or ideological traditions. However, not everyone in the Mari republic cared about doctrinal conformity. As Galina Lindquist (2008: 154) notes for Tuva, another multireligious region within the Russian Federation, many of the ways in which people engage with powerful nonhuman forces occur "on the margins" of established religious systems. These margins often incorporate not only various religious traditions, but also Soviet science, inverting its purpose from demystifying the world to controlling the mysterious. Some people carried out such interstitial practices occasionally, for instance by visiting a church in the hope of soaking up cosmic energy. Others were highly engaged religious virtuosi, such as the yoga master and psychic healer with whom some of my Chimarij interlocutors had studied.

The attraction of a new-age synthesis of scientific paradigms and religious traditions has been noted in Russia (Akhmetova 2005; Lindquist 2006) and in other parts of the world undergoing rapid social and technological change (Gombrich and Obeyesekere 1988: 452; Stewart 1991: 131). In post-Soviet Russia, the quest for empowerment through occult knowledge resonates in peculiar ways with atheist understandings of religion and science. In an influential formulation from his *Critique of Hegel's Philosophy of Right*, Marx called religion the "inverted world consciousness" that reflects the "inverted world" of social inequalities which denies people access to the truth about social and natural relations (Marx 1957 [1844]: 378). Soviet atheist propaganda simplified the idea of inverted consciousness to present religion as a system of explanations that came into play when experiential knowledge failed to provide convincing answers. In the words of Knowledge Society lecturer Nikolaj Sofronov: "only in those instances when the rural toiler encounters unknown, incomprehensible forces of nature and society beyond his control, does he take them to be something foreign and even hostile to him. Only then does he turn to god for 'help'" (1973: 9). But it is doubtful if this understanding of religion as an explanation of the unexplainable captured what was most important to local religious practitioners. In the 1985 sociological survey of beliefs and traditions in the Mari ASSR, declared religious believers were asked what they saw as the positive functions of religion. Although the statement that religion "explains many questions of life" was the first option given to respondents, only 6.4 percent chose this answer. Far more believers maintained that religion helped them get through difficult moments in life (30.6 percent), prevented people from committing reprehensible actions (15.3), kept them safe from misfortune and illness (14.8), or promoted the preservation of ethnic traditions and culture (7.5 percent; Solov'ev 1987: 132–133). Still, the idea that religion equaled faulty knowledge about the world shaped didactic responses like the Evenings of Miracles without Miracles, which were designed to promote popular knowledge of science in order to counter religiosity.

Though it may not have resonated much with committed religious practitioners, the idea that religion was a mode of knowledge structurally similar to science proved convincing to people who had assimilated the methods and truth standards of scientific inquiry. Toward the end of its existence, even the Knowledge Society showed an increasing fascination with the occult knowledge which it suspected in religion. In the year of the breakup of the Soviet Union, the brochure series *Znak voprosa* (Question Mark), inaugurated during perestroika to popularize debate on controversial themes, covered such topics as "Fortune telling: Superstition or . . . ?" and "Will there be an end of the world?"

The answers were no longer the clear-cut denunciations of superstition which such lectures as "Should one believe the cards?" or "Religious prophecy and scientific prediction" had provided for decades. Instead, readers learned that since people had strong connections to their environment, certain bodily characteristics such as the lines of the hand or the shape of the cranium could very well predict something about their future impact on the world (Rostsius 1991). Another volume argued that the biblical book of Revelation not only contained facts about a past ecological catastrophe, but also useful warnings about what would happen in the future if the kind of technological development that had brought about the nuclear disaster in Chernobyl continued (Barashkov 1991). In these "post-atheist" publications, science appears to have triumphed as the ultimate authority, but takes on some of the resigned fatalism of which Knowledge Society lecturers had long accused religion.

For religious methodicians in Marij El, the unquestioned authority of popularized science provided a lens through which to understand the effects of ritual objects and actions. A Mari cultural entrepreneur involved in the Chimarij revival explained that only pure beeswax candles should be used for prayer, never the cheap paraffin ones sold in church, because beeswax shared the same cell structure as the universe and the human body. A burning beeswax candle spread the energy of this cell structure, endowing the prayer with its force. The cell-structure model of the universe was popularized through lectures in the Knowledge Society's planetarium, an important venue for atheist propaganda that remained in operation until 2006. Seeking to explain the many stories about communal employees and party activists who had fatal accidents after felling trees or disrupting ceremonies in sacred groves, the retired Mari teacher from Shorun'zha drew on information from a television program about Siberia that claimed that ritual sites had special magnetic properties whose energies affected those who disturbed them.[8] Both the teacher and the entrepreneur mentioned a local adept of raja yoga as a source of their interest in the sacred energies behind natural phenomena.

When I found this yogi in his office in the culture palace of the armed forces, it turned out that he considered himself to be a scientist unaffiliated with any religion. His career path was closely connected with Soviet networks of lifelong learning and their transformations through perestroika and beyond. As a medical student in Astrakhan' in the 1970s, the young man had started practicing autogenic training, a concentration technique with inspirations from Indian yoga that was publicized in 1932 by the German psychiatrist Johannes Heinrich Schulz (1884–1970). The yogi left medical school when his father, an army officer, was transferred to Joshkar-Ola (a city with no medical training facilities), and received a degree in biology instead. With the onset of perestroika in the 1980s, books on yoga by Soviet authors started to appear, and he read the work of the Leningrad biologist Vladimir Vasil'evich Antonov, *The Art of Being Happy (Iskusstvo byt' schastlivym)*.[9] During visits to Antonov, he learned additional techniques, while also developing an interest in psychology. In 1985, on the initiative of the factory's Komsomol cell, he was invited to organize an "office of psychological relaxation" (*kabinet psikhologicheskoj razgruzki*) at Joshkar-Ola's electronics factory. The possibility of forming private "medical cooperatives" emerged soon after, and he found a partner with whom he developed similar offices of relaxation on a fee-for-service basis. Adapting the techniques of autogenic training, these offices employed music, slides of natural scenes, and texts that suggested specific "thought-images" that would arise before the mind and relax the brain.

As factories and social services fell apart, the yogi shifted his practice to energy field therapy and began teaching raja yoga out of an office in the army's culture palace, obtained through personal connections. Although the Russian word for psychic healer, *ekstra-sens*, indicates a spiritual quest to move beyond sense perception, every detail in the office spoke of the yogi's methodical expertise in using color, sound, and gestures to achieve particular psychological effects. Discussing Mari ritual clothing, he remarked that "the color white is a source of light, it embodies the fact that humans are drawn to light," an insight he had obviously taken to heart for his own professional presentation: the off-white color of his coat matched that of the soft carpeting. The photographic wallpaper behind his desk depicted a life-size birch grove, and every one of his sentences ended with an upward cadence of the voice, punctuated with a short smile.

This yogi based his attention to ambient detail on the theory that informational energy emanates from every object, organ, and person (Lemon 2008; Lindquist 2006: 54–55). He had traveled to India several times and claimed that Indian civilization had first refined many of these ideas, which were now being confirmed by science. However, one should not "cross over" into Indian civilization, because it was "a civilization of the past. It has already been replaced." Instead, "one must take the most important things from it, one must understand and interpret it in a contemporary fashion, on the level of contemporary science." By seeking to influence psychological states through a mix of what he understood to be ancient Indian knowledge and contemporary science, this yogi took theories of multisensory education back to some sources that Brezhnev era methodicians would never have acknowledged: the quests of reform pedagogues in the nineteenth and early twentieth centuries, whose reflections on the role of sensory impressions for developing human potentials also drew inspiration from European occultism and its encounters with Hindu practices (Maydell 1997; Zander 2008).

Like any atheist scientist, the yogi had little good to say about organized religion, particularly Christianity, which he considered to stand in particularly stark contradiction to science. But he also used the language of "spirituality" to refer to those human potentials that escaped ordinary science, which needed to be developed through disciplines of self-improvement (*samosovershenstvovanie*). Priests, he said, presented themselves as the only source of spiritual development, but much of organized religion really just reflected the vision of the "mentally disturbed." Yoga, by contrast, united spirit, mind, and body, enabling adepts to gain control over aspects of life that the ignorant accepted as given. The yogi claimed, for instance, that he and his students were able to take illnesses upon themselves and to materialize objects out of cosmic energy. Because "a person who possesses knowledge of raja yoga has colossal spiritual possibilities," even the Soviet government was afraid of its consequences and prohibited pursuit of this discipline, he added.

By no means unique to Russia (e.g., Langford 1999), the yogi's inversion of science into an occult discipline might be seen as the outcome of a gradual decline of the emancipatory aims of Soviet science education. Whereas in 1972, Nekhoroshkov proclaimed on Mari radio that science made the Soviet people "creators of their own fortune, their own fate,"[10] by 1991 the Knowledge Society published brochures treating both scientific and religious knowledge as keys to long-determined destinies. Yoga and other esoteric disciplines, in turn, promised post-Soviet citizens that they could regain control over their fate through spiritual powers that trumped natural laws.

The fascination with seeing and unlocking hidden destinies can thus be read as a reaction to the failed promises of secularist development (Comaroff and Comaroff 2000; West and Sanders 2003). However, following Theodor Adorno's observations on astrology in the postwar U.S., we might also say that this psychic healer picked up on key features of the didactic networks that had popularized socialist science. Adorno argues that the "naturalist supernaturalism" of astrological columns—which emphasize the "merciless" immutability of prediction—is indicative of the fact that, for most people, science constitutes an "abstract authority" that has to be accepted rather than understood (1994 [1974]: 46, 51, 57). In the Soviet context, this authority was perhaps not so much abstract as located in very concrete institutions. The yogi, for instance, claimed that the Soviet and Bulgarian governments had conducted mass experiments with hypnosis through television. In a context where scientific findings regularly served as tools for persuading citizens to adopt a materialist outlook on life and to work for a socialist future, the idea that science provided the power to know and control the destiny of others even without their consent was only a step away. The instrumental understanding of insight as a key to power was already there, as was the idea that those higher up in the chain of authority reserved crucial bits of information for themselves.

Dispersion, Old and New

If many people in post-Soviet Marij El equate scientific and religious epistemologies when they engage with nonhuman forces, this reveals more than a failure of Soviet scientific optimism. It is also a phase in the ongoing relationship between atheist and religious didacticism. Lived religions have come to more closely resemble the image in which atheist propagandists saw them: systems of explanation and attempts to govern forces and circumstances commonly thought to be out of human control. But while atheist science remade religion in its own image, post-Soviet religious practice has reinvigorated the dynamics of spirit that late Soviet methodicians tried so hard to keep under control.

The three clusters of examples in this chapter focus on what may seem to be very different issues: the common problems of cultural and religious activists to make room for their work in the calendar of productive activities; the place of religious practice in the life course and the succession of generations; and the intertwining of science and religion in popular approaches to nonhuman forces. But all are united by the theme of the dispersal of religion across other areas of human life. Contrary to what some people have argued about "dispersed" or "invisible" religion (Höhn 2007; Luckmann 1991), the intermittent, contingent, and socially marginal nature of religious practice in rural Russia does not appear to be entirely a consequence of secularization. Rather, the established traditions of compartmentalizing religious practice in accordance with season, age, and gender facilitated its survival through successive waves of social change. At the same time, perceived affinities between religious epistemologies and other ways of approaching the extraordinary encouraged people to develop personal syntheses under the heading of "spirituality," rather than abandoning religion for the newly propagated "scientific world view."

The changes that the Soviet period did bring to the relationship between religious and secular commitments revolved around novel approaches to learning. State-prescribed didactic methods aimed at a constant, rapid, and verifiable acquisition of new knowledge and skills, replacing the slower, more socially and temporally circumscribed transformations involved in a father's silent prayer over bread or an aging woman's immersion in scriptural recitation in preparation for death. Secular didacticism was far less modest than rural religiosity in its demands for commitment and attention, but its promise of limitless transformations eventually undermined its own goal of creating good citizens for an increasingly static society. By applying Soviet promises of methodical self-improvement to the development of extrasensory capacities, post-Soviet religious seekers are recovering the dynamism of the concept of spirit that was almost lost in late Soviet moral education. Pushing the quest for knowledge beyond the boundaries of the humanly possible, they show how difficult it is for secularism to remain settled in its self-imposed limitations.

Conclusion: Affinity and Discernment

In the preface, I told the story of an Orthodox priest who was convinced that the devil guided Karl Marx's hand in writing *Capital*. When I told a young icon painter in Joshkar-Ola about this encounter, she neither derided the priest nor joined in his condemnation of the father of communism. Instead, she briefly paused to think, then asked if I thought Marx would have known. Another priest had once told her that a "spiritual person" (*dukhovnyj chelovek*) always knew "where his thoughts come from, which ones are his own, and which ones are induced from outside [*vnushajutsja*]." By implication, she was asking if I would credit Marx with the gift of spiritual discernment. If the devil had attempted to suggest ideas to him, would he have noticed, or would he have mistaken them for his own?

Few readers of this book are likely to worry about the devil's capacity to infiltrate their thoughts. But the problem of discernment still stands as a challenge to any analysis that searches for similarities and changes across time periods or cultural domains. Borrowing Weber's and Goethe's concept of "elective affinity," I have pursued the spirit of didacticism through secularist and religious quests for transformation. As a way of mobilizing people into social activity through relationships of teaching and learning, didacticism involves a view of human beings as capable of the speedy and unlimited change of attitudes and behavior, and an understanding of objects, words, and practices as tools to induce such changes. Driven by activists who imbibed these principles during their Soviet secular training, religious revival in the post-Soviet era sometimes seeks to emulate and recreate Soviet educational networks, and sometimes keeps a tension-ridden distance. Throughout, it is clear that the religious and secular spheres are not governed by fundamentally different ethics or rationalities, but intersect in the lives of individuals and communities.

Acknowledging that the question of historical causality remains open, the point of positing an elective affinity between such phenomena as Protestant cell groups and Soviet study groups has been less to claim that one grows out of the other, than to look at how practices that have very different origins (or remote common roots) converge and give new meaning to each other. The Protestant-communist encounter in post-Soviet Russia is a new phase in a long dialogue between religious and political models for groups that are able to grow under legally, economically, or morally precarious conditions. In the cases of Russian Orthodoxy and Chimarij Paganism, by contrast, the didactic approaches that gained currency in Soviet secular culture influence religious traditions to which they had previously been less central, coming into friction with core assumptions about the means and ends of personal change. Understanding elective affinity as an ongoing interaction thus helps us to move away from the common narrative of the functional replacement of religious by secular elements and vice versa, asking instead what each sphere might owe to the other in a given situation.

In all cases, affinity is no harmonious give-and-take, but unfolds in a context of unequal relations between different religious communities and shifting secular powers. Even though the bloody persecutions ceased in the aftermath of the Second World War, the regulation of religious communities and intimidation of their members remained an integral part of Soviet secularism. And after the collapse of socialism, religious groups had very unequal room for maneuver when it came to deciding which elements of Soviet secular culture to use and to discard. But this is not a story of any one side imposing its standards and approaches on the others. Facilitated by a shared commitment to the human potential to grow over the course of a lifetime, transformational terms such as "spirit," "promise," and "hope" travel across multiple religious-secular boundaries. In different historical traditions, they accumulate different meanings and values, but the common terms also create a field of intertextuality that makes conversations—including creative misunderstandings—possible.

Spirit is one of these traveling terms that stands simultaneously for the condition and the goal of transformation in a variety of traditions. For religious as well as secularist specialists, judgments about spirit are always to some extent open to doubt, because they require attention to the interplay of elements that make up a particular style. This is where the dilemmas of discernment experienced by religious and anti-religious practitioners intersect with those of less committed observers (Pels 2003). For example, when Weber asserts that the same "spirit" characterizes Protestant and capitalist asceticisms, he engages in a practice of discernment. When he first introduces the term "spirit of capitalism" in *The Protestant Ethic*, he characterizes it with the help of a "provisional illustration [*provisorischen Veranschaulichung*]" from the writings of Benjamin Franklin, but only after having noted that any representation of this spirit will necessarily be a creation of the scholar, "composed gradually out of its separate parts, which are to be taken from historical reality" (1922: 30). Later, Weber further decouples "spirit" from observable form by admitting that "the 'capitalist' form of an economy and the spirit in which it is conducted generally stand in an 'adequate' relation to each other, but not in a 'law-bound' dependency" (49). Spirit is thus neither an abstract end point nor an observable fact, but a complex of qualities that scholars attempt to discern with something of the morphological interest which Goethe applies to plants, or church musicians to the unity of movement, mood, and purpose which they want a congregation to achieve.

Discerning a common spirit is always subject to disagreement, and such disagreements are as important an aspect of elective affinities as are resemblances. Throughout this book, we have encountered people who insisted that things that formally resembled each other were infused with a different spirit and, conversely, that outwardly very different things were manifestations of the same qualities. Where I saw a resemblance between communist study circles and Charismatic cell groups, church members insisted that the latter fostered qualities of leadership and responsibility that were the opposite of Soviet values. Where outsiders hailed ritual activity in Shorun'zha as an expression of the village's enduring communal spirit, the collective farm chairman declared it to be a sad substitute for the cultural activities that once enlivened the Soviet countryside. Where atheist activists claimed that all religious liturgies equally overwhelmed the rational defenses of participants with a barrage of sensory stimuli, Orthodox theologians grouped Soviet events and Protestant worship together under the common label of "soulfulness," in opposition to the spiritual serenity of Orthodox gatherings. From the perspective of engaged participants, affinity and perversion can lie very close together.

The distinctions made in these judgments can suggest alternative ways of drawing religious-secular boundaries. For example, where academic literature on secularism tends to treat it as an outgrowth of rationalistic modernity, some religious practitioners discern the spirit of secularism in the free rein it gives to the sensual imagination and the emotional attachment to human leaders. And while scholars sometimes shy away from criticizing religious commitments because this might distract from their aim to be self-critical about the social sciences' own roots in secularist paradigms, the vibrant interreligious debates of the post-Soviet Volga region call into question the logic of that self-imposed restraint. Religious practitioners of various stripes can disagree with one another as vehemently as with their atheist opponents—and often on the subject of the "hows" of desirable transformations as much as the "whys" of doctrine. In this field of crisscrossing debate, scholars who reserve their critical faculties for the secularist side seem to absolutize the very division between secularity and religion they set out to question.

Among the concerns that unite all sides are the difficulties of learning discernment and of replicating this skill. Recall the Orthodox priest who bluntly stated that there was no way to teach someone to see the difference between a Chimarij sacrifice and an Orthodox liturgy through verbal explanation alone. Two converts between religious traditions—the bereaved mother who left the Baptist Church to become a Charismatic, and the Mari school principal who converted to Islam—mentioned a new capacity to discern the spiritual state of others as a sudden gift they received on conversion, through no learning effort of their own. From a secularist point of view, Theodor Adorno wrote that true learning consists of such skills as associating Henri Bergson's philosophy with impressionist art, skills that are almost impossible to teach. Learning, for Adorno, has "no proper customs," but depends most of all on the quality of "openness [*Aufgeschlossenheit*]" in the learner, "the ability to let something intellectual come close" (1971: 40).

If it is true that discernment defies methodical learning and explanation, but is always open to dispute, where does that leave the social scientist interested in how things diverge and converge over time? One could insist that historians and ethnographers only make analytic distinctions, while value judgments should be left to the lived worlds of our hosts and to the theologians of all sides. There were many moments during my research when I gratefully resorted to such professional self-limitation. It allowed me, for instance, to plead ignorance on the question of whether Marx would have known devilish whispers from his own thoughts.

But the boundary between the descriptive and the normative aspects of scholarly discernment is not always easy to maintain, and both secularist and religious movements often provoke more committed responses. The title of one history of Soviet science suggests that the Knowledge Society's politically motivated popularizations constituted a "perversion of knowledge" (Birstein 2001). With the help of the deliberately mixed metaphors of "millennial capitalism" and "occult economies," John and Jean Comaroff (2000) identify affinities between emergent religious phenomena and neoliberal economies as based in a common perversion of previous ideals of social and economic emancipation. Whether the aim is a simple defense of the idea of scientific rationality or a dialectical critique of its shaky foundations, none of these scholars is afraid to evaluate the outcome of a transformative process nor to judge it for betraying important ideals.

Among scholars of postsecular religion, many are wary of such normativity. In their understanding, the unexpected resurgence of public religion forces them to distrust their own capacities for discernment, because it challenges common narratives of modernity. Encounters with "the repugnant cultural other" (Harding 1991), the "docile agent" (Mahmood 2001), or with people who seem "at once too similar to anthropologists to be worthy of study and too meaningfully different to be easily made sense of" (Robbins 2003: 192), have led a number of anthropologists to adopt a stance of methodical distrust against their own intuitions.

Before falling into the extremes of either normative confidence in one's own discerning capacities or systematic distrust of them, it may bear repeating that discernment is a difficult virtue in religious as well as secular traditions. One possible reason that it eludes methodical directives is that it depends on a kind of attention that does not result from being invited into a didactic public. The way of being attentive that Adorno calls "openness" is a virtue incumbent on the observer, not a response to active solicitation. Such uncalled-for attention can lead to observations that a historically informed anthropology is well equipped to make, such as noticing not-so-obvious connections across geographical and temporal divides, or looking for relevant differences behind claims of persistence.

In approaching materials from atheist and religious mobilizations, being attentive means questioning if secularism is always adequately described when it is equated with liberal modernity, and searching for broader comparative contexts among twentieth-century secularist projects. It means changing focus from general contrasts between secular and religious publics toward noting how atheist aspirations were transformed by the multireligious landscape of the Soviet Union even as they reshaped that landscape in their own image. Or, switching the scope of comparison once again, we might ask what happens to religious practice in various parts of the world as religious communities and religious entrepreneurs become the bearers of the transformative hopes that previous generations associated with secular institutions. Considering the powerful role that various forms of religious commitments play in politics both within and outside of North American academia, it may be justified to ask if some of the energy that currently goes into interrogating secularism would be better spent developing an equally sophisticated critique of the varieties of religious practice.

What follows from attention is not necessarily normative judgment, but rather interest, or, in the words of one of the characters who discuss chemical affinities in Goethe's novel, the sympathetic sense of "participation" (*Teilnahme*) which grows in the process of attentive observation (1956 [1809]: 38). One might think of Hirokazu Miyazaki's study of the hope of Fijian indigenous activists, where he warns that if the investigator simply seeks to replicate the hope of those studied, its forward movement becomes preempted into retrospective repetition (2004: 127). I have been pursuing the spirit of methodical didacticism through its fits and misfits with religious practices, above all because I place some hope in the human capacity to learn, a hope that I share with many of the people I encountered in the Mari republic, both in archival documents and in the flesh. If secular methodicians produced a distorted understanding of their religious competitors, one reason may be this very paradox of shared, but separate hope: in portraying the methods and goals of religious transformations as both overly similar and completely opposed to their own concerns, atheists strove to sustain the differences that would keep hope moving forward.

Glossary

akathistos (Greek; pl. *akathistoi*), *akafist* (Russian): Orthodox Christian hymn in praise of a saint, Jesus Christ, or an icon of Mary; may be performed as part of a church service or by laypeople in private

agavajrem, aga pajrem (Mari): spring plowing festival involving meatless sacrifices in a small grove at the edge of the village fields

ASSR (Russian): Autonomous Soviet Socialist Republic; an administrative unit providing ethnic autonomy within the RSFSR or another part of the Soviet Union

batjushka (Russian): lit. "little father"; term of address for a Russian Orthodox priest

bozhnitsa (Russian, colloquial): derived from *bog* (God); shelf in a corner of a house where icons and other sacred objects are kept; often closed off by a curtain in the Volga region

Charismatic: in a general sense (usually lowercase), any movement within a Christian church that practices spiritual gifts, such as speaking in tongues. In this book, the term is used more specifically for a subgroup of Pentecostal churches with origins in late twentieth-century North America, associated with prosperity theology, a selective appropriation of contemporary popular culture and media, and an emphasis on systematic church growth.

chastushka (Russian; pl. *chastushki*): genre of teasing four-line verses whose texts are improvised to a set tune

Chimarij (Mari): lit. "pure Mari"; a term used for unbaptized Mari and, by extension, Mari who practice traditional sacrificial rituals

dukh, dukhovnost' (adj. *dukhovnyj*) (Russian): spirit, spirituality (adj. spiritual)

jachejka (Russian): lit. "cell"; the basic unit that made up local organizations of the Communist Party and the Komsomol during the Soviet period; later, transferred to small, face-to-face study groups in evangelical churches

joltash (Mari): friend; used as translation for Russian *tovarishch*

225

Joshkar-Ola (Mari): Red City, the capital of Marij El

jumo (Mari): god; can be applied to Mari and Christian divinities and saints

jumyn jüla (Mari): lit. "god's custom"; Mari neologism for "catechism" or "religion"; title of a book on Chimarij ritual by the high priest Aleksandr Tanygin and the ethnographer Nikandr Popov

kart (Tatar): lit. "elder"; term used in Russian for Chimarij priests

kolkhoz (Russian): short for *kollektivnoe khozjajstvo*; collective farm

kolkhoznik, fem. *kolkhoznitsa* (Russian): collective farm worker

Komsomol (Russian): short for Kommunisticheskij Sojuz Molodëzhi; communist youth league

Kugu Sorta (Mari): lit. "big candle"; Mari reform movement of the late nineteenth and early twentieth centuries whose members rejected Christianity, but also animal and food sacrifices, and sought to present a rationalized and codified Mari religion. The movement was wiped out under Stalin.

kumaltysh (Mari): lit. "prayer"; term used for a ritual gathering, such as a sacrificial ceremony

Marij El (Mari): lit. "Mari country"; official name of the Mari republic since 1991

Mari Ushem (Mari): lit. "Union of Maris"; association representing Mari cultural and political interests, founded in April 1990

medrese (Tatar/Arabic): Islamic religious school

mer kumaltysh (Mari): lit. "world prayer" or "communal prayer"; prayer ceremony to which Maris are invited regardless of their residence

metodist (Russian): expert in didactic methods, events, and program planning at a cultural institution; rendered as "methodician" in this book

nagljadka (Russian, antiquated): informal learning by emulation, through watching others

nagljadnost' (Russian): visuality, visual teaching aids

onaeng (Mari): lit. "holy person"; a Chimarij priest

otpevanie (Russian): lit. "singing off"; Russian Orthodox funeral mass

peledysh pajrem (Mari): lit. "festival of flowers"; Soviet holiday created for the Maris in the 1920s and revived in the 1960s; also known as *joshkar peledysh pajrem,* the Festival of Red Flowers *poklon* (Russian): bow, prostration

poklonjat'sja (verb), *poklonenie* (n.) (Russian): to bow down, to worship; worship (n.)

poshkudo (Mari): neighbor

proslavlenie (Russian): praise

rodo-tukym (Mari): relatives

RSFSR (Russian): Russian Soviet Federal Socialist Republic; one of the republics of the Soviet Union, known today as the Russian Federation

rural council (Russian: *sel'sovet*): lowest level of elected government in the Soviet and post-Soviet countryside. The rural council chairperson is comparable to a village mayor.

sabantuj (Tatar): festival of spring sowing held around the same time as the Mari *agavajrem*, involving wrestling and horse-racing competitions and ritual meals. Since the 1920s, it was promoted as a secularized ethnic festival analogous to the Mari *peledysh pajrem*.

semik (Russian), *semyk* (Mari): in the Russian and Mari folk calendar, a day for commemorating the dead seven weeks after Easter

shymaksh (Mari): pointed headdress worn by married Mari women on the left bank of the Volga; consists of an embroidered scarf placed over a birchbark cone on a woman's forehead and covers the back of her head and her hair

soroka (Mari, Russian derivation): married woman's headdress worn in the western parts of the Mari region; consists of a rectangular box of birchbark placed on a woman's head and covered by an embroidered scarf tied under the chin

subbotnik (Russian): derived from *subbota* (Saturday); unpaid community workday, typically devoted to cleaning up and beautifying public spaces

sürem (Mari): summer festival with animal sacrifices, celebrated around haying time

tamada (Georgian): Soviet term for toastmaster; master of ceremonies at a banquet

tovarishch (Russian): comrade

znanie (Russian): knowledge

Notes

Introduction

1. GARME, f. R-836, op. 1, d. 11a, l. 144 (Minutes of a workers assembly in the shoe factory, Joshkar-Ola, August 15, 1960). For more on the context of this archival file, see chapter 3.

2. For critical discussions of the so-called secularization thesis, see Bruce 1992; Smith 2003. But compare Brown 2001 and Pollack 2003 for evidence of the overall decline of religious commitments in twentieth-century Europe, West as well as East.

3. In anthropology, the work of Talal Asad (2003, 2006) has been of seminal influence, spawning works on secularism in the Middle East (Mahmood 2005, 2006) and Western Europe (Keane 2009; Scott 2007). For more detailed explorations of the varieties of liberal secularism, compare the work of Charles Taylor (2007) on the Anglo-Saxon world, and Jean Baubérot (2004) and John Bowen (2008) on France.

4. For a comparative argument about empires as polities built around the governance of difference, see Burbank and Cooper 2010. For studies of the Ottoman and Russian Empires, and of British colonial approaches to religious diversity in India, see Barkey 2008; Burbank 2006; van der Veer 1994.

5. Suggesting the potential for comparative research across socialist and nonsocialist secularisms, Yang (2008) develops an argument about secularism as part of a postcolonial state-building project in Maoist China, and Buturovic (2007) presents a discussion of socialist (in this case, Yugoslav) atheism in an edited volume largely devoted to South Asia.

6. This charge was popularized by prominent Russian and continental European émigrés before and after the Second World War, often in the context of arguments for the essential similarity of the "totalitarian" movements of Bolshevism, fascism, and Nazism (Berdyaev 1932; Gurian 1952; Voegelin 1993 [1938]).

7. E.g., Pivovarov 1976: 4. This definition of religion can be traced to nineteenth-century evolutionist theorists such as Edward Burnett Tylor. On Tylor's approach to religion and its Durkheimian critiques, see Stringer 1999.

8. E.g., GARF, f. A-561, op. 1, d. 400 (Transcript of a theoretical conference on "The causes of the vitality of religious survivals in the USSR," Moscow, January 18–21, 1960).

9. Antonina Aleksandrova, *Priglashaem k razgovoru,* April 23, 1972, Mari Republican Radio sound archives, Joshkar-Ola, tape 810.

10. These percentages are on the low end of Russia-wide averages. In the surveys conducted by a Russian-Finnish team under Dmitrij Furman and Kimmo Kääriäinen, the combined categories of unbelievers and atheists made up 42 percent of the Russian population in 1991, 35 percent in 1993, and 20 percent in 2004 (Furman and Kääriäinen 2006: 48).

11. Literally, "pure Mari"—a Mari term denoting unbaptized people that some adherents of the Mari rituals claim for themselves. When speaking Russian, most use the term *jazychestvo* (Paganism), others prefer to speak of the "traditional Mari religion" (*traditsionnaja marijskaja religija*).

I. Neighbors and Comrades

1. See, for example, Baubérot 2004 on France, Bhargava 1998 on India, Buturovic 2007 on Yugoslavia, Özyürek 2006 on Turkey, and Yang 2008 on China.

2. Particularly well known among Soviet authors were Marx's dictum on religion as "the opium of the people" (1957 [1844]: 378) and Engels's critique of the religiously sanctified patriarchal family as an archetype of social inequality (Engels 1962b [1884]).

3. Linguistic convergences between the (genetically unrelated) Slavic, Finno-Ugric, and Turkic languages of the Volga region furnished some of the material for the concept of the "language alliance" as elaborated by Nikolaj Trubetskoj and Roman Jakobson (Jakobson 1931; Sériot 1999). For linguistic and folkloric data on mutual borrowings between Finno-Ugric and Turkic speakers, see Akhmet'ianov 1981, 1989; Suleymanova 1996. On shared religious sites, see Frank 1988.

4. Although I visited the Lutheran congregation in Ljupersola on several occasions in 2005, I was not present at this council meeting. My account of the speeches is based on a tape recording provided by one of the Lutheran clergy present. Although a building permit was eventually granted, the official designation of the building remained in flux at the time of my last visit in 2008. In an effort to avoid being seen as exerting pressure in the matter, I made no attempt to contact the district administration or village officials to hear the story from their perspective.

5. *V chuzhoj monastyr' so svoim ustavom ne khodjat.* This proverb is roughly equivalent to the English "When in Rome, do as the Romans do" and can be used to make a point about proper behavior in unfamiliar settings not connected to religion. But given the religious metaphor, it is not surprising that it often came up in conversations about interactions between people of different faiths.

6. By 2005, a Chimarij organization under changed leadership was beginning to see some success with a new strategy of registration. Instead of first seeking registration at the level of the republic, they were registering organizations in individual districts where Chimarij rituals had a strong presence. By the end of 2005, they had achieved registration in two districts. A staff member of the Mari Cultural Center was optimistic about the chances for republic-wide registration once a few more districts were added.

7. In fact, the woman in charge of teaching Quranic reading at the mosque in Joshkar-Ola, who was often invited to recite passages from the Quran at funerals, frequently complained about how many Tatars were following what she considered to be "Russian" customs of holding funeral and commemorative feasts at gravesites.

8. Russia is not the only place where Protestant conversion poses problems for participation in ritual commemorations of the dead. For cases from southeastern Africa and Indonesia, see Bond 1987; Keane 2007.

9. Note his wavering between the more colloquial "faith" (*vera*) and the official "religion" (*religija*), his frequent false starts and tautological word choices (to be "faithful" to one's "faith"), as well as the absence of stock official phrases, such as

"freedom of religious confession" (*svoboda veroispovedanija*), which he replaces by saying that in Finland "everything is permitted" (*vse razresheno*).

10. All instances of "his own" in this quote are translations of the Mari *shkezhe*, a third-person reflexive possessive pronoun that, like all Mari pronouns, is gender-neutral and could also be understood as "her own." I thank Veronika Semënova for assisting me in translating the Mari passages on the tape.

11. On the shifting scales of us-them distinctions in multiethnic Russia, see Lemon 2000: 211–214. More generally on the relationship between linguistic distinctions (and indistinctions) and political identification, see Gal and Woolard 2001.

12. Commitment to this discourse includes a policy of nonconfrontation with other religions recognized as "traditional" to particular regions and ethnic groups, such as Islam in the Volga region and Central Asia (Filatov 2002; Mitrokhin 2004: 451–455).

13. For example, when Patriarch Aleksij II visited Marij El in 1993 for the installation of the first bishop in Russia's youngest diocese, he stressed the Orthodox Church's intention not to oppose the "traditional Mari faith," but to live in "harmonious coexistence, mutual understanding" (*Marijskaja Pravda*, July 27, 1993, p. 1).

14. As listed in a draft copy of the letter provided to me by its author, these violations included: the meeting's agenda had not been announced in advance, the presence of a quorum of village residents had not been ascertained, the vote had been by open ballot without giving people the option of first voting to keep it secret, the presence of representatives of the Russian Orthodox Church violated the separation of church and state, and some statements made by the district head contradicted the federal law on freedom of conscience—for instance, the assertion that converts would not be buried in the village graveyard and the claim that only some religions were appropriate for residents of the republic.

15. For a searing exploration of the ways in which everyday neighborly relations and intercommunal violence fold into each other, see Das 2007; on troubled coexistence in Russia's North Caucasus, see Tishkov 2001.

16. In the Khanate, only Muslims were part of the tax-collecting nobility, to the exclusion of nobles and chiefs of the non-Muslim subject peoples (Bakhtin 1998: 41). In Muscovy, unbaptized peasants paid tribute (*jasak*) in kind instead of monetary taxes until the early eighteenth century (Kappeler 1982: 259).

17. The Udmurts are a group of Finno-Ugric speakers living to the north of the Mari. In 2005–2006, I heard Russian residents and Orthodox clergy perpetuate similar rumors about human sacrifice at Chimarij rituals, possibly as a result of reading about this incident, which is known as the Multan case. A middle-aged Russian woman who had grown up in an ethnically mixed railroad settlement also warned me that Maris were skilled at sorcery, making it dangerous to accept food in their villages.

18. Like many days on which Mari villagers commemorate their dead, this date is a borrowing from the Orthodox Christian calendar. Since at least the nineteenth century, Mari ceremonies have been timed to coincide with Orthodox feast days in many villages (Kalinina 2003).

19. GARME, f. R-118, op. 1, d. 23, l. 220 (Presentation by the chairman of the Mari organization of the League of the Militant Godless, Radajkin, at a seminar of Komsomol propagandists, December 20, 1940). The recommended replacement was

a simple white or flowered headscarf, folded into a triangular shape and tied either under the chin or behind the neck, which became part of the generic image of the Soviet *kolkhoznitsa* and is still widely worn by rural women.

20. GARF, f. R-6991, op. 3, d. 570, l. 151 (Report from Nabatov for the second quarter of 1951, July 10, 1951).

21. Ibid., d. 571, ll. 27–28 (Report from Nabatov for the second quarter of 1952, July 11, 1952). Nabatov added that the head of the district's financial division had some success in his attempts to stop this practice when he started to tax the mullahs for the gifts.

22. Ibid., d. 570, l. 26 (Report from Nabatov for the second quarter of 1949, July 16, 1949).

23. Ibid., d. 569, l. 96 (Report from Nabatov for the second quarter of 1948, July 13, 1948).

24. In 1951, a Mari *kart* asked Nabatov why Tatars were allowed to celebrate *sabantuj*, while Maris were prohibited from celebrating *semyk*. Ibid., d. 570, l. 151 (Report from Nabatov for the second quarter of 1951, July 10, 1951).

25. GARME, f. P-1, op. 26, d. 23, l. 37 (Minutes of the bureau meeting of the regional party committee, April 28, 1965).

26. Examples include Navroz, a purportedly pre-Islamic New Year celebration of Caucasus mountaineers (Sadomskaya 1990: 249), and summer solstice celebrations such as the Latvian Ligo and Russian Ivan Kupala, promoted to reclaim the Christian feast of St. John the Baptist for atheist folk culture (Powell 1975: 69). The introduction of fir trees for New Year from 1935 onward was also justified with the argument that putting them up was a Pagan winter custom that had been appropriated by the church for Christmas (Petrone 2000: 86). For a more general discussion of the Soviet politics of finding Pagan survivals in folk religion, see Levin 1993.

27. See Clark 1995 on early Soviet experiments with mass outdoor spectacles and the hopes of social transformation attached to them.

28. GARME, f. P-14, op. 18, d. 5, ll. 5–6 (Resolution of the Novyj-Tor"jal district committee on the organization of the festival *peledysh pajrem*, May 12, 1965); *Marijskaja Pravda*, June 22, 1965, p. 1; Humphrey 1998: 380–381.

29. A search of the indexes in party, government, and KGB personnel files in Joshkar-Ola did not yield a file on Nabatov that provided information on his ethnicity, education, and prior residence and work experience. In his reports he occasionally refers to "us Maris" and quotes Mari terms, suggesting that he was an ethnic Mari and had at least some command of the language. GARF, f. R-6991, op. 3, d. 570, l. 74 (Report from Nabatov on the fourth quarter of 1949, January 14, 1950); ibid., l. 94 (Report from Nabatov on the second quarter of 1950, July 17, 1950). In terms of his professional training, his correspondence shows that he was also in charge of supervising logging operations in the republic. At one point, the council chairman reproached him that his reports were not at the level expected of a man of his "general and political erudition," suggesting that he may have had some postsecondary education and/or a prior career in the party bureaucracy. Ibid., d. 569, l. 71 (Letter from council chairman Poljanskij to Nabatov, November 26, 1947). As historians have observed, it was common for commissioners of religious affairs to be recruited either from the party bureaucracy or from the KGB (Chumachenko 2002: 24–25; Kolymagin 2004: 115).

30. GARF, f. R-6991, op. 3, d. 569, l. 1 (Report by commissioner Nabatov to the council for the fourth quarter of 1945, received January 22, 1946).

31. Ibid., l. 2.

32. Ibid., ll. 7–8 (Report of council member Fil'chenkov on a voyage of inspection to the Mari ASSR, March 6, 1946).

33. Examples of such petitions were attached to Fil'chenkov's report and a later report from Nabatov. See ibid., l. 16 (Petition from citizens of the village of Bol'shaja Orsha to commissioner Nabatov, November 30, 1945); ibid., d. 571, ll. 9–13 (Petitions and supporting documents from citizens of Pektubaevo district and Uspenka village to commissioner Nabatov, September 15 and October 19, 1951).

34. Ibid., d. 569, l. 12.

35. Ibid., l. 19 (Draft of a report from council chairman Poljanskij to the Central Committee, n.d.).

36. Ibid., l. 23 (Letter from the vice chairmen of the Councils for the Affairs of Religious Cults and the Affairs of the Russian Orthodox Church to the commissioners, January 22, 1946).

37. Ibid., l. 19.

38. Ibid., l. 22 (Draft of a letter from Nabatov to the district executive committees, ca. January 1946).

39. Ibid., ll. 8–9. During the fall sacrificial season of 1951, according to Nabatov's reports, a number of collective farms did contribute calves and sheep from collective ownership. This may have been an unintended consequence of the reduction of privately owned livestock as a result of restrictive taxation during the last years of Stalin's life. Ibid., d. 571, l. 7 (Report from Nabatov on the fourth quarter of 1951, January 7, 1952).

40. Ibid., d. 569, l. 52 (Report from Nabatov for the first quarter of 1947, April 21, 1947).

41. Ibid., l. 52v.

42. Ibid., d. 570, l. 5 (Report from Nabatov for the fourth quarter of 1948, January 18, 1949).

43. Ibid., l. 8.

44. Ibid., d. 571, l. 41 (Report from Nabatov for the third quarter of 1952, October 7, 1952).

45. This term appears in a marginal note by a Moscow reader, written in red pencil on one of Nabatov's reports, beside a paragraph referring to local authorities permitting *sabantuj* after the completion of the plowing of the fields for winter grain, and Mari sacrificial ceremonies in the fall after the fulfillment of the state's grain delivery quotas. Ibid., d. 570, l. 31 (Report from Nabatov for the second quarter of 1949, July 16, 1949).

46. Ibid., d. 569, l. 97 (Report from Nabatov for the second quarter of 1948, July 13, 1948). This is the only mention of a horse as a sacrificial animal in Nabatov's correspondence, although precollectivization sources mention horses as common sacrifices for high-ranking gods. The use of an old horse unfit for work seems to be a compromise with the economic and legal constraints of the post-collectivization era, since older ethnographic sources as well as late twentieth-century Chimarij writings emphasize that sacrificial animals should be young and without blemish (Popov and Tanygin 2003: 202–209; Sebeok and Ingemann 1956: 166–167).

47. GARF, f. R-6991, op. 3, d. 570, ll. 26–27 (Report from Nabatov for the second quarter of 1949, July 16, 1949).

48. Ibid., d. 569, l. 52v (Report from Nabatov for the first quarter of 1947, April 21, 1947). The same village had gone to considerable lengths to forestall the closing of the mosque before the war: when an order came to close it and use the building as a school and rural council office, villagers built both a schoolhouse and a council hall. Ibid., l. 27 (Report from Nabatov for the second quarter of 1946, July 5, 1946). Shortly before its closure in 1940, the mosque was one of only five functioning houses of worship in the republic. GARME, f. R-118, op. 1, d. 24, l. 31 (Information on the uses of closed prayer buildings in districts of the republic, ca. 1940).

49. GARF, f. R-6991, op. 3, d. 569, l. 75 (Report from Nabatov for the fourth quarter of 1947, January 19, 1948).

50. Ibid., l. 79 (Letter from council chairman Poljanskij to Nabatov, February 24, 1948).

51. Ibid., d. 570, l. 127 (Report from Nabatov on the fourth quarter of 1950, January 9, 1951).

52. Ibid., d. 571, l. 39.

53. Nabatov's discharge is documented ibid., d. 571, l. 44 (Note on the margin of Nabatov's report for the third quarter of 1952, October 7, 1952). A complete reconstruction of personnel arrangements for both councils during the following years is difficult, because most of the Khrushchev era records were still classified in the Russian state archives in Moscow during my research in 2005, and several files were missing in Marij El's republican archives. Sometime between 1953 and 1960, Aleksej Grigor'evich Smirnov succeeded the first commissioner for Russian Orthodox Church affairs, Kuz'ma Alekseevich Shikin. Smirnov occasionally appears on lists of commissioners of religious cults for the Mari ASSR. See, for example, ibid., d. 1360, l. 141 (List of commissioners of both councils invited to a meeting of both councils); ibid., d. 1387, l. 80 (Mailing list for a presentation of council chairman Puzin, October 1962). From around 1963, Viktor Ivanovich Savel'ev served as the commissioner of Russian Orthodox Church affairs, becoming commissioner of the unified Council for Religious Affairs in 1965. Savel'ev was replaced in 1984 by Vasilij Aleksandrovich Isakov, who held the position until the council was disbanded in 1990. GARME, f. R-836, op. 1, d. 4, ll. 207–208 (Letter from Bishop Mikhail of Gor'kij to V. I. Savel'ev, May 10, 1963); interview with Isakov, July 2, 2003.

54. Literally, "birch tree," this festival was created in the 1970s to replace Pentecost; see Paxson 2005: 335–337.

55. See Bhargava 2007 for a discussion of the ways in which Indian secularism both drew on European models and altered them in response to the multireligious situation in India.

2. "Go Teach"

1. See, for instance, the debates at a 1963 conference devoted to a projected book on "the spiritual life of communist society." GARF, f. R-9547, op. 1, d. 1314 (Transcript of the scholarly conference "Laws of formation and development of the spiritual life of communist society," May 9–11, 1963); Stepanian 1966.

2. GARF, f. R-6991, op. 3, d. 570, ll. 23–23v (Council chairman Poljanskij to Nabatov, May 25, 1949); ibid., l. 125 (Council chairman Poljanskij to Nabatov, Janu-

ary 9, 1951); GARF, f. R-9547, op. 1, d. 443, l. 3 (Minutes of the Mari division of the Society for the Dissemination of Political and Scientific Knowledge, January 11, 1950); ibid., l. 118 (Minutes of July 10, 1950).

3. Even in 1955, at the height of Khrushchev's first call to renew atheist assaults on religion, only 6.3 percent of all lectures in the RSFSR were devoted to atheist topics, and this percentage fell to 3.5 the following year. GARF, f. A-561, op. 1, d. 375, l. 35 (Report on atheist propaganda conducted by regional organizations of the society, 1956). In 1969, just over one-fourth of all lectures devoted to the natural sciences—itself only one among many fields covered by the society—were classified as atheist propaganda. Ibid., d. 1294, l. 1 (Resolution of the presidium of the All-Russian Knowledge Society, January 15, 1971).

4. On the society's recruitment difficulties, see ibid., d. 65, l. 190 (Transcript of the all-Russian seminar meeting of the chairpersons of the scientific atheist and natural scientific sections in the regional and ASSR divisions of the society, January 10–11, 1956); GARF, f. R-9547, op. 1, d. 1377, ll. 11–12 (Transcript of an all-union seminar on questions of aid to propaganda in rural areas, February 29, 1964).

5. GARF, f. A-561, op. 1, d. 65, l. 168.

6. GARF, f. R-9547, op. 1, d. 1377, l. 34.

7. GARF, f. A-561, op. 1, d. 65, l. 116.

8. Ibid., l. 116.

9. Ibid., l. 82.

10. Ibid., l. 96. On the promotion of corn during the Khrushchev era, see Medvedev 1987.

11. GARME, f. R-737, op. 2, d. 115, l. 64 (Lecture text by A. M. Gluzman, Joshkar-Ola, 1962).

12. Ibid., ll. 65–66.

13. GARF, f. A-561, op. 1, d. 283, l. 91 (Transcript of a seminar for lecturers on scientific atheist topics, Moscow, June 15–16, 1959).

14. Ibid., d. 65, l. 194.

15. Ibid., d. 283, ll. 27–28.

16. Ivanov is one of the most common Russian surnames, so the implication is that anyone can accomplish this feat.

17. GARME, f. R-737, op. 2, d. 161, ll. 3–4 (Report from secretary Chistjakov of the Knowledge Society to the chairman of the ideological department of the Mari regional committee of the CPSU, November 20, 1963); sound archives of Mari Republican Radio, tape 810 (Antonina Aleksandrova, *Priglashaem k razgovoru,* April 23, 1972).

18. GARF, f. A-561, op. 1, d. 283, l. 62.

19. Scholars at the 1963 conference on the spiritual life of communism referred to the privileging of philosophy over empirical social sciences as a Stalinist legacy akin to those denounced by the Twentieth Party Congress (GARF, f. R-9547, op. 1, d. 1314, ll. 82, 156). They thus link Stalin's "personality cult" not so much with mass irrationality but with a faulty understanding of the sources of rational understanding.

20. Ibid., d. 1312, l. 130 (Lecture by E. A. Adamov, "On the art of oratory," held at the all-union seminar on problems of the moral code of the builder of communism, Moscow, February 20–23, 1963).

21. GARME, f. P-8, op. 7, d. 495, l. 47 (Minutes of the bureau of the Joshkar-Ola city committee of the CPSU, December 2, 1960).

22. The phrase "carry knowledge to the people" (*nesti znanija narodu*) was the slogan of the Knowledge Society, with roots in the enlightenment ethos of prerevolutionary reformers.

23. Technically, St. Peter and Paul's Day, in Mari *Petro pajrem*, in Russian *Petrov den'*. While this is a feast day of the Orthodox Christian calendar, Maris venerate St. Peter as *Petro jumo* (the god Peter).

24. Matthew 21:12–13; Luke 19:45–46.

25. Literally, "little father"—an affectionately respectful term of address for an Orthodox priest.

26. *Dukhovnoe obrazovanie*, i.e., the education given in a theological seminary or other ecclesiastical educational institution, as opposed to the term *mirskoe obrazovanie*, which I had used to ask about his secular, or literally "worldly education."

27. Contemporary Russian Orthodox believers often refer to the nineteenth-century *startsy* as the perfect embodiment of this ideal of saintliness. *Startsy* were monks living in withdrawal from the world who attracted a large following of pilgrims and were often considered to have spiritual gifts such as second sight or the power to work miracles by their prayers (Treadgold 1978: 38). As charismatic figures, contemporary *startsy* can wield an influence that goes far beyond their formal standing in the church hierarchy, and they are sometimes viewed with suspicion by the leadership of the Orthodox Church (Mitrokhin 2004). But, at least in their conversations with me as a heterodox Christian, priests and lay believers referred to such saintly hermit monks and ascetic priests as evidence for the overall holiness of the Orthodox Church as a community.

28. See S. Coleman 2000 on the place of neo-Charismatic churches (a late twentieth-century movement often associated with a theology of prosperity) in the older Pentecostal movement.

29. GARME, f. P-8, op. 7, d. 506, l. 107 (Information about a visit to the study circle on political economy, for the party bureau of the Maksim Gor'kij Polytechnical Institute, January 28, 1960).

30. Sunday Adelaja [Sandej Adeladzha], *Lichnoe razvitie v liderakh* [tape from a leadership seminar] (Kiev: Fares, April 2, 1999). Adelaja's disdain notwithstanding, I saw the Russian translation of Hagin's *How to Be Led by the Spirit of God* (1997 [1978]) on the bookshelves of several members of the Christian Center.

3. Church Closings and Sermon Circuits

1. The figures of 110 enterprises and 17,000 employees come from the report of Commissioner Smirnov to the Council for Orthodox Church Affairs, September 1960 (GARME, f. R-836, op. 1, d. 3, ll. 240–243). The collected minutes of the meetings make up a file of 265 pages (ibid., d. 11a).

2. Ibid., l. 237 (Excerpt from the minutes of the meeting of the Council for Russian Orthodox Church Affairs, November 19, 1960).

3. *Pravda*, January 10, 1960.

4. GARME, f. R-836, op. 1, d. 3, l. 5 (Resolution of the Council of People's Commissars of the Mari ASSR, April 6, 1944). See also Starikov and Levenshtein 2001: 19.

5. GARME, f. R-275, op. 1, d. 140, l. 7 (Resolution of the Tsarevokokshajsk regional executive committee, January 16, 1919), published in Tarasova et al. 2004: 191.

6. GARME, f. R-836, op. 1, d. 3, l. 246 (Report on the situation of churches in Joshkar-Ola, commissioner for Russian Orthodox Church affairs Smirnov, October 1, 1960). A similar struggle over historical perspective between Orthodox believers and Soviet officials is apparent in correspondence from 1973, when citizens of Joshkar-Ola petitioned for permission to use "the former building of the Church of the Ascension, which is occupied by the beer brewery," for divine services. In the negative response from the city government, the building was pointedly referred to not as a former church, but as "the industrial building of the factory for beer and nonalcoholic drinks." GARME, f. R-836, op. 2, d. 18, ll. 13–14 (Families from the city of Joshkar-Ola to the chairman of the council of ministers of the USSR, January 2, 1973); ibid., l. 27 (Joshkar-Ola city executive committee to E. A. Chemodanova, July 17, 1973).

7. GARME, f. P-1, op. 18, d. 149, ll. 153–154 (Resolution of the Mari regional committee of the CPSU, April 13, 1960), published in Tarasova et al. 2004: 292–293; on Khrushchev era housing policies, see Ruble 1993.

8. GARME, f. R-836, op. 1, d. 11a, ll. 204–205 (Minutes of the assembly of the committee for radio and television in the Council of Ministers of the Mari ASSR, August 18, 1960).

9. Ibid., ll. 54–56 (Minutes of the workforce assembly at the repair shop, August 15, 1960).

10. Ibid., ll. 206–208 (Minutes of the workforce assembly at the Mari publishing house, August 16, 1960).

11. Ibid., d. 3, ll. 240–243.

12. Ibid., d. 11a, ll. 189–194 (Minutes of the workforce assembly at the production and storage units of the Mari factory for civil machine construction, August 16, 1960).

13. Ibid., d. 3, ll. 283–285 (Believers from Joshkar-Ola to N. S. Khrushchev, December 30, 1960).

14. V. Alekseev, "Potasovka v khrame 'bozh'em'," *Marijskaja Pravda*, August 12, 1960, p. 3. The assembly of pensioners is mentioned in the minutes of the workers assembly at the vitamin factory, August 16, 1960 (GARME, f. R-836, op. 1, d. 11a, ll. 20–21).

15. Ibid., l. 23 (Minutes of the assembly of dairy and cooling facility workers, August 16, 1960); ibid., ll. 36–37 (Minutes of the assembly of workshops 27 and 42, August 16, 1960).

16. Disturbance of the public order (*narushenie obshchestvennogo porjadka*) is referred to ibid., ll. 15–16 (Minutes of the general trade union assembly of pharmacy employees, August 15, 1960) and ll. 64–65 (Minutes of the assembly of the collective of the republican library of the Mari ASSR, August 15, 1960). Hooliganism is mentioned ibid., ll. 3–4 (Minutes of the assembly of the collective of the passenger transport facility, August 16, 1960) and ll. 36–37 (Minutes of the assembly of the workers and employees of the automatic telephone exchange, August 16, 1960).

17. V. Alekseev, "Potasovka v khrame 'bozh'em'," p. 3. On anti-hooliganism campaigns during the Khrushchev era, see LaPierre 2006.

18. "Propovedi i dela ottsov dukhovnykh," cited in GARME, f. R-836, op. 1, d. 11a, l. 66 (Resolution of the collective of the republican library of the Mari ASSR, August 15, 1960).

19. Ju. Kuprijanov and Ju. Nikolaev, "Kazanskie ottsy dukhovnye i ikh dela grekhovnye," *Marijskaja Pravda,* May 11, 1960, p. 4; Ju. Kuprijanov and Ju. Nikolaev, "Jumyn engzhe-vlak da nunyn sulykan pashasht," *Marij Kommuna,* May 11, 1960, p. 4. The Mari-language article is longer, probably an unabridged version of the original article from *Sovetskaja Tatarija.* The story of Archbishop Iov's trial and deposition is told in "Sud zal gych: Arkhiepiskop Iovym razoblachatlyme," *Marij Kommuna,* June 24, 1960, p. 4, also translated from *Sovetskaja Tatarija.* It is possible that the longer and more complete coverage of the matter in the Mari-language paper reflects the editors' perception that Mari speakers were more likely to hold religious sympathies, but it may also be that religious issues were not seen as important enough to take up much space in the Russian-language paper, which had the larger print run and wider distribution.

20. GARME, f. R-836, op. 1, d. 11a, l. 52 (Minutes of the assembly of workers at the brick factory "12 years of October," August 15, 1960); ibid., ll. 54–56.

21. Ju. Kuprijanov and Ju. Nikolaev, "Kazanskie ottsy dukhovnye i ikh dela grekhovnye," *Marijskaja Pravda,* May 11, 1960, p. 4.

22. GARME, f. R-836, op. 1, d. 11a, ll. 54–56.

23. Ibid., d. 3, ll. 201–202 ([A named member of the congregation of Resurrection Church] to the commissioner in the house of soviets, April 4, 1960); ibid., ll. 229–234 (Believers of the city of Joshkar-Ola to the commissioner for church affairs of the Mari ASSR, June 27, 1960).

24. Ibid., l. 279 (Orthodox Christians of the Resurrection Cathedral Joshkar-Ola to N. S. Khrushchev, December 22, 1960).

25. For instance, ibid., d. 11a, l. 27 (Minutes of the meeting of workers of the state bank and construction bank, August 16, 1960).

26. For instance, one resolution calls for the building to be turned into a club. Ibid., l. 30 (Minutes of the assembly at the asphalt-concrete works and garage of the city repair trust, August 16, 1960). Another also calls for stronger measures against Baptists. Ibid., l. 57 (Minutes of the assembly at the Joshkar-Ola repair factory, August 15, 1960). Both points take up suggestions made in the recorded discussion.

27. GARME, f. P-8, op. 7, d. 484, l. 75 (Appendix 2, Minutes of the bureau of the city committee, March 3, 1960).

28. Chistjakov's role in both organizations, and as a liaison between them, is documented ibid., d. 492, ll. 7–11 (Minutes of the bureau of the city committee, August 25, 1960), where he is named as a staff member of the department for propaganda and agitation responsible for atheist work, and GARME, f. R-737, op. 2, d. 69, ll. 9–11 (Minutes of the meeting of the section for scientific atheism of the Mari division of the Knowledge Society, November 3, 1960), where he participates as a member and reports on the above meeting of the city committee bureau.

29. GARME, f. R-836, op. 1, d. 11a, l. 99 (Minutes of the assembly of workers in produce store no. 2, August 16, 1960). In Russian, the sentence reads "Professor Bogoslov pisal poslednee izdatel'stvo biblii, no on otrësja [*sic*] ot religii." The remainder of the minutes from this store is also full of orthographic and grammatical errors, indicating that the problem may have been more with the note taker than with the lecturer.

30. Ibid., ll. 206-208.

31. Ibid., l. 32 (Minutes of the assembly of workers in the children's hospital, August 15, 1960).

32. Ibid., ll. 10-11 (Minutes of the assembly of workers in the sewing workshop "Truzhenitsa," August 16, 1960).

33. Ibid., ll. 39-40 (Minutes of the assembly of workers in workshop 26, August 16, 1960).

34. Ibid., ll. 39-40 (7 votes against, 330 in favor); ibid., ll. 144-145 (Minutes of the assembly of workers in the shoe factory, August 15, 1960 [2 votes against, 156 in favor]); ibid., ll. 171-171v (Minutes of the assembly of workers in the city hospital, n.d. [1 vote against, 1 abstention, 198 in favor]); ibid., ll. 177-178 (Minutes of the assembly of workers in workshop 8, n.d. [6 votes against, 176 in favor]); ibid., ll. 220-221 (Minutes of the assembly of workers at Joshkar-Ola station, August 17, 1960 [2 votes against, 7 abstentions, 63 in favor]).

35. Examples of methodological literature from the Mari republican library containing lecture titles are in Nekhoroshkov 1964: 52-54; Nekhoroshkov 1967a: 21-23. The latter work also contains sample "plans" of lectures and sample invitations to evenings of questions and answers; Novoselova 1959 contains plans for such evenings and the full text of a lecture by A. Krasnov, "The origin and essence of Mari religious cults."

36. The 1958-1975 minutes of the meetings of the scientific methodical council on scientific atheism of the RSFSR division of the Knowledge Society, which I surveyed (GARF, f. A-561, op. 1, passim), most typically involved the discussion of one or two lecture texts that had been recommended for publication.

37. GARME, f. 737, op. 2, d. 69, ll. 89-92 (Exemplary topics for lectures on questions of scientific atheist propaganda for 1955).

38. GARF, f. A-561, op. 1, d. 284, l. 1v (*Primernaja tematika lektsij po nauchnomu ateizmu* [Moscow: Znanie, 1959]).

39. A comparison between the number of recommended lecture titles and the number of brochures printed per year makes it very unlikely that full texts could have been available for all lectures. For 1958, for instance, the publication plan of the RSFSR division of the Knowledge Society included ten brochures on scientific atheism, when, as noted above, a year later there were seventy-one recommended lecture titles. Ibid., d. 183, ll. 3-4 (Transcript of a meeting in the office of the vice chairman of the society, March 22, 1958).

40. Ibid., d. 22, l. 8 (Information on the state of scientific atheist propaganda for the year 1955, A. S. Vasil'ev, director of the division for scientific atheist propaganda).

41. GARME, f. R-737, op. 2, d. 78, ll. 54-55 (Certificate of inspection of the work of the Zvenigovo district division of the Knowledge Society, June 19, 1960).

42. Ibid., d. 98, l. 166 (List of recommended lecture topics, Mari regional division of the Knowledge Society, 1961).

43. GARME, f. P-1, op. 18, d. 245, l. 33 (Information on the state of party education as of the beginning of the 1959-1960 academic year, regional committee instructor Putilova, November 1959); GARME, f. P-22, op. 1, d. 33, ll. 46-62 (Report on the work of nine-month training courses for party and state workers under the Mari regional committee for 1951-1952).

44. GARF, f. R-9547, op. 1, d. 443, l. 225 (Minutes of the board meeting of the Mari regional division of the Knowledge Society, December 19, 1950).

45. GARME, f. R-737, op. 2, d. 307, l. 48v (Evaluation of the lecture "Crimes of minors" by comrade Kirillov, member of the Knowledge Society, factory for semi-conductors, Joshkar-Ola, 1971).

46. GARF, f. A-561, op. 1, d. 22, ll. 11–12 (Report on the state, tasks, and means for the improvement of scientific atheist propaganda in the divisions of the Knowledge Society RSFSR, December 1955); GARME, f. R-737, op. 2, d. 69, ll. 64–65 (Review of the lecture text "Origin and life of ancient man" by comrade S. Reshetov, member of the Knowledge Society, reviewed by N. A. Pomrjaskinskaja, January 1963).

47. GARF, f. A-561, op. 1, d. 65, l. 20.

4. Marginal Lessons

1. GARME, f. P-12, op. 14, d. 13, ll. 1–2 (Information on the course of public presentations by the district group of political informers, leading workers of the district, and the group of lecturers of the CPSU district committee in Morki district, September 20, 1971); "Vneshtatnye instruktory—upora rajkoma," *Marijskaja Pravda*, August 21, 1960, p. 2; "Rajonnyj smotr agitbrigad," *Put' k kommunizmu*, March 11, 1972, p. 1; "K vam priekhal agitpoezd," *Marijskaja Pravda*, August 16, 1972, pp. 2–3.

2. Technically, the organization was no longer a collective farm (*kollektivnoe khozjajstvo*, or *kolkhoz* for short) but an agricultural work group (*sel'sko-khozjajst-vennaja artel'*, or *sel'khozartel'*), one of several forms of voluntary agricultural association that replaced the mandatory state or collective farms after Yeltsin's 1993 land reform (Wegren 2005: 67–69). But, as in other villages, people referred to the new entity by the Soviet term *kolkhoz* except in very formal contexts, and I follow them in this usage.

3. Talal Asad's (1993) critique of Clifford Geertz's notion of religion as a cultural system can be read as an instance of this debate.

4. This was a little over US$10 in 2005, a sum that might well equal the entire monthly salary of a farm worker, or about half or one-third of the pay of a rural cultural worker. The chairman somewhat exaggerates the actual ticket prices in Joshkar-Ola's cinemas, which were closer to 100–150 rubles, or US$3–5, at that time. Even that price presented a significant expense for rural and city dwellers alike.

5. Visual Aid

1. V. Vasil'ev, "Nagljadnost' na zanjatijakh," *Put' k kommunizmu*, September 7, 1972, p. 2.

2. For archival examples of such evaluations, see GARME, f. P-8, op. 7, d. 507, ll. 7–8 (Information on the work of the agit-brigade and the state of visual agitation in the Joshkar-Ola candy factory, April 5, 1960); GARME, f. R-737, op. 2, d. 307, ll. 27–27v (Certificate of inspection of the Morki district organization of the Knowledge Society, ca. 1970).

3. GARF, f. R-6991, op. 6, d. 80, l. 219 (Report on the state of religiosity among women from commissioner of religious affairs Savel'ev to the first secretary of the Mari regional committee and the chairman of the council of ministers of the Mari ASSR, June 16, 1967). Viktor Solov'ev's study of religious belief in the Mari ASSR

(conducted in 1972) found that 40 percent of Komsomol members lived in households with icons (Solov'ev 1977: 108).

4. But see Plamper 2010 on Stalin era ideas that the Soviet leader's ubiquitous portrait could see what was going on in offices and homes.

5. Transcript of an audio recording of the discussion (ca. 2003) provided by the Missionary Department, Orthodox Diocese of Joshkar-Ola and Marij El.

6. Lacking a centralized authority comparable to the Vatican for deciding doctrinal questions, the Orthodox churches accommodate quite a broad diversity of opinion, and Orthodox print culture in contemporary Russia reflects this. Until an editorial council was instituted at the Moscow Patriarchate in 2009, individual diocesan bishops and metropolitans had the right to authorize publications. Under that system, the imprint "With the blessing of . . . " (followed by the name and title of the church hierarch) and the fact that a book was sold in a church or an Orthodox store were the only indications for a lay reader that its contents were theologically acceptable. Individual bishops vary in the range of theological tendencies to which they give their blessing (Mitrokhin 2004: 174–208), and Dukhanin's brochure certainly only reflects a fraction of the spectrum of opinion among Russian Orthodox Christians, and is not a work of academic theology. I quote from it because it resonates with opinions about images, imaginaries, and prayer expressed by engaged Orthodox laypeople in Marij El, and with treatments of spirituality and sensuality in other Orthodox publications.

7. In spite of reservations, even Russian icon painting did not remain untouched by this trend, as attested by eighteenth-century icons of St. Catherine with the face of Empress Catherine I (Marker 2008).

8. Evagrios the Solitary (ca. AD 345–399), "On Prayer: One Hundred and Fifty-Three Texts," §§ 117, 120, quoted from the English edition of the *Philokalia* (Palmer, Sherrard, and Ware 1979–1995, vol. 1: 68).

6. The Soul and the Spirit

1. GARF, f. R-9547, op. 1, d. 1314, l. 34 (Transcript of the scholarly conference "Laws of the formation and development of the spiritual life of communist society," May 9–11, 1963).

2. For example, campaigns against the alcohol use associated with rural religious holidays made no effort to distinguish concerns with public health and decorum from concerns with economic productivity. See GARME, f. P-14, op. 26, d. 7, l. 115 (Resolution of the Novyj Tor"jal district committee, "On the celebration of the festival of St. Elijah's Day by the workers of avant-garde collective farm," August 24, 1973); Mari Republican Radio sound archives, tape 810 (*Priglashaem k razgovoru*, April 23, 1972).

3. See 1 Thessalonians 5:23; Hebrews 4:12. On the division in the *Philokalia* and later Russian Orthodox elaborations, see Palmer, Sherrard, and Ware 1979–1995, vol. 4: 76–77, 107–108; Luka 2006 [1978].

4. Caroline Humphrey (1998: 417) makes a related argument about Siberian shamanism as offering responses to the unacknowledged tensions of late Soviet society.

5. Simon Coleman (2000) and Joel Robbins (2004: 256–257) give insightful descriptions of the repetitive structure behind the apparent spontaneity of Pen-

tecostal and Charismatic services, raising intriguing questions about the intended and unintended effects of liturgical actions. Tanya Luhrmann (2004) recognizes the crucial role of liturgy for sustaining members' commitment to Charismatic-type megachurches, but sees their effect largely in the triggering of individual imaginative processes.

6. The Russian word is *sila*, which translates both as "strength" and "power" in English. I use "strength" to distinguish *sila* from *vlast'* (power, authority, used both in an institutional sense, as in *sovetskaja vlast'*, Soviet power, and in terms of control over others, such as *vlast' diavola*, the power of the devil). This translation also emphasizes the everyday nature of many of the tasks for which Pentecostals rely on this gift of the Holy Spirit (Shaull and Cesar 2000: 65–71).

7. Course 3: "Life and spirit of praise." Materials written and provided by the leader of the praise-and-worship band, Joshkar-Ola Christian Center.

8. In Slavonic: "Priidite, poklonimsja Tsarevi nashemu Bogu / Priidite, poklonimsja i pripadem Khristu, Tsarevi nashemu Bogu / Priidite, poklonimsja i pripadem Samomu Khristu, Tsarevi i Bogu nashemu / Priidite, poklonimsja i pripadem Emu" (Vsenoshchnoe bdenie 2001: 15).

9. This is Psalm 103 in the Russian Synodal Bible translation, which follows the numbering of the classical Greek translation of the Hebrew Bible (Septuagint).

10. For the teachings about praise, power, and changes in the world that I outline below, an important influence seems to be Myles Munroe (see Munroe 2000), a U.S.-trained Jamaican preacher who has made several visits to the Embassy of God and whose books have been published in Russian translation by its Kievan publishing house, Fares.

11. Note that the three stages she identifies differ from those given earlier in this section, which were praise, worship, and entry into the holiest of holies. The terminology in which the congregation discussed their liturgy was quite fluid, and at other times the bandleader distinguished between "worship" and "entry into the holiest of holies." The phrase "entering the courtyard" was used to describe the introductory part of the service.

12. GARF, f. A-561, op. 1, d. 282, l. 28.

13. Ibid., l. 29.

14. For an earlier, but similar list of prohibited groups, see GARF, f. R-6991, op. 3, d. 1417, l. 175 (Circular from the Council for Religious Affairs on "Strengthening the work of inhibiting the illegal activities of sectarians," June 1963).

15. GARME, f. R-836, op. 2, d. 21, ll. 20–21 (Notes, in commissioner for religious affairs Savel'ev's hand, on the achievements of Soviet power in the Mari republic and the dangers of Pentecostalism, evidently prepared for a conversation with members of this group, ca. 1977); l. 18 in the same file contains a handwritten report on a conversation held December 13, 1977, which follows the same basic points.

7. Lifelong Learning

1. For example, in the Mari ASSR in 1965, 33.7 percent of all newborn children were baptized; 2.3 percent of couples had a church marriage; and 37.3 percent of all deceased received a funeral service, although mainly in the "absentee" form where a service was held without the presence of the corpse (*zaochnoe otpevanie*). Only 9.7 percent were actually buried by a priest. GARF, f. R-6991, op. 2, d. 572, l. 73 (Data

on religious rituals and the income and expenses of religious organizations in the Mari ASSR for 1965, compiled by commissioner for religious affairs Savel'ev). For 1973, Savel'ev reported that the percentages had dropped to 24.2 for baptisms and remained at 2.3 for weddings. He did not mention funerals, perhaps because their rate continued to be high. Ibid., op. 6, d. 634, l. 99 (Report from commissioner Savel'ev to council chairman Kuroedov, October 21, 1974). The preponderance of funerals and baptisms over religious weddings is consistent with union-wide trends. Generalizing from Soviet sociological literature, Christel Lane (1978: 60) concludes that the reported rates for baptisms and Christian funerals were stable at around 50 percent throughout the 1960s, while the rates were between 1 and 15 percent for church weddings, depending on the region and with trends declining over time (see also Merridale 2000: 278). The figures from the Mari ASSR are on the low end of these trends, and this may be because of the tenuous influence of Christianity among the Mari population. Muslim life-cycle rituals do not seem to be factored into these percentages, and the numbers of rites recorded at the sole legally functioning mosque of the republic offer limited insight into the practices that may have been performed by knowledgeable Muslims without state registration. But mosque records also suggest a preponderance of funerals. In 1970, for instance, the mullah in Kul'bash performed two naming ceremonies, two weddings, and four funerals. GARF, R-6991, op. 6, d. 302, l. 70.

2. There is a large literature on the significance of the possessive pronoun "ours" (*nash*) in Russian discourses and practices of collectivity. For examples, see Pesmen 2000; Ransel 2000: 176; on the related reflexive possessive pronoun *svoj* (one's own), see Paxson 2005: 82–85.

3. GARF, f. R-6991, op. 6, d. 643, l. 75 (Report from commissioner Savel'ev to the Council for Religious Affairs, October 22, 1974). See also ibid., d. 80, l. 219 (Report from commissioner Savel'ev to the Mari regional party committee on the state of religiosity among women, June 16, 1967), where Savel'ev claimed that religiosity was highest among Mari women with low levels of education, giving an ethnic dimension to the association between religion and social marginality.

4. Ibid., d. 470, l. 219 (Information on the state of religiosity and control over the observance of the law on religious cults in the Gornomari district from February 28 to March 6, 1972, commissioner Savel'ev to the district committee of the CPSU).

5. GARF, f. R-6991, op. 3, d. 569, ll. 83–84 (Report from commissioner Nabatov for the first quarter of 1948, April 19, 1948).

6. GARME, f. R-836, op. 2, d. 15, ll. 84–85 (Savel'ev to the executive committee of Lenin district and the city executive committee of Joshkar-Ola, January 12, 1977).

7. GARF, f. R-6991, op. 3, d. 571, l. 26 (Report from commissioner Nabatov for the second quarter of 1952, July 11, 1952).

8. On a comparable interest in quasi-scientific explanations of ritual efficacy among people who identify as Orthodox Christians, see Barchunova 2007; Kormina 2006; Lindquist 2006.

9. Antonov now markets his books on spiritual development on the website of the scientific-spiritual ecological center "Swami," Saint Petersburg. See www.swami-center.org/en/text/about_us.html, accessed June 6, 2008.

10. *Priglashaem k razgovoru,* produced by Antonina Aleksandrova, Mari Republican Radio sound archives, Joshkar-Ola, tape 810 (April 23, 1972).

Bibliography

Archival Collections

STATE ARCHIVES OF THE RUSSIAN FEDERATION, MOSCOW (GARF)
A-561, Knowledge Society of the RSFSR, 1949–1975.
R-6991, Council for Religious Affairs of the USSR, 1947–1975.
R-9547, Knowledge Society of the USSR, 1948–1963.

STATE ARCHIVES OF THE REPUBLIC OF MARIJ EL, JOSHKAR-OLA (GARME)
P-1, Mari Regional Committee of the Communist Party (*Obkom*), 1960–1975.
P-8, Joshkar-Ola City Committee of the Communist Party (*Gorkom*), 1960–1975.
P-12, Morki District Committee of the Communist Party (*Raikom*), 1960–1975.
P-14, Novyj Tor"jal District Committee of the Communist Party, 1960–1975.
P-22, Higher Party Courses of the Mari Regional Committee, 1950–1962.
R-118, League of the Militant Godless, Mari Republican Division, 1937–1944.
R-737, Knowledge Society, Mari Republican Division, 1952–1975.
R-836, Commissioner for Religious Affairs in the Mari ASSR, 1946–1980.

Published Sources

Adler, Jeremy. 1987. *Eine fast magische Anziehungskraft: Goethes Wahlverwandtschaften und die Chemie seiner Zeit*. Munich: Beck.
Adorno, Theodor W. 1971. *Erziehung zur Mündigkeit*. Edited by Gerd Kadelbach. Frankfurt: Suhrkamp.
———. 1994 [1974]. The Stars Down to Earth: The Los Angeles Times Astrology Column. In his *The Stars Down to Earth and Other Essays on the Irrational in Culture*, edited by Stephen Crook. London: Routledge, 46–171.
Agadjanian, Alexander. 2003. Breakthrough to Modernity, Apologia to Traditionalism: The Russian Orthodox View of Society and Culture in Comparative Perspective. *Religion, State and Society* 31(4): 327–346.
Akhmet'ianov, Rifkat Gazizianovich. 1981. *Obshchaia leksika dukhovnoi kul'tury narodov srednego Povolzh'ia*. Moscow: Nauka.
———. 1989. *Obshchaia leksika material'noi kul'tury narodov srednego Povolzh'ia*. Moscow: Nauka.
Akhmetova, M. V., ed. 2005. *Sovremennaia rossiiskaia mifologiia*. Moscow: Rossiiskii gosudarstvennyi gumanitarnyi universitet.
Aktar, Ayhan. 2003. Homogenising the Nation, Turkifying the Economy: The Turkish Experience of Population Exchange Reconsidered. In *Crossing the Aegean: An Appraisal of the 1923 Compulsory Population Exchange between Greece and Turkey*, edited by Renée Hirschon. New York: Berghahn, 79–95.

Aleksandrova, Antonina Petrovna. 1978. *Velenie vremeni.* Ioshkar-Ola: Mariiskoe knizhnoe izdatel'stvo.

Anderson, Benedict. 1983. *Imagined Communities: Reflections on the Origin and Spread of Nationalism.* London: Verso.

Andrews, James T. 2003. *Science for the Masses: The Bolshevik State, Public Science, and the Popular Imagination in Soviet Russia, 1917–1934.* College Station: Texas A&M University Press.

Anonymous. 1963. Sotsialisticheskoe pereustroistvo byta i bor'ba za novye traditsii (mimeographed typescript of a lecture presented for discussion to the scientific-methodological council on the propaganda of scientific atheism of the All-Union Knowledge Society). Copy in the Russian State Library, Moscow.

Arutiunian, Iurii Vartanovich, L. M. Drobizheva, M. N. Kuz'min, N. S. Polishchuk, and S. S. Savoskul. 1992. *Russkie: Etnosotsiologicheskie ocherki.* Moscow: Nauka.

Asad, Talal. 1993. *Genealogies of Religion: Discipline and Reasons of Power in Christianity and Islam.* Baltimore, MD: Johns Hopkins University Press.

———. 2003. *Formations of the Secular: Christianity, Islam, Modernity.* Stanford, CA: Stanford University Press.

———. 2006. Trying to Understand French Secularism. In *Political Theologies: Public Religions in a Post-Secular World,* edited by Hent de Vries and Lawrence Sullivan. New York: Fordham University Press, 494–526.

Ash, Mitchell G. 1995. *Gestalt Psychology in German Culture, 1890–1967: Holism and the Quest for Objectivity.* Cambridge: Cambridge University Press.

Assmann, Jan. 2002. *Herrschaft und Heil: Politische Theologie in Altägypten, Israel und Europa.* Frankfurt: Fischer.

Austin, John L. 1965. *How to Do Things with Words.* Edited by J. O. Urmson. New York: Oxford University Press.

Bakhtin, Aleksandr Gennad'evich. 1998. *XV–XVI veka v istorii mariiskogo kraia.* Ioshkar-Ola: Mariiskii poligrafichesko-izdatel'skii kombinat.

Balzer, Marjorie Mandelstam. 2005. Whose Steeple Is Higher? Religious Competition in Siberia. *Religion, State and Society* 33(1): 57–69.

Barashkov, Aleksandr Igorevich. 1991. *Budet li konets sveta?* Moscow: Znanie.

Barchunova, Tatiana V. 2007. Downloading Cosmic Energy: Intersection of Faith-Based and Health-Care Practices (the Novosibirsk Case). In *Cosmologies of Suffering: Post-Communist Transformation, Sacral Communication, and Healing,* edited by Agita Lūse and Imre Lázár. Newcastle, England: Cambridge Scholars, 54–67.

Barinskaia, A. P., and V. I. Savel'ev. 1973. *Sovetskoe zakonodatel'stvo o religioznykh kul'takh.* Ioshkar-Ola: Mariiskoe knizhnoe izdatel'stvo.

Barkey, Karen. 2008. *Empire of Difference: The Ottomans in Comparative Perspective.* Cambridge: Cambridge University Press.

Bartholomew, Richard. 2006. Publishing, Celebrity, and the Globalisation of Conservative Protestantism. *Journal of Contemporary Religion* 21(1): 1–13.

Baubérot, Jean. 2004. *Laïcité 1905–2005, entre passion et raison.* Paris: Seuil.

Bauman, Richard. 1983. *Let Your Words Be Few: Symbolism of Speaking and Silence among Seventeenth-Century Quakers.* Cambridge: Cambridge University Press.

Bazykin, V., and V. Komarov. 1961. *Put' v kosmos otkryt.* Moscow: Sovetskaia Rossiia.

Bellah, Robert N. 1967. Civil Religion in America. *Daedalus* 96(1): 1–21.

Belting, Hans. 2000 [1990]. *Bild und Kult: Eine Geschichte des Bildes vor dem Zeit-alter der Kunst.* 5th ed. Munich: Beck.

———. 2001. Bild und Tod: Verkörperung in frühen Kulturen. In his *Bild-Anthropo-logie: Entwürfe für eine Bildwissenschaft.* Munich: Wilhelm Fink, 143–188.

Benn, David Wedgwood. 1989. *Persuasion and Soviet Politics.* Oxford: Basil Blackwell.

Berdyaev, Nicholas. 1932. *The Russian Revolution: Two Essays on Its Implications in Religion and Psychology.* London: Sheed & Ward.

Berglund, Bruce, and Brian Porter-Szűcs, eds. 2010. *Christianity and Modernity in Eastern Europe.* Budapest: Central European University Press.

Berkhoff, Karel C. 2004. *Harvest of Despair: Life and Death in Ukraine under Nazi Rule.* Cambridge, MA: Harvard University Press.

Bernshtam, T. A. 2005. *Prikhodskaia zhizn' russkoi derevni: Ocherki po tserkovnoi etnografii.* Saint Petersburg: Peterburgskoe vostokovedenie.

Berzonsky, Vladimir. 2004. Are Eastern Orthodoxy and Evangelicalism Compat-ible? No. An Orthodox Perspective. In *Three Views on Eastern Orthodoxy and Evangelicalism,* edited by James J. Stamoolis. Grand Rapids, MI: Zondervan, 169–181.

Bhargava, Rajeev. 1998. What Is Secularism For? In *Secularism and Its Critics,* edited by Rajeev Bhargava. Delhi: Oxford University Press, 486–542.

———. 2007. The Distinctiveness of Indian Secularism. In *The Future of Secularism,* edited by T. N. Srinivasan. Oxford: Oxford University Press, 20–53.

Birstein, Vadim J. 2001. *The Perversion of Knowledge: The True Story of Soviet Sci-ence.* Boulder, CO: Westview.

Bloch, Alexia. 2004. *Red Ties and Residential Schools: Indigenous Siberians in a Post-Soviet State.* Philadelphia: University of Pennsylvania Press.

Bond, George C. 1987. Ancestors and Protestants: Religious Coexistence in the Social Field of a Zambian Community. *American Ethnologist* 14(1): 55–72.

Bornkamm, Günther. 1968. Lobpreis, Bekenntnis und Opfer: Eine alttestamentliche Studie. In *Geschichte und Glaube: Gesammelte Aufsätze,* vol. 3. Munich: Christian Kaiser, 122–139.

Bouchard, Michel. 2004. Graveyards: Russian Ritual and Belief Pertaining to the Dead. *Religion* 34: 345–362.

Bourdeaux, Michael. 1995. Glasnost and the Gospel: The Emergence of Religious Pluralism. In *The Politics of Religion in Russia and the New States of Eurasia,* edited by Michael Bourdeaux. Armonk, NY: Sharpe, 113–127.

Bourdieu, Pierre, and Jean-Claude Passeron. 1970. *La reproduction: Éléments pour une théorie du système d'enseignement.* Paris: Minuit.

Bowen, John. 2008. *Why the French Don't Like Headscarves: Islam, the State, and Public Space.* Princeton, NJ: Princeton University Press.

Bowman, Glenn. 2010. Orthodox-Muslim Interactions at "Mixed Shrines" in Mace-donia. In *Eastern Christians in Anthropological Perspective,* edited by C. M. Hann and Hermann Goltz. Berkeley: University of California Press, 195–219.

Boyer, Dominic. 2005. *Spirit and System: Media, Intellectuals, and the Dialectic in Modern German Culture.* Chicago: University of Chicago Press.

Breidbach, Olaf. 2006. *Goethes Metamorphosenlehre.* Munich: Wilhelm Fink.

Breslauer, George. 1982. *Khrushchev and Brezhnev as Leaders: Building Authority in Soviet Politics.* London: George Allen & Unwin.

Brittain, Christopher Craig. 2005. The "Secular" as a Tragic Category: On Talal Asad, Religion and Representation. *Method and Theory in the Study of Religion* 17(2): 149–165.

Brooks, Jeffrey. 1985. *When Russia Learned to Read: Literacy and Popular Culture, 1861–1917.* Princeton, NJ: Princeton University Press.

Brown, Callum. 2001. *The Death of Christian Britain: Understanding Secularisation 1800–2000.* London: Routledge.

Broz, Ludek. 2009. Conversion to Religion? Negotiating Continuity and Discontinuity in Contemporary Altai. In *Conversion after Socialism: Disruptions, Modernisms and Technologies of Faith in the Former Soviet Union,* edited by Mathijs Pelkmans. New York: Berghahn, 17–37.

Bruce, Steve, ed. 1992. *Religion and Modernization: Sociologists and Historians Debate the Secularization Thesis.* Oxford: Clarendon.

Buchli, Victor. 1999. *An Archaeology of Socialism.* Oxford: Berg.

Buckser, Andrew S. 1996. *Communities of Faith: Sectarianism, Identity, and Social Change on a Danish Island.* Providence, RI: Berghahn.

Burbank, Jane. 2006. An Imperial Rights Regime: Law and Citizenship in the Russian Empire. *Kritika,* n.s., 7(3): 397–431.

Burbank, Jane, and Frederick Cooper. 2010. *Empires in World History: Power and the Politics of Difference.* Princeton, NJ: Princeton University Press.

Burston, David, and Rebecca Denova, eds. 2005. *Passionate Dialogues: Critical Perspectives on Mel Gibson's "The Passion of the Christ."* Pittsburgh, PA: Mise.

Burwick, Frederick. 1986. *The Damnation of Newton: Goethe's Color Theory and Romantic Perception.* Berlin: de Gruyter.

Buturovic, Amila. 2007. When Secularism Opposes Nationalism: The Case of the Former Yugoslavia. In *The Future of Secularism,* edited by T. N. Srinivasan. Oxford: Oxford University Press, 284–304.

Caldwell, Melissa. 2008. Social Welfare and Christian Welfare: Who Gets Saved in Post-Soviet Christian Charity Work? In *Religion, Morality, and Community in Post-Soviet Societies,* edited by Mark D. Steinberg and Catherine Wanner. Washington, DC: Woodrow Wilson Center Press, 179–214.

Casanova, José. 1994. *Public Religions in the Modern World.* Chicago: University of Chicago Press.

Chakrabarty, Dipesh. 2000. *Provincializing Europe: Postcolonial Thought and Historical Difference.* Princeton, NJ: Princeton University Press.

Chernykh, Iu. A. 1967. *Disput: Kak ego prigotovit' i provesti.* Moscow: Obshchestvo Znanie RSFSR.

Christian, William A. 1972. *Person and God in a Spanish Valley.* New York: Seminar Press.

Chumachenko, Tatiana A. 2002. *Church and State in Soviet Russia: Russian Orthodoxy from World War II to the Khrushchev Years.* Edited and translated by Edward E. Roslof. Armonk, NY: Sharpe.

Clark, Katerina. 1995. *Petersburg: Crucible of Cultural Revolution.* Cambridge, MA: Harvard University Press.

Cody, Francis. 2009. Inscribing Subjects to Citizenship: Petitions, Literacy Activism, and the Performativity of Signature in Rural Tamil India. *Cultural Anthropology* 24(3): 347–380.

Coleman, Heather. 2005. *Russian Baptists and Spiritual Revolution, 1905–1929.* Bloomington: Indiana University Press.

———. 2007. Tales of Violence against Religious Dissidents in the Orthodox Village. In *Sacred Stories: Religion and Spirituality in Modern Russia,* edited by Mark Steinberg and Heather Coleman. Bloomington: Indiana University Press, 200–221.

Coleman, Simon. 2000. *The Globalization of Charismatic Christianity: Spreading the Gospel of Prosperity.* Cambridge: Cambridge University Press.

———. 2006. Materializing the Self: Words and Gifts in the Construction of Charismatic Protestant Identity. In *The Anthropology of Christianity,* edited by Fenella Cannell. Durham, NC: Duke University Press, 163–184.

Collier, Stephen J. 2001. Post-Socialist City: The Government of Society in Neoliberal Times. Ph.D. diss., Department of Anthropology, University of California, Berkeley.

Collins, James. 1996. Socialization to Text: Structure and Contradiction in Schooled Literacy. In *Natural Histories of Discourse,* edited by Michael Silverstein and Greg Urban. Chicago: University of Chicago Press, 203–228.

———. 2003. Language, Identity, and Learning in the Era of "Expert-Guided" Systems. In *Linguistic Anthropology of Education,* edited by S. Wortham and B. Rymes. Westport, CT: Praeger, 31–60.

Comaroff, Jean, and John Comaroff. 1997. *Of Revelation and Revolution.* Vol. 2: *The Dialectics of Modernity on a South African Frontier.* Chicago: University of Chicago Press.

———. 2000. Millennial Capitalism: First Thoughts on a Second Coming. *Public Culture* 12(2): 291–343.

Corley, Felix. 1996. *Religion in the Soviet Union: An Archival Reader.* New York: New York University Press.

Cox, Harvey. 1984. *Religion in the Secular City: Toward a Postmodern Theology.* New York: Simon and Schuster.

Crapanzano, Vincent. 2000. *Serving the Word: Literalism in America from the Pulpit to the Bench.* New York: New Press.

Das, Veena. 2006. Secularism and the Argument from Nature. In *Powers of the Secular Modern: Talal Asad and His Interlocutors,* edited by David Scott and Charles Hirschkind. Stanford, CA: Stanford University Press, 93–112.

———. 2007. *Life and Words: Violence and the Descent into the Ordinary.* Berkeley: University of California Press.

David-Fox, Michael. 1997. *Revolution of the Mind: Higher Learning among the Bolsheviks, 1918–1929.* Ithaca, NY: Cornell University Press.

Davie, Grace. 1994. *Religion in Britain since 1945: Believing without Belonging.* Oxford: Blackwell.

Davies, R. W., and Stephen G. Wheatcroft. 2004. *The Years of Hunger: Soviet Agriculture, 1931–1933.* New York: Palgrave Macmillan.

Derluguian, Georgi M. 2005. *Bourdieu's Secret Admirer in the Caucasus: A World-System Biography.* Chicago: University of Chicago Press.

de Vries, Hent. 2006. Introduction: Before, Around, and Beyond the Theologico-Political. In *Political Theologies: Public Religions in a Post-Secular World,* edited by Hent de Vries and Lawrence Sullivan. New York: Fordham University Press, 1–88.

Dombrowski, Kirk. 2001. *Against Culture: Development, Politics, and Religion in Indian Alaska.* Lincoln: University of Nebraska Press.

Dragadze, Tamara. 1993. The Domestication of Religion under Soviet Communism. In *Socialism: Ideals, Ideologies, and Local Practice,* edited by C. M. Hann. London: Routledge, 148–156.

Dukhanin, Valerii. 2005. *Pravoslavie i mir kino.* Moscow: Drakkar.

Dumont, Louis. 1966. *Homo hiérarchicus: Essai sur le système des castes.* Paris: Gallimard.

———. 1983. De l'individu-hors-du monde à l'individu-dans-le-monde. In his *Essais sur l'individualisme: Une perspective anthropologique sur l'idéologie moderne.* Paris: Seuil, 33–67.

Durkheim, Emile. 1998 [1914]. *Les formes élémentaires de la vie religieuse.* Paris: Quadrige/Presses universitaires de France.

Eickelman, Dale. 1992. Mass Higher Education and the Religious Imagination in Contemporary Arab Societies. *American Ethnologist* 19(4): 643–655.

Eklof, Ben, ed. 1993. *School and Society in Tsarist and Soviet Russia.* New York: St. Martin's.

Elliott, Mark, and Sharyl Corrado. 1999. The 1997 Russian Law on Religion: The Impact on Protestants. *Religion, State and Society* 27(1): 109–134.

Engelhardt, Jeffers. 2009. Right Singing and Conversion to Orthodox Christianity in Estonia. In *Conversions after Socialism: Disruptions, Modernisms and Technologies of Faith in the Former Soviet Union,* edited by Mathijs Pelkmans. New York: Berghahn, 85–106.

Engelke, Matthew. 2007. *A Problem of Presence: Beyond Scripture in an African Church.* Berkeley: University of California Press.

Engels, Friedrich. 1962a [1878]. Anti-Dühring. In Karl Marx and Friedrich Engels, *Werke,* vol. 20. Berlin: Dietz, 5–303.

———. 1962b [1884]. Der Ursprung der Familie, des Privateigentums und des Staates. In Karl Marx and Friedrich Engels, *Werke,* vol. 21. Berlin: Dietz, 25–173.

Engelstein, Laura. 1999. *Castration and the Heavenly Kingdom: A Russian Folktale.* Ithaca, NY: Cornell University Press.

Erlmann, Veit. 1982. Trance and Music in the Hausa Bòorii Spirit Possession Cult in Niger. *Ethnomusicology* 26(1): 49–58.

Erzen, Tanya. 2006. *Straight to Jesus: Sexual and Christian Conversions in the Ex-Gay Movement.* Berkeley: University of California Press.

Felmy, Karl Christian. 1984. *Die Deutung der göttlichen Liturgie in der russischen Theologie: Wege und Wandlungen russischer Liturgie-Auslegung.* Berlin: de Gruyter.

Feofan (Govorov, aka Zatvornik), Saint. 1991. *Chto est' dukhovnaia zhizn' i kak na nee nastroit'sia? Pis'ma.* Leningrad: Leningradskoe otdelenie obshchestva Znanie.

Feuerbach, Ludwig. 1841. *Das Wesen des Christentums.* Leipzig: Wigand.

Field, Deborah. 2007. *Private Life and Communist Morality in Khrushchev's Russia.* New York: Peter Lang.

Filatov, Sergei. 2002. Religioznaia zhizn' Povolzh'ia: Pragmatichnoe khristianstvo. In *Religiia i obshchestvo: Ocherki religioznoi zhizni sovremennoi Rossii,* edited by S. V. Filatov. Moscow: Letnii sad, 58–74.

Filatov, Sergei, and Roman Lunkin. 2006. Statistics on Religion in Russia: The Reality behind the Figures. *Religion, State and Society* 34(1): 33–49.

Fitzpatrick, Sheila. 1970. *The Commissariat of the Enlightenment: Soviet Organization of Education and the Arts under Lunacharsky, October 1917–1921.* Cambridge: Cambridge University Press.

———. 1979. *Education and Social Mobility in the Soviet Union, 1921–1934.* Cambridge: Cambridge University Press.

———. 1994. *Stalin's Peasants: Resistance and Survival in the Soviet Village after Collectivization.* New York: Oxford University Press.

———. 2006. Social Parasites: How Tramps, Idle Youth and Busy Entrepreneurs Impeded the Soviet March to Communism. *Cahiers du Monde Russe* 47(1–2): 377–408.

Florovsky, Georges. 1991 [1937]. *Les voies de la théologie russe.* Vol. 1. Translated by J. C. Roberti. Paris: Desclée de Brouwer.

———. 2003 [1963]. The Function of Tradition in the Ancient Church. In *Eastern Orthodox Theology: A Contemporary Reader,* edited by Daniel B. Clendenin. 2nd ed. Grand Rapids, MI: Baker Academic, 97–114.

Frank, Allen. 1988. The Veneration of Muslim Saints among the Maris of Russia. *Eurasian Studies Yearbook* 70: 79–84.

Froese, Leonhard. 1963. *Ideengeschichtliche Triebkräfte der russischen und sowjetischen Pädagogik.* 2nd ed. Heidelberg: Quelle & Meyer.

Froese, Paul. 2008. *The Plot to Kill God: Findings from the Soviet Experiment in Secularization.* Berkeley: University of California Press.

Furman, Dmitrii Efimovich, and Kimmo Kääriäinen. 2006. *Religioznost' v Rossii v 90e gody XX-nachale XXI veka.* Moscow: OGNI TD.

Gal, Susan, and Kathryn Woolard. 2001. *Languages and Publics: The Making of Authority.* Manchester, England: St. Jerome Publishing.

Garrard, John, and Carol Garrard. 2008. *Russian Orthodoxy Resurgent: Faith and Power in the New Russia.* Princeton, NJ: Princeton University Press.

Geertz, Clifford. 1973. "Internal Conversion" in Contemporary Bali. In his *The Interpretation of Cultures.* London: Hutchinson, 170–189.

Gell, Alfred. 1998. *Art and Agency: An Anthropological Theory.* Oxford: Oxford University Press.

Geraci, Robert P. 2001. *Window on the East: National and Imperial Identities in Late Tsarist Russia.* Ithaca, NY: Cornell University Press.

Ghodsee, Kristen. 2009. *Muslim Lives in Eastern Europe: Gender, Ethnicity, and the Transformation of Islam in Postsocialist Bulgaria.* Princeton, NJ: Princeton University Press.

Goethe, Johann Wolfgang von. 1956 [1809]. *Die Wahlverwandtschaften.* Stuttgart: Reclam.

Goffman, Erving. 1983. Felicity's Condition. *American Journal of Sociology* 89(1): 1–53.

———. 1986 [1974]. *Frame Analysis: An Essay on the Organization of Experience.* Boston: Northeastern University Press.

Goltz, Hermann. 1974. *Hiera mesiteia: Zur Theorie der hierarchischen Societät im corpus areopagiticum.* Erlangen: Lehrstuhl für Geschichte und Theologie des christlichen Ostens.

——. 1979. Antihäretische Konsequenzen: "Monismus" und "Materialismus" in der orthodoxen Tradition. In *Studien zum Menschenbild in Gnosis und Manichäismus,* edited by Peter Nagel. Halle: Martin-Luther-Universität, 253–274.

Gombrich, Richard F., and Gananath Obeyesekere. 1988. *Buddhism Transformed: Religious Change in Sri Lanka.* Princeton, NJ: Princeton University Press.

Gorfunkel', P. L. 1976. *Psikhologicheskie osnovy nagliadnosti v lektsionnoi propagande: V pomoshch' lektoru.* Izhevsk: Udmurtiia.

Gorokhov, M. S. 1974. Formy i metody individual'noi raboty propagandista. In *Piatiletka i propagandist: Materialy respublikanskoi nauchno-prakticheskoi konferentsii propagandistov,* edited by Dom politicheskogo prosveshcheniia Mariiskogo obkoma KPSS. Ioshkar-Ola: Mariiskoe knizhnoe izdatel'stvo, 50–51.

Gorsuch, Anne E. 2000. *Youth in Revolutionary Russia: Enthusiasts, Bohemians, Delinquents.* Bloomington: Indiana University Press.

Graham, Loren. 1972. *Science and Philosophy in the Soviet Union.* New York: Knopf.

Grant, Bruce. 1995. *In the Soviet House of Culture: A Century of Perestroikas.* Princeton, NJ: Princeton University Press.

——. 2009. *The Captive and the Gift: Cultural Histories of Sovereignty in Russia and the Caucasus.* Ithaca, NY: Cornell University Press.

Grossman, Gregory. 1977. The "Second Economy" of the USSR. *Problems of Communism* 26(5): 25–40.

Gunn, T. Jeremy. 1999. The Law of the Russian Federation on the Freedom of Conscience and Religious Associations from a Human Rights Perspective. In *Proselytism and Orthodoxy in Russia: The New War for Souls,* edited by John Witte and Michael Bourdeaux. Maryknoll, NY: Orbis, 239–264.

Gurian, Waldemar. 1952. Totalitarian Religions. *Review of Politics* 14(1): 3–14.

Habermas, Jürgen. 1988. *Theorie des kommunikativen Handelns.* Frankfurt: Suhrkamp.

——. 2005. Vorpolitische Grundlagen des demokratischen Rechtsstaates? In Jürgen Habermas and Joseph Ratzinger, *Dialektik der Säkularisierung: Über Religion und Vernunft.* Freiburg: Herder, 15–37.

Hagin, Kenneth [Kennet Khegin]. 1997 [1978]. *Kak byt' vedomym Dukhom Bozh'im.* Saint Petersburg: Khristianskii vzgliad.

Harding, Susan Friend. 1987. Convicted by the Holy Spirit: The Rhetoric of Fundamental Baptist Conversion. *American Ethnologist* 14(1): 167–181.

——. 1991. Representing Fundamentalism: The Problem of the Repugnant Cultural Other. *Social Research* 58(2): 373–393.

——. 2000. *The Book of Jerry Falwell.* Princeton, NJ: Princeton University Press.

Hawley, John Stratton. 1987. Morality beyond Morality in the Lives of Three Hindu Saints. In *Saints and Virtues,* edited by John Stratton Hawley. Berkeley: University of California Press, 52–72.

Hawn, C. Michael. 2003. Form and Ritual: Sequential and Cyclic Musical Structures and Their Use in Liturgy. In his *Gather into One: Praying and Singing Globally.* Grand Rapids, MI: Eerdmans, 224–240.

Hayden, Robert M. 2002. Antagonistic Tolerance: Competitive Sharing of Religious Sites in South Asia and the Balkans. *Current Anthropology* 43(2): 205–231.

Headley, Stephen C. 2010. *Christ after Communism: Spiritual Authority and Its Transmission in Moscow Today.* Rollinsford, NH: Orthodox Research Institute.

Hemment, Julie. 2009. Soviet-Style Neoliberalism? *Nashi,* Youth Voluntarism, and the Restructuring of Social Welfare in Russia. *Problems of Post-Communism* 56(6): 36–50.

Hervieu-Léger, Danièle. 1997. Faces of Catholic Transnationalism in and beyond France. In *Transnational Religion and Fading States,* edited by Susanne Hoeber Rudolph and James Piscatori. Boulder, CO: Westview, 104–118.

Hirsch, Francine. 2005. *Empire of Nations: Ethnographic Knowledge and the Making of the Soviet Union.* Ithaca, NY: Cornell University Press.

Hirschkind, Charles. 2006. *The Ethical Soundscape: Cassette Sermons and Islamic Counterpublics.* New York: Columbia University Press.

Hirschon, Renée. 1989. *Heirs of the Greek Catastrophe: The Social Life of Asia Minor Refugees in Piraeus.* Oxford: Clarendon.

Höhn, Hans-Joachim. 2007. *Postsäkular: Gesellschaft im Umbruch—Religion im Wandel.* Paderborn: Schöningh.

Honko, Lauri. 1987. Die Authentizität des Kalevala. In *Authentizität und Betrug in der Ethnologie,* edited by H. P. Duerr. Frankfurt: Suhrkamp, 357–392.

Hornsby, Bill. 2000. *The Cell-Driven Church.* Houston, TX: Touch Publications.

Humphrey, Caroline. 1989. Janus-Faced Signs: The Political Language of a Soviet Minority before *Glasnost'.* In *Social Anthropology and the Politics of Language,* edited by Ralph Grillo. London: Routledge, 145–175.

———. 1997. Exemplars and Rules: Aspects of the Discourse of Moralities in Mongolia. In *The Ethnography of Moralities,* edited by Signe Howell. London: Routledge, 25–47.

———. 1998. *Marx Went Away, but Karl Stayed Behind* [updated edition of *The Karl Marx Collective,* 1983]. Ann Arbor: University of Michigan Press.

Hunt, Stephen. 2004. *The Alpha Enterprise: Evangelism in a Post-Christian Era.* Aldershot, England: Ashgate.

Hurston, Karen. 2001. *Breakthrough Cell Groups.* Houston, TX: Touch Publications.

Husband, William B. 2000. *"Godless Communists": Atheism and Society in Soviet Russia, 1917–1932.* DeKalb: Northern Illinois University Press.

Iantemir, Mikhail Nikolaevich. 2006 [1928]. *Mariiskaia Avtonomnaia Oblast': Ocherk.* Ioshkar-Ola: String.

Iarygin, Nikolai N. 2004. *Evangel'skoe dvizhenie v Volgo-Viatskom regione.* Moscow: Akademicheskii proekt.

Ignatii (Brianchaninov), Saint. 2000. *Uchenie Pravoslavnoi Tserkvi o molitve Iisusovoi.* Edited by S. E. Molotkov. Saint Petersburg: Satis.

Ignatov, P. I. 1963. Prichiny zhivuchesti religioznykh perezhitkov v SSSR i puti ikh preodoleniia. In *Ateisticheskie znaniia—narodu: Stenogrammy lektsii, prochitannykh na respublikanskikh seminarakh i v narodnykh universitetakh ateizma,* edited by N. V. Fedorovich. Leningrad: Obshchestvo po rasprostraneniiu politicheskikh i nauchnykh znanii RSFSR, 198–229.

Jaffe, Alexandra. 2003. "Imagined Competence": Classroom Evaluation, Collective Identity, and Linguistic Authenticity in a Corsican Bilingual Classroom. In *Linguistic Anthropology of Education,* edited by S. Wortham and B. Rymes. Westport, CT: Praeger, 151–184.

Jakobson, Roman. 1931. *K kharakteristike evraziiskogo iazykovogo soiuza.* Paris: Izdatel'stvo evraziitsev.

Jakobson, Roman, with Krystyna Pomorska. 1983 [1980]. *Dialogues*. Cambridge, MA: MIT Press.

Jay, Martin. 1993. *Downcast Eyes: The Denigration of Vision in Twentieth-Century French Thought*. Berkeley: University of California Press.

Johnson, Emily D. 2006. *How St. Petersburg Learned to Study Itself: The Russian Idea of Kraevedenie*. University Park: Pennsylvania State University Press.

Kalinina, Ol'ga Aleksandrovna, ed. 2003. *Kalendarnye prazdniki i obriady mariitsev*. Ioshkar-Ola: MarNIIIaLI.

Kappeler, Andreas. 1982. *Rußlands erste Nationalitäten: Das Zarenreich und die Völker der Mittleren Volga vom 16. bis 19. Jahrhundert*. Vienna: Böhlau.

———. 1992. *Rußland als Vielvölkerreich: Entstehung, Geschichte, Zerfall*. Munich: Beck.

Kats, Rustam Sviatoslavovich. 2004 [1986]. *Istoriia sovetskoi fantastiki*. 3rd ed. Saint Petersburg: Izdatel'stvo S.-Peterburgskogo universiteta.

Keane, Webb. 2007. *Christian Moderns: Freedom and Fetish in the Mission Encounter*. Berkeley: University of California Press.

———. 2009. Freedom and Blasphemy: On Indonesian Press Bans and Danish Cartoons. *Public Culture* 21(1): 47–76.

Keller, Eva. 2005. *The Road to Clarity: Seventh-Day Adventism in Madagascar*. New York: Palgrave Macmillan.

Kelly, Catriona. 2001. *Refining Russia: Advice Literature, Polite Culture, and Gender from Catherine to Yeltsin*. Oxford: Oxford University Press.

———. 2002. "A Laboratory for the Manufacture of Proletarian Writers": The *Stengazeta* (Wall Newspaper), *Kul'turnost'* and the Language of Politics in the Early Soviet Period. *Europe-Asia Studies* 54(4): 573–602.

Kenez, Peter. 1985. *The Birth of the Propaganda State: Soviet Methods of Mass Mobilization, 1917–1929*. Cambridge: Cambridge University Press.

Kenworthy, Scott. 2008. To Save the World or to Renounce It: Modes of Moral Action in Russian Orthodoxy. In *Religion, Morality, and Community in Post-Soviet Societies*, edited by Mark D. Steinberg and Catherine Wanner. Washington, DC: Woodrow Wilson Center Press, 21–54.

Kerr, Stephen T. 2005. The Experimental Tradition in Russian Education. In *Educational Reform in Post-Soviet Russia: Legacies and Prospects*. London: Frank Cass, 102–128.

Khalid, Adeeb. 2006. Backwardness and the Quest for Civilization: Early Soviet Central Asia in Comparative Perspective. *Slavic Review* 65(2): 231–251.

———. 2007. *Islam after Communism: Religion and Politics in Central Asia*. Berkeley: University of California Press.

Kharkhordin, Oleg. 1999. *The Collective and the Individual in Russia: A Study of Practices*. Berkeley: University of California Press.

Kirsanov, Aleksei Vasil'evich. 1976. *K ubezhdeniiu cherez interes: Zametki lektora— Opyt, analiz, razmyshleniia*. Moscow: Moskovskii rabochii.

Kirschenbaum, Lisa A. 2001. *Small Comrades: Revolutionizing Childhood in Soviet Russia, 1917–1932*. New York: Routledge Falmer.

Kivelson, Valerie A., and Joan Neuberger. 2008. Seeing into Being: An Introduction. In *Picturing Russia: Explorations in Visual Culture*, edited by Valerie A. Kivelson and Joan Neuberger. New Haven, CT: Yale University Press, 1–11.

Kligman, Gail. 1988. *The Wedding of the Dead: Ritual, Poetics, and Popular Culture in Transylvania.* Berkeley: University of California Press.

Klimó, Árpád von, and Malte Rolf, eds. 2006. *Rausch und Diktatur: Inszenierung, Mobilisierung und Kontrolle in totalitären Systemen.* Frankfurt: Campus.

Knight, Nathaniel. 1998. Science, Empire, and Nationality: Ethnography in the Russian Geographical Society, 1845–1855. In *Imperial Russia: New Histories for the Empire,* edited by J. Burbank and D. L. Ransel. Bloomington: Indiana University Press, 108–141.

Kolymagin, Boris. 2004. *Krymskaia ekumena: Religioznaia zhizn' poslevoennogo Kryma.* Saint Petersburg: Aleteiia.

Kormina, Zhanna V. 2006. Religioznost' russkoi provintsii: K voprosu o funktsii sel'skikh sviatyn'. In *Sny bogoroditsy: Issledovaniia po antropologii religii,* edited by Zh. V. Kormina, A. A. Panchenko, and S. A. Shtyrkov. Saint Petersburg: Izdatel'stvo Evropeiskogo universiteta, 130–150.

Kornai, János. 1992. *The Socialist System: The Political Economy of Communism.* Princeton, NJ: Princeton University Press.

Korobov, Stepan Alekseevich. 1957. *Proshloe mariiskogo naroda.* Ioshkar-Ola: Mariiskoe knizhnoe izdatel'stvo.

Kotkin, Stephen. 1995. *Magnetic Mountain: Stalinism as a Civilization.* Berkeley: University of California Press.

Kozelsky, Mara. 2010. *Christianizing Crimea: Shaping Sacred Space in the Russian Empire and Beyond.* DeKalb: Northern Illinois University Press.

Krasnov, A. 1959. Proiskhozhdenie i sushchnost' mariiskikh religioznykh kul'tov. In *Nauchno-ateisticheskaia propaganda v kul'turno-prosvetitel'skikh uchrezhdeniiakh,* edited by I. V. Novoselova. Ioshkar-Ola: Ministerstvo kul'tury Mariiskoi ASSR, 46–53.

Kudriavtseva, A. 2002. Chudotvornyi sekret. *Vo!* May 21–28: 12.

Kurilla, Ivan. 2002. Civil Activism without NGOs: The Communist Party as a Civil Society Substitute. *Demokratizatsiya* 10(3): 392–400.

Kuteinikova, Nina Sergeevna. 2005. *Ikonopisanie Rossii vtoroi poloviny XX veka.* Saint Petersburg: Znaki.

Lalukka, Seppo. 1997. *Vostochno-Finskie narody Rossii: Analiz etnodemograficheskikh protsessov.* Saint Petersburg: Evropeiskii dom.

Lane, Christel. 1978. *Christian Religion in the Soviet Union: A Sociological Study.* London: George Allen and Unwin.

———. 1981. *The Rites of Rulers: Ritual in Industrial Society—The Soviet Case.* Cambridge: Cambridge University Press.

Lang, Bernhard. 1997. *Sacred Games: A History of Christian Worship.* New Haven, CT: Yale University Press.

Langford, Jean. 1999. Medical Mimesis: Healing Signs of a Cosmopolitan "Quack." *American Ethnologist* 26(1): 24–46.

LaPierre, Brian. 2006. Making Hooliganism on a Mass Scale: The Campaign against Petty Hooliganism in the Soviet Union, 1956–1964. *Cahiers du Monde Russe* 47(1–2): 349–376.

Lemon, Alaina. 2000. *Between Two Fires: Gypsy Performance and Romani Memory from Pushkin to Postsocialism.* Durham, NC: Duke University Press.

———. 2008. Hermeneutic Algebra: Solving for Love, Time/Space, and Value in Putin-Era Personal Ads. *Journal of Linguistic Anthropology* 18(2): 236–267.

Levin, Eve. 1993. *Dvoeverie* and Popular Religion. In *Seeking God: The Recovery of Religious Identity in Orthodox Russia, Ukraine, and Georgia*, edited by S. K. Batalden. DeKalb: Northern Illinois University Press, 31–52.

Lincoln, Bruce. 1994. A Lakota Sundance and the Problematics of Sociocosmic Reunion. *History of Religions* 34(1): 1–14.

Lindquist, Galina. 2006. *Conjuring Hope: Healing and Magic in Contemporary Russia*. New York: Berghahn.

———. 2008. Allies and Subordinates: Religious Practice on the Margins between Buddhism and Shamanism in Southern Siberia. In *On the Margins of Religion*, edited by Frances Pine and João de Pina-Cabral. New York: Berghahn, 153–168.

Löwy, Michael. 2004. Le concept d'affinité élective chez Max Weber. *Archives de Sciences sociales des religions* 127: 93–103.

Luckmann, Thomas. 1991. *Die unsichtbare Religion*. Frankfurt: Suhrkamp.

Luehrmann, Sonja. 2005. Recycling Cultural Construction: Desecularisation in Postsoviet Mari El. *Religion, State and Society* 33(1): 35–56.

———. 2010. A Dual Struggle of Images on Russia's Middle Volga: Icon Veneration in the Face of Protestant and Pagan Critique. In *Eastern Christians in Anthropological Perspective*, edited by C. M. Hann and Hermann Goltz. Berkeley: University of California Press, 56–78.

———. 2011. The Modernity of Manual Reproduction: Soviet Propaganda and the Creative Life of Ideology. *Cultural Anthropology* 26(3): 363–388.

Luhrmann, Tanya M. 2004. Metakinesis: How God Becomes Intimate in Contemporary U.S. Christianity. *American Anthropologist* 106(3): 518–528.

Luka (Voino-Iasenetskii), Saint. 2006 [1978]. *Dukh, dusha i telo: Izbrannye poucheniia*. Moscow: Dar".

Madan, T. N. 1998. Secularism in Its Place. In *Secularism and Its Critics*, edited by Rajeev Bhargava. Delhi: Oxford University Press, 297–320.

Mahmood, Saba. 2001. Feminist Theory, Embodiment, and the Docile Agent: Some Reflections on the Egyptian Islamic Revival. *Cultural Anthropology* 6(2): 202–236.

———. 2005. *Politics of Piety: The Islamic Revival and the Feminist Subject*. Princeton, NJ: Princeton University Press.

———. 2006. Secularism, Hermeneutics, and Empire: The Politics of Islamic Reformation. *Public Culture* 18(2): 323–347.

———. 2008. Is Critique Secular? A Symposium at UC Berkeley. *Public Culture* 20(3): 447–452.

Malia, Martin. 1965. *Alexander Herzen and the Birth of Russian Socialism*. New York: Grosset and Dunlap.

Manchester, Laurie. 2008. *Holy Fathers, Secular Sons: Clergy, Intelligentsia, and the Modern Self in Revolutionary Russia*. DeKalb: Northern Illinois University Press.

Marker, Gary. 2008. An Icon of Female Authority: The St. Catherine Image of 1721. In *Picturing Russia: Explorations in Visual Culture*, edited by Valerie A. Kivelson and Joan Neuberger. New Haven, CT: Yale University Press, 63–66.

Martin, David. 1990. *Tongues of Fire: The Explosion of Protestantism in Latin America*. Oxford: Basil Blackwell.

———. 2002. *Pentecostalism: The World Their Parish*. Oxford: Blackwell.

Martin, Terry. 2001. *The Affirmative Action Empire: Nations and Nationalism in the Soviet Union, 1923–1939*. Ithaca, NY: Cornell University Press.

Martynov, V. I. 1997. *Penie, igra i molitva v russkoi bogosluzhebnopevcheskoi sisteme.* Moscow: Filologiia.

Marx, Karl. 1957 [1844]. Zur Kritik der Hegelschen Rechtsphilosophie: Einleitung. In Karl Marx and Friedrich Engels, *Werke,* vol. 1. Berlin: Dietz, 378–391.

Massell, Gregory J. 1974. *The Surrogate Proletariat: Moslem Women and Revolutionary Strategies in Soviet Central Asia.* Princeton, NJ: Princeton University Press.

Maydell, Renata von. 1997. Anthroposophy in Russia. In *The Occult in Russian and Soviet Culture,* edited by Bernice Glatzer Rosenthal. Ithaca, NY: Cornell University Press, 153–167.

Mazower, Mark. 2004. *Salonica, City of Ghosts: Christians, Muslims and Jews, 1430–1950.* New York: Knopf.

Mazzarella, William. 2003. *Shoveling Smoke: Advertising and Globalization in Contemporary India.* Durham, NC: Duke University Press.

McCawley, Martin. 1976. *Khrushchev and the Development of Soviet Agriculture: The Virgin Land Programme 1953-1964.* London: Macmillan.

McDermott, R. P., and Henry Tylbor. 1995. On the Necessity of Collusion in Conversation. In *The Dialogic Emergence of Culture,* edited by Dennis Tedlock and Bruce Mannheim. Urbana: University of Illinois Press, 218–236.

Medvedev, Zhores A. 1987. *Soviet Agriculture.* New York: Norton.

Merridale, Catherine. 2000. *Night of Stone: Death and Memory in Twentieth-Century Russia.* New York: Penguin.

Mertz, Elizabeth. 2007. *The Language of Law School: Learning to "Think Like a Lawyer."* Oxford: Oxford University Press.

Messick, Brinkley. 1993. *The Calligraphic State: Textual Domination and History in a Muslim Society.* Berkeley: University of California Press.

Meyendorff, John. 2001a [1964]. Byzantine Views of Islam. In his *The Byzantine Legacy in the Orthodox Church.* Crestwood, NY: St. Vladimir's Seminary Press, 89–114.

———. 2001b [1982]. The "Defense of the Holy Hesychasts" by St. Gregory Palamas. In his *The Byzantine Legacy in the Orthodox Church.* Crestwood, NY: St. Vladimir's Seminary Press, 167–194.

Meyer, Birgit. 1998. "Make a Complete Break with the Past": Memory and Post-Colonial Modernity in Ghanaian Pentecostalist Discourse. *Journal of Religion in Africa* 28(3): 316–349.

———. 1999. *Translating the Devil: Religion and Modernity among the Ewe in Ghana.* Edinburgh: Edinburgh University Press.

———. 2006. Impossible Representations: Pentecostalism, Vision, and Video Technology in Ghana. In *Religion, Media, and the Public Sphere,* edited by Birgit Meyer and Annelies Moors. Bloomington: Indiana University Press, 290–312.

Mitchell, W. J. T. 1994. *Picture Theory.* Chicago: University of Chicago Press.

Mitrofanov, Georgii. 2002. *Istoriia Russkoi Pravoslavnoi Tserkvi, 1900-1927.* Saint Petersburg: Satis.

Mitrokhin, Nikolai L. 2004. *Russkaia Pravoslavnaia Tserkov': Sovremennoe sostoianie i aktual'nye problemy.* Moscow: Novoe literaturnoe obozrenie.

Miyazaki, Hirokazu. 2004. *The Method of Hope: Anthropology, Philosophy, and Fijian Knowledge.* Stanford, CA: Stanford University Press.

Möckel, Christian. 2003. *Anschaulichkeit des Wissens und kulturelle Sinnstiftung: Beiträge aus Lebensphilosophie, Phänomenologie und symbolischem Idealismus zu einer Goetheschen Fragestellung.* Berlin: Logos.

Moiseevskaia, O. 1961. Ob aktivizatsii uchashchikhsia na uroke. In *Prepodavanie politicheskikh distsiplin v professional'no-tekhnicheskikh uchebnykh zavedeniiakh,* edited by Tsentral'nyi uchebno-metodicheskii kabinet professional'no-tekhnicheskikh uchilishch. Moscow: Proftekhizdat, 36–42.

Molotova, Tamara Lavrent'evna. 1992. *Mariiskii narodnyi kostium.* Ioshkar-Ola: Mariiskoe knizhnoe izdatel'stvo.

Moore, Sally, and Barbara Myerhoff. 1977. Secular Ritual: Forms and Meanings. In *Secular Ritual,* edited by Sally Moore and Barbara Myerhoff. Assen, Netherlands: Van Gorcum, 3–24.

Mueggler, Erik. 2001. *The Age of Wild Ghosts: Memory, Violence, and Place in Southwest China.* Berkeley: University of California Press.

Munroe, Myles. 2000. *The Purpose and Power of Praise and Worship.* Shippensburg, PA: Destiny Image.

Navaro-Yashin, Yael. 2002. *Faces of the State: Secularism and Public Life in Turkey.* Princeton, NJ: Princeton University Press.

Nekhoroshkov, Mikhail Fedorovich. 1964. *Vliiat' na soznanie i chuvstva: Iz opyta raboty kluba ateistov Mariiskogo gosudarstvennogo pedagogicheskogo instituta im. N. K. Krupskoi.* Ioshkar-Ola: Mariiskoe knizhnoe izdatel'stvo.

———. 1967a. *Nauchno-ateisticheskaia propaganda v uchrezhdeniiakh kul'tury.* Ioshkar-Ola: Mariiskoe knizhnoe izdatel'stvo.

———. 1967b. *Sem'ia i religiia.* Ioshkar-Ola: Mariiskoe knizhnoe izdatel'stvo.

Northrop, Douglas. 2004. *Veiled Empire: Gender and Power in Stalinist Central Asia.* Ithaca, NY: Cornell University Press.

Nove, Alec. 1982 [1969]. *An Economic History of the U.S.S.R.* Rev. ed. Harmondsworth, England: Penguin.

Novoselova, I. V., ed. 1959. *Nauchno-ateisticheskaia propaganda v kul'turnoprosvetitel'skikh uchrezhdeniiakh: Sbornik metodicheskikh i bibliograficheskikh materialov.* Ioshkar-Ola: Ministerstvo kul'tury Mariiskoi ASSR.

O'Neill, Kevin. 2010. *City of God: Christian Citizenship in Postwar Guatemala.* Berkeley: University of California Press.

Ong, Walter J. 1982. *Orality and Literacy: The Technologizing of the Word.* London: Methuen.

Osipov, A. A. 1963. Kritika pravoslavnogo propovednichestva. In *Ateisticheskie znaniia—narodu: Stenogrammy lektsii, prochitannykh na respublikanskikh seminarakh i v narodnykh universitetakh ateizma,* edited by N. V. Fedorovich. Leningrad: Obshchestvo po rasprostraneniiu politicheskikh i nauchnykh znanii RSFSR, 71–103.

Osipov, A. I. 2001. Sviatitel' Ignatii ob osnovakh dukhovnoi zhizni. In his *Pravoslavnoe ponimanie smysla zhizni.* Kiev: Obshchestvo liubitelei pravoslavnoi literatury, 97–126.

Oushakine, Serguei Alex. 2004. The Flexible and the Pliant: Disturbed Organisms of Soviet Modernity. *Cultural Anthropology* 19(3): 392–429.

Ozouf, Jacques, and Mona Ozouf. 1992. *La République des instituteurs.* Paris: Seuil.

Özyürek, Esra. 2006. *Nostalgia for the Modern: State Secularism and Everyday Politics in Turkey.* Durham, NC: Duke University Press.

Paert, Irina. 2004. Demystifying the Heavens: Women, Religion, and Khrushchev's Anti-Religious Campaign, 1954–64. In *Women in the Khrushchev Era,* edited by Melanie Ilič, Susan E. Reid, and Lynne Attwood. Basingstoke, England: Palgrave Macmillan, 203–221.

Palmer, G. E. H., Philip Sherrard, and Kallistos Ware, eds. and trans. 1979–1995. *The Philokalia: The Complete Text Compiled by St. Nikodimos of the Holy Mountain and St. Makarios of Corinth.* 4 vols. London: Faber and Faber.

Panchenko, Aleksandr. 2004. *Khristovshchina i skopchestvo: Fol'klor i traditsionnaia kul'tura russkikh misticheskikh sekt.* 2nd ed. Moscow: OGI.

Pandey, Gyanendra. 2003. *Remembering Partition: Violence, Nationalism, and History in India.* Cambridge: Cambridge University Press.

Papkova, Irina. 2007. The Russian Orthodox Church and Political Party Platforms. *Journal of Church and State* 49(1): 117–134.

Paxson, Margaret. 2005. *Solovyovo: The Story of Memory in a Russian Village.* Bloomington: Indiana University Press.

Pelikan, Jaroslav. 1993. *Christianity and Classical Culture: The Metamorphosis of Natural Theology in the Christian Encounter with Hellenism.* New Haven, CT: Yale University Press.

Pelkmans, Mathijs. 2006. *Defending the Border: Identity, Religion, and Modernity in the Republic of Georgia.* Ithaca, NY: Cornell University Press.

Pelkmans, Mathijs, ed. 2009. *Conversions after Socialism: Disruptions, Modernisms and Technologies of Faith in the Former Soviet Union.* New York: Berghahn.

Pels, Peter. 2003. Spirits of Modernity: Alfred Wallace, Edward Tylor, and the Visual Politics of Fact. In *Magic and Modernity: Interfaces of Revelation and Concealment,* edited by Birgit Meyer and Peter Pels. Stanford, CA: Stanford University Press, 241–271.

Peris, Daniel. 1998. *Storming the Heavens: The Soviet League of the Militant Godless.* Ithaca, NY: Cornell University Press.

———. 2000. "God Is Now on Our Side": The Religious Revival on Unoccupied Soviet Territory during World War II. *Kritika* 1: 97–118.

Pesmen, Dale. 2000. *Russia and Soul: An Exploration.* Ithaca, NY: Cornell University Press.

Petrone, Karen. 2000. *Life Has Become More Joyous, Comrades: Celebrations in the Time of Stalin.* Bloomington: Indiana University Press.

Petrov, Petâr. 2003. Sotsialisticheskite trudovi praznitsi i rituali—kontseptsiia i potreblenie. In *Sotsializmât: Realnost i iliuzii: Etnologichni aspekti na vsekidnevnata kultura,* edited by Radost Ivanova, Ana Luleva, and Rachko Popov. Sofia: Institute of Ethnography, Bulgarian Academy of Sciences, 133–149.

Philips, Susan. 1982. *The Invisible Culture: Communication in Classroom and Community on the Warm Springs Indian Reservation.* Highland Park, IL: Waveland.

Phillips, Sarah. 2008. *Women's Social Activism in the New Ukraine: Development and the Politics of Differentiation.* Bloomington: Indiana University Press.

Pivovarov, Viktor Grigor'evich. 1971. *Byt, kul'tura, natsional'nye traditsii i verovaniia naseleniia Checheno-ingushskoi ASSR (Osnovnye zadachi, instrumentarii, protse-*

dury i nauchno-organizatsionnyi plan konkretno-sotsiologicheskogo issledovaniia). Groznyi: Checheno-ingushskoe knizhnoe izdatel'stvo.

———. 1974. *Na etapakh sotsiologicheskogo issledovaniia (Teoriia i praktika sotsiologicheskikh issledovanii problem ateizma i religii).* Groznyi: Checheno-ingushskoe knizhnoe izdatel'stvo.

———. 1976. *Religioznost': Opyt i problemy izucheniia.* Ioshkar-Ola: Mariiskoe knizhnoe izdatel'stvo.

Plaggenborg, Stefan. 1996. *Revolutionskultur: Menschenbilder und kulturelle Praxis in Sowjetrussland zwischen Oktoberrevolution und Stalinismus.* Vienna: Böhlau.

Plamper, Jan. 2010. *Alkhimiia vlasti: Kul't Stalina v izobrazitel'nom iskusstve.* Moscow: Novoe literaturnoe obozrenie.

Pollack, Detlef. 2003. *Säkularisierung—ein moderner Mythos? Studien zum religiösen Wandel in Deutschland.* Tübingen: Mohr-Siebeck.

Popov, Nikandr Semenovich. 1987. *Pravoslavie v mariiskom krae.* Ioshkar-Ola: Mariiskoe knizhnoe izdatel'stvo.

———. 1996. Na mariiskom iazycheskom molenii. *Etnograficheskoe obozrenie* 1996(3): 130–145.

———. 2005. Religioznye verovaniia. In *Mariitsy: Istoriko-etnograficheskie ocherki,* edited by N. S. Popov et al. Ioshkar-Ola: MarNIIIaLI, 215–227.

Popov, Nikandr Semenovich, and Aleksandr Ivanovich Tanygin. 2003. *Iumyn iüla.* Ioshkar-Ola: Ministerstvo kul'tury i mezhnatsional'nykh otnoshenii.

Pospielovsky, Dimitry V. 1987a. *A History of Marxist-Leninist Atheism and Soviet Antireligious Policies.* Vol. 1. New York: St. Martin's.

———. 1987b. *Soviet Antireligious Campaigns and Persecutions.* Vol. 2. New York: St. Martin's.

Powell, David E. 1975. *Antireligious Propaganda in the Soviet Union: A Study of Mass Persuasion.* Cambridge, MA: MIT Press.

Ransel, David L. 2000. *Village Mothers: Three Generations of Change in Russia and Tataria.* Bloomington: Indiana University Press.

Reddy, William M. 2001. *The Navigation of Feeling: A Framework for the History of Emotions.* Cambridge: Cambridge University Press.

Reid, Susan E. 2004. Women in the Home. In *Women in the Khrushchev Era,* edited by Melanie Ilič, Susan E. Reid, and Lynne Attwood. Basingstoke, England: Palgrave Macmillan, 149–176.

Reinhard, Kenneth. 2005. Toward a Political Theology of the Neighbor. In *The Neighbor: Three Inquiries in Political Theology,* by Slavoj Žižek, Eric L. Santner, and Kenneth Reinhard. Chicago: University of Chicago Press, 11–75.

Ries, Nancy. 2009. Potato Ontology: Surviving Postsocialism in Russia. *Cultural Anthropology* 24(2): 181–212.

Riles, Annelise. 2000. *The Network Inside Out.* Ann Arbor: University of Michigan Press.

Robbins, Joel. 2003. What Is a Christian? Notes Toward an Anthropology of Christianity. *Religion* 33: 191–199.

———. 2004. *Becoming Sinners: Christianity and Moral Torment in a Papua New Guinea Society.* Berkeley: University of California Press.

Rogers, Douglas J. 2009. *The Old Faith and the Russian Land: A Historical Ethnography of Ethics in the Urals.* Ithaca, NY: Cornell University Press.

Rolf, Malte. 2006. *Das sowjetische Massenfest.* Hamburg: Hamburger Edition.

Rosenthal, Bernice Glatzer. 1997. Introduction. In *The Occult in Russian and Soviet Culture*, edited by B. G. Rosenthal. Ithaca, NY: Cornell University Press, 1–32.

Rossiiskaia Federatsiia—Federal'naia Sluzhba Gosudarstvennoi Statistiki. 2004. *Itogi Vserossiiskoi Perepisi 2002 goda*. Vol. 4: *Natsional'nyi sostav i vladenie iazykami, grazhdanstvo*. Moscow: Statistika Rossii.

Rostsius, Iurii Vladimirovich. 1991. *Gadanie: Sueverie ili . . . ?* Moscow: Znanie.

Ruble, Blair. 1990. *Leningrad: Shaping a Soviet City*. Berkeley: University of California Press.

———. 1993. From *Khrushcheby* to *Korobki*. In *Russian Housing in the Modern Age: Design and Social History*, edited by William C. Brumfield and Blair A. Ruble. Cambridge: Cambridge University Press, 232–270.

Rubskii, Viacheslav. 2003. *Posobie po razgovoru s sektantami: Protivosektantskii bloknot*. Pochaev, Ukraine: Pochaevskaia lavka.

Rudnyckyj, Daromir. 2009. Spiritual Economies: Islam and Neoliberalism in Contemporary Indonesia. *Cultural Anthropology* 24(1): 104–141.

Sadomskaya, Natalya. 1990. Soviet Anthropology and Contemporary Rituals. *Cahiers du monde russe et soviétique* 31(2–3): 245–254.

Sahlins, Marshall. 1985. *Islands of History*. Chicago: University of Chicago Press.

Sanukov, Ksenofont N. 2000. *Iz istorii Marii El: Tragediia 30x godov*. Ioshkar-Ola: Mariiskii gosudarstvennyi universitet.

Sanukov, Ksenofont N., G. N. Aiplatov, A. G. Ivanov, and A. S. Kasimov. 2004. Vchera. In *Ioshkar-Ola: Vchera, segodnia, zavtra*, edited by Ioshkar-Olinskaia gorodskaia administratsiia. Ioshkar-Ola: LIK, 13–92.

Sawatsky, Walter. 1981. *Soviet Evangelicals since World War II*. Kitchener, ON: Herald.

Scherrer, Jutta. 1978. Les écoles du Parti de Capri et de Bologne: La formation de l'intelligentsia du Parti. *Cahiers du monde russe et soviétique* 19: 258–284.

Schmemann, Alexander. 1966 [1961]. *Introduction to Liturgical Theology*. Translated by Asheleigh E. Moorehouse. Portland, ME: American Orthodox Press.

Schmitt, Carl. 2002 [1932]. *Der Begriff des Politischen*. Berlin: Duncker & Humblot.

———. 2004 [1922]. *Politische Theologie: Vier Kapitel zur Lehre von der Souveränität*. Berlin: Duncker & Humblot.

Schweidler, Walter. 2007. *Postsäkulare Gesellschaft: Perspektiven interdisziplinärer Forschung*. Munich: Karl Alber.

Scott, Joan Wallach. 2007. *The Politics of the Veil*. Princeton, NJ: Princeton University Press.

Sebeok, Thomas A., and Frances J. Ingemann. 1956. *Studies in Cheremis: The Supernatural*. New York: Wenner-Gren Foundation.

Sériot, Patrick. 1999. *Structure et totalité: Les origines intellectuelles du structuralisme en Europe centrale et orientale*. Paris: Presses universitaires de France.

Shabykov, V. I., S. N. Isanbaev, and E. A. Ozhiganova, eds. 2005. *Religioznoe soznanie naseleniia Respubliki Marii El (Materialy sotsiologicheskikh issledovanii 1994 i 2004 godov)*. Ioshkar-Ola: MarNIIIaLi.

Shaull, Richard, and Waldo Cesar. 2000. *Pentecostalism and the Future of the Christian Churches: Promises, Limitations, Challenges*. Grand Rapids, MI: Eerdmans.

Shchipanov, Aleksandr Semenovich. 1961. *Plakat v klube*. Moscow: Ministerstvo kul'tury RSFSR.

Shchipkov, Aleksandr. 1998. *Vo chto verit Rossiia: Religioznye protsessy v postpere-stroechnoi Rossii: Kurs lektsii.* Saint Petersburg: Izdatel'stvo Russkogo Khristians-kogo gumanitarnogo instituta.

Sherel', Aleksandr. 2004. *Audiokul'tura XX veka: Istoriia, esteticheskie zakonomer-nosti, osobennosti vliianiia na auditoriiu.* Moscow: Progress-Traditsiia.

Shevzov, Vera. 2004. *Russian Orthodoxy on the Eve of Revolution.* Oxford: Oxford University Press.

———. 2007. Scripting the Gaze: Liturgy, Homilies, and the Kazan Icon of the Moth-er of God in Late Imperial Russia. In *Sacred Stories: Religion and Spirituality in Modern Russia,* edited by Mark Steinberg and Heather Coleman. Bloomington: Indiana University Press, 61–92.

Shkarovskii, Mikhail V. 1995. *Russkaia pravoslavnaia tserkov' i sovetskoe gosudarstvo v 1943–1964 gg.: Ot peremiriia k novoi voine.* Saint Petersburg: DEAN-ADIA-M.

Shterin, Marat, and James Richardson. 1998. Local Laws Restricting Religion in Russia: Precursors of Russia's New National Law. *Journal of Church and State* 40(2): 319–341.

Slezkine, Yuri L. 1994. The USSR as a Communal Apartment; or, How a Socialist State Promoted Ethnic Particularism. *Slavic Review* 53(2): 414–452.

Smith, Christian. 2003. Introduction: Rethinking the Secularization of American Public Life. In *The Secular Revolution: Power, Interests, and Conflict in the Secu-larization of American Public Life,* edited by Christian Smith. Berkeley: Univer-sity of California Press, 1–96.

Smolitsch, Igor. 1953. *Russisches Mönchtum: Enstehung, Entwicklung und Wesen, 988–1917.* Würzburg: Augustinus.

Smolkin, Victoria [Viktoriia Smolkin]. 2009. "Sviato mesto pusto ne byvaet": Atei-sticheskoe vospitanie v Sovetskom Soiuze, 1964–1968. *Neprikosnovennyi zapas* 65: 36–52.

Sofronov, Nikolai Sergeevich. 1973. *Ateisticheskoe vospitanie kolkhoznogo krest'ianstva.* Ioshkar-Ola: Mariiskoe knizhnoe izdatel'stvo.

Sokolovskii, Sergei Valer'evich. 2006. Eshche raz o sud'bakh "finno-ugorskikh naro-dov": Kommentarii k dokumentam PASE o kul'turakh "ural'skikh menshinstv." *Etnograficheskoe obozrenie* 2006(1): 6–13.

Solomonik, A. G. 1977. *Metody ustnoi massovoi propagandy.* Moscow: Obshchestvo Znanie RSFSR.

Solov'ev, Viktor Stepanovich. 1966. *Peledysh pairem (natsional'nyi prazdnik mariis-kogo naroda).* Ioshkar-Ola: Mariiskoe knizhnoe izdatel'stvo.

———. 1977. *Sotsiologicheskie issledovaniia—v praktiku ideologicheskoi raboty: Neko-torye itogi izucheniia problem byta, kul'tury, traditsii i verovanii naseleniia Ma-riiskoi ASSR.* Ioshkar-Ola: Mariiskoe knizhnoe izdatel'stvo.

———. 1982. Nekotorye osobennosti formirovaniia ateisticheskoi ubezhdennosti cheloveka. In *Ateizm i sotsialisticheskaia kul'tura: Materialy nauchnoi konferentsii "Ateizm i dukhovnaia kul'tura razvitogo sotsializma,"* edited by V. S. Solov'ev. Ioshkar-Ola: Mariiskoe knizhnoe izdatel'stvo, 56–67.

———. 1987. *Po puti dukhovnogo progressa: Nekotorye itogi povtornogo sotsiologiche-skogo issledovaniia problem byta, kul'tury, natsional'nykh traditsii, ateizma i ver-ovanii naseleniia Mariiskoi ASSR.* Ioshkar-Ola: Mariiskoe knizhnoe izdatel'stvo.

———. 1991. *Mnogonatsional'nost'—nashe bogatstvo*. Ioshkar-Ola: Mariiskoe knizhnoe izdatel'stvo.

Sorabji, Cornelia. 2008. Bosnian Neighborhoods Revisited: Tolerance, Commitment and *Komšiluk* in Sarajevo. In *On the Margins of Religion*, edited by Frances Pine and João de Pina-Cabral. New York: Berghahn, 97–112.

Sretenskii monastyr', ed. 2004. *Akafist Presviatoi Bogoroditse v chest' ikony Ee Kazanskoi*. Moscow: Izdanie Sretenskogo monastyria.

Starikov, Sergei Valentinovich, and Oleg Genrikhovich Levenshtein. 2001. *Pravoslavnye khramy i monastyri mariiskogo kraia*. Ioshkar-Ola: Periodika Marii El.

Stepanian, Tsolak Aleksandrovich, ed. 1966. *Stroitel'stvo kommunizma i dukhovnyi mir cheloveka*. Moscow: Nauka.

Stewart, Charles. 1991. *Demons and the Devil: Moral Imagination in Modern Greek Culture*. Princeton, NJ: Princeton University Press.

Stewart, Charles, and Rosalind Shaw, eds. 1994. *Syncretism/Anti-Syncretism: The Politics of Religious Synthesis*. London: Routledge.

Stites, Richard. 1987. The Origins of Soviet Ritual Style: Symbol and Festival in the Russian Revolution. In *Symbols of Power: The Esthetics of Political Legitimation in the Soviet Union and Eastern Europe*, edited by Claes Arvidsson and Lars Erik Blomqvist. Stockholm: Almqvist & Wiksell, 23–42.

———. 1989. *Revolutionary Dreams: Utopian Vision and Experimental Life in the Russian Revolution*. New York: Oxford University Press.

Stöckl, Kristina. 2006. Modernity and Its Critique in 20th Century Russian Orthodox Thought. *Studies in East European Thought* 58: 243–269.

Stockstill, Larry [Lerri Stokstill]. 2001 [1998]. *Iacheechnaia tserkov': Model' dlia sluzheniia kazhdomu chlenu tela khrista*. Moscow: Slovo zhizni.

Stone, Andrew B. 2008. "Overcoming Peasant Backwardness": The Khrushchev Antireligious Campaign and the Rural Soviet Union. *Russian Review* 67(2): 296–320.

Stringer, Martin D. 1999. Rethinking Animism: Thoughts from the Infancy of Our Discipline. *Journal of the Royal Anthropological Institute* 5(4): 541–555.

Stronski, Paul. 2010. *Tashkent: Forging a Soviet City, 1930–1966*. Pittsburgh, PA: University of Pittsburgh Press.

Suleymanova, Rita N. 1996. Die Geisterwelt der Baschkiren. In *Muslim Culture in Russia and Central Asia from the 18th to the Early 20th Centuries*, edited by M. Kemper, A. von Kügelgen, and D. Yermakov. Berlin: Klaus Schwarz, 5–36.

Sullivan, Winnifred F. 2009. *Prison Religion: Faith-Based Reform and the Constitution*. Princeton, NJ: Princeton University Press.

Tarasova, V. M., A. G. Ivanov, V. P. Shomina, and G. A. Lapteva, eds. 2004. *Ioshkar-Ole—420 let (1584–2004): Dokumenty i materialy po istorii goroda*. 2nd ed. Ioshkar-Ola: State Archive of the Republic of Marii El.

Taubman, William. 2003. *Khrushchev: The Man and His Era*. New York: Norton.

Taylor, Charles. 2004. *Modern Social Imaginaries*. Durham, NC: Duke University Press.

———. 2007. *A Secular Age*. Cambridge, Mass.: Belknap.

Tiapkin, N. K. 1970. *Zainteresovat', raz"iasnit', ubedit'*. Moscow: Znanie.

Tishkov, Valerii Aleksandrovich. 2001. *Obshchestvo v vooruzhennom konflikte: Etnografiia chechenskoi voiny*. Moscow: Nauka.

Todes, Daniel. 2001. *Pavlov's Physiology Factory: Experiment, Interpretation, Labora-tory.* Baltimore, MD: Johns Hopkins University Press.

Treadgold, Donald W. 1978. Russian Orthodoxy and Society. In *Russian Orthodoxy and the Old Regime*, edited by Robert L. Nichols and Theofanis G. Stavrou. Min-neapolis: University of Minnesota Press, 21–43.

Trotsky, Leon. 1973 [1923]. *Problems of Everyday Life: Creating the Foundations for a New Society in Revolutionary Russia.* New York: Pathfinder.

Tsekhanskaia, Kira Vladimirovna. 2004. *Ikonopochitanie v russkoi traditsionnoi kul'ture.* Moscow: Institut etnologii i antropologii RAN.

Tumarkin, Nina. 1983. *Lenin Lives! The Lenin Cult in Soviet Russia.* Cambridge, MA: Harvard University Press.

———. 1994. *The Living and the Dead: The Rise and Fall of the Cult of World War II in Russia.* New York: Basic.

Urazmanova, Raufa Karimovna. 2009. "Musul'manskie" obriady v bytu tatar. *Etnograficheskoe obozrenie,* no. 1: 13–26.

Urban, Greg. 2001. *Metaculture: How Culture Moves through the World.* Minneapo-lis: University of Minnesota Press.

Uvarov, Anatolii. 2000. Liuteranstvo blizko Finno-Ugram. *Vestnik,* August 2000: 15.

Uzzell, Lawrence. 1997. Religious Freedom in Russia. Washington, DC: Commission on Security and Cooperation in Europe.

Valtchinova, Galia. 2004. Constructing the Bulgarian Pythia: Intersecting Religion, Memory, and History in the Seer Vanga. In *Memory, Politics, and Religion: The Past Meets the Present in Europe,* edited by Deema Kaneff, Frances Pine, and Haldes Haukanen. Münster: Lit, 179–198.

van der Veer, Peter. 1992. Playing or Praying: A Sufi Saint's Day in Surat. *Journal of Asian Studies* 51(3): 545–565.

———. 1994. *Religious Nationalism: Hindus and Muslims in India.* Berkeley: Uni-versity of California Press.

Veniamin (Milov), Bishop. 2002. *Pastyrskoe bogoslovie s asketikoi.* Moscow: Izdatel'stvo Moskovskogo podvor'ia Sviato-Troitskoi Sergievoi Lavry.

Vershlovskii, S. G., and L. N. Lesokhina. 1968. *Eticheskaia beseda i disput v vechernei shkole: Metodicheskie rekomendatsii.* Leningrad: Akademiia pedagogicheskikh nauk SSSR.

Viola, Lynne. 1996. *Peasant Rebels under Stalin: Collectivization and the Culture of Peasant Resistance.* New York: Oxford University Press.

Vitz, Paul C., and Arnold B. Glimcher. 1984. *Modern Art and Modern Science: The Parallel Analysis of Vision.* New York: Praeger.

Voegelin, Eric. 1993 [1938]. *Die politischen Religionen,* edited by Peter J. Opitz. Munich: Wilhelm Fink.

Vsenoshchnoe bdenie. 2001. *Vsenoshchnoe bdenie: Bozhestvennaia liturgiia.* Sergiev Posad: Sviato-Troitskaia Sergieva Lavra.

Walters, Philip [Filip Uolters]. 2002. Religiia v Tyve. In *Religiia i obshchestvo: Ocherki religioznoi zhizni sovremennoi Rossii,* edited by S. B. Filatov. Moscow: Letnii sad, 213–232.

Wanner, Catherine. 2007. *Communities of the Converted: Ukrainians and Global Evangelism.* Ithaca, NY: Cornell University Press.

Ware, Kallistos. 1985. Ways of Prayer and Contemplation, part I: Eastern. In *Christian Spirituality: Origins to the Twelfth Century*, edited by Bernard McGinn, John Meyendorff, and Jean Leclercq. New York: Crossroad, 395–414.

Warner, Michael. 2002. *Publics and Counterpublics*. New York: Zone.

Warren, Rick. 2002. *The Purpose Driven Life*. Grand Rapids, MI: Zondervan.

Weber, Max. 1922. *Die protestantische Ethik und der Geist des Kapitalismus*. Tübingen: Mohr-Siebeck.

———. 1972 [1921]. *Wirtschaft und Gesellschaft: Grundriss der verstehenden Soziologie*. 5th ed. Edited by Johannes Winckelmann. Tübingen: Mohr-Siebeck.

Wegren, Stephen K. 2005. *The Moral Economy Reconsidered: Russia's Search for Agrarian Capitalism*. New York: Palgrave Macmillan.

Weiner, Amir. 2001. *Making Sense of War: The Second World War and the Fate of the Bolshevik Revolution*. Princeton, NJ: Princeton University Press.

Werth, Paul. 2000. From "Pagan" Muslims to "Baptized" Communists: Religious Conversion and Ethnic Particularity in Russia's Eastern Provinces. *Comparative Studies in Society and History* 42(3): 497–523.

———. 2001. Big Candles and "Internal Conversion": The Mari Animist Reformation and Its Russian Appropriations. In *Of Religion and Empire: Missions, Conversion, and Tolerance in Tsarist Russia*, edited by Robert P. Geraci and Michael Khodarkovsky. Ithaca, NY: Cornell University Press, 144–172.

———. 2002. *At the Margins of Orthodoxy: Mission, Governance, and Confessional Politics in Russia's Volga-Kama Region, 1827–1905*. Ithaca, NY: Cornell University Press.

West, Harry, and Todd Sanders, eds. 2003. *Transparency and Conspiracy: Ethnographies of Suspicion in the New World Order*. Durham, NC: Duke University Press.

White, Anne. 2000. Social Change in Provincial Russia: The Intelligentsia in a *Raion* Centre. *Europe-Asia Studies* 52(4): 677–694.

Whitehouse, Harvey. 2000. *Arguments and Icons: Divergent Modes of Religiosity*. Oxford: Oxford University Press.

Wichmann, Julie. 1913. *Beiträge zur Ethnographie der Tscheremissen*. Helsinki: Société finno-ougrienne.

Wichmann, Yrjö. 1932. Über eine Reformbewegung der heidnischen Tscheremissen. *Journal de la société finno-ougrienne* 45: 21–46.

Wiesing, Lambert. 2005. Virtuelle Realität: Die Angleichung des Bildes an die Imagination. In his *Artifizielle Präsenz: Studien zur Philosophie des Bildes*. Frankfurt: Suhrkamp, 107–124.

Willis, Paul E. 1981. *Learning to Labor: How Working Class Kids Get Working Class Jobs*. New York: Columbia University Press.

Wolfe, Thomas C. 2005. *Governing Soviet Journalism: The Press and the Socialist Person after Stalin*. Bloomington: Indiana University Press.

Wood, Elizabeth. 2005. *Performing Justice: Agitation Trials in Revolutionary Russia, 1920–1933*. Ithaca, NY: Cornell University Press.

Wortham, Stanton. 1994. *Acting out Participant Examples in the Classroom*. Amsterdam: John Benjamins.

Yang, Mayfair Mei-hui. 2004. Spatial Struggles: Postcolonial Complex, State Disenchantment, and Popular Reappropriation of Space in Rural Southeast China. *Journal of Asian Studies* 63(3): 719–755.

———. 2008. Introduction. In *Chinese Religiosities: Afflictions of Modernity and State Formation*, edited by Mayfair Mei-hui Yang. Berkeley: University of California Press, 1–40.

Yazykova, Irina. 2010. *Hidden and Triumphant: The Underground Struggle to Save Russian Iconography*. Translated by Paul Grenier. Brewster, MA: Paraclete.

Yurchak, Alexei. 2006. *Everything Was Forever, until It Was No More: The Last Soviet Generation*. Princeton, NJ: Princeton University Press.

Zander, Helmut. 2008. *Anthroposophie in Deutschland*. 2 vols. Göttingen: Vandenhoeck & Ruprecht.

Zankov, L. V., ed. 1958. *Sochetanie slova uchitelia i sredstv nagliadnosti v obuchenii: Didakticheskoe issledovanie*. Moscow: Izdatel'stvo Akademii pedagogicheskikh nauk RSFSR.

Zigon, Jarrett. 2011. *HIV Is God's Blessing: Rehabilitating Morality in Neoliberal Russia*. Berkeley: University of California Press.

Zil'berberg, L. 1956. *Ispol'zovanie kino v nauchno-ateisticheskoi propagande*. Moscow: Gosudarstvennoe izdatel'stvo kul'turno-prosvetitel'skoi literatury.

Žižek, Slavoj, Eric L. Santner, and Kenneth Reinhard. 2005. *The Neighbor: Three Inquiries in Political Theology*. Chicago: University of Chicago Press.

Index

Sonja Luehrmann is Assistant Professor of Anthropology at Simon Fraser University. She is the author of *Alutiiq Villages under Russian and U.S. Rule*.